T0219408

Medical Malpractice on Trial

Medical Malpractice on Trial

PAUL C. WEILER

HARVARD UNIVERSITY PRESS
Cambridge, Massachusetts
London, England
1991

Library of Congress Cataloging-in-Publication Data
Weiler, Paul C.
    Medical malpractice on trial / Paul C. Weiler.
        p.   cm.
    Includes indexes.
    ISBN 0-674-56120-1 (alk. paper)
    1. Physicians—Malpractice—United States.   I. Title.
    [DNLM: 1. Insurance, Physicians' liability—United States.
2. Malpractice—United States—legislation. W 32.5 AA1 W35m]
KF2905.3.W37 1991
346.7303'32—dc20
[347.306332]
DNLM/DLC
for Library of Congress   90–15600
                                                       CIP

To my parents, Bernie and Marcella Cronin Weiler

Contents

Preface

In early 1990, addressing a crowd gathered to celebrate the centennial of the Johns Hopkins Medical School, President Bush expressed his empathy with the medical profession's fear of malpractice litigation. He observed that this anxiety had chilled the spirit of medical voluntarism in the nation, was inducing increasingly costly defensive medicine, and threatened the future prospects of life-saving medical research and innovation. The President told his receptive audience that he had instructed the Domestic Policy Council to investigate what might be done to alleviate the specter of litigation and "to restore common sense and fairness to America's medical malpractice system." A White House spokesman said later that what the President had in mind were measures to reduce excessive litigation and escalating damage awards.

It may seem ironic that this presidential reform initiative appeared in 1990, a year in which malpractice insurance premiums around the country were dropping from the peaks they had reached a year or two earlier. The simple explanation is that nationally malpractice premiums had surged from just $60 million in 1960 to more than $7 billion by 1990. Much of this huge increase had taken place in two bursts in the mid-seventies and the mid-eighties, when total premiums *more than doubled*. Situated as it was at the eye of the storm over tort litigation, medical malpractice law was the subject in the seventies of a variety of pioneering legislative changes to common law doctrines and judicial practices that were applied more generally in the eighties. Tort reform in this area consistently aimed to cut back on the legal rights of injured victims in order to contain the burden of liability imposed on doctors, hospitals, and enterprises generally. Although there was a sense of uneasy calm by the end of the eighties, leaders of the medical profession were under no illusion that a stable equilibrium had been reached. Consequently, the American Medical

Association and other specialty groups continued to press for more fundamental reforms, some of which would take malpractice claims entirely out of the civil justice system.

Like President Bush, I empathize with the plight of America's doctors, who are subjected with increasing frequency to the ministrations of a legal system that is neither kind nor gentle. Indeed, unlike the typical corporate defendant in a lawsuit, a doctor feels a distinctively emotional as well as financial trauma during tort litigation. A patient to whom a doctor has been giving personal care and treatment is publicly challenging the doctor's professional competence and reputation because something has gone wrong. I would certainly feel extremely aggrieved if I were regularly sued by my students on account of mistakes I made in the law school classroom. I understand, then, why medical practitioners so passionately insist that something must be done to remove this looming tort threat from their everyday working lives.

To understand that sentiment, though, is not to wholeheartedly endorse it. In fact, my book rests on a premise quite different from the one endorsed by President Bush and most other politicians who have grappled with the malpractice "crisis" in the last two decades. Even though tort suits do inflict considerable harm on doctors, medical injuries inflict much greater harm on patients. Indeed, far more patient injuries—even negligently inflicted patient injuries—occur every day in America's hospitals than ever find their way into America's legal system, let alone obtain redress there. Medical malpractice actually provides the best source of evidence for those dissenters from the tort reform movement who assert that the real tort crisis consists in too few, not too many, tort claims.

Still, recognition that patients who are injured have bigger problems than doctors who are sued is not a basis for a ringing endorsement of the legal status quo, despite the protestations of trial lawyers' associations. To the contrary, in this book I argue for major reforms in tort law, primarily in the area of damages rather than liability. Channeling more of tort's scarce funds to compensate all the economic losses of patients by paying less for pain and suffering and other psychological harms would rationalize and improve the fairness of our malpractice system (as the President wants). I am persuaded, though, that even more fundamental changes are needed if we are to secure equitable compensation for past medical injuries and effective prevention of future injuries. To that end, rather than simply cut back on the patient's right to secure redress under existing law, we must broaden the liability of health care organizations to cover all patient injuries, whether the injuries are caused by a doctor's fault or not. Such a system would be a much better arrangement for patients and doctors alike.

The formation of my legal policy views on this subject and the impetus for writing this book arose largely from my participation over the last five years in two complementary studies of medical injuries and tort reform. The first of these projects, the Harvard Medical Practice Study, was undertaken in New York State at the invitation in 1986 of Governor Mario Cuomo's administration, in particular of Dr. David Axelrod, the commissioner of health for the state of New York. This empirical study was led by Dr. Howard Hiatt, of the Harvard Medical School and the Harvard School of Public Health, Professor Joseph Newhouse, of the Harvard Medical School, the Harvard School of Public Health, and the Kennedy School of Government, and me (of Harvard Law School).

Along with a number of colleagues from a variety of specialties we undertook the first comprehensive empirical study of the relationship between medical injuries and tort litigation. Through systematic analysis of a large sample of hospital records we determined how many patients were being injured as a result of medical treatment and how many of these injuries were attributable to the negligence of doctors or other health care providers. After collecting and examining litigation and insurance records, we determined how many patients filed malpractice claims and how the filing of a claim by a patient's attorney squared with our judgment about the patient's injury and the doctor's negligence. Through in-depth interviews with the injured patients in our sample and a matched control group of noninjured patients, we determined the size of financial losses suffered by patients as a result of medical injury (as distinct from the underlying disease), how much of the losses were being compensated by other nontort sources such as health or disability insurance, and how much additional loss still required redress through the tort system or a no-fault liability alternative. Finally, through surveys of practicing doctors and econometric analysis of the impact of state-by-state variation in tort claims on variations in medical injuries we assessed the deterrent effect of tort litigation on medical care.

The results of the Harvard study were first published in a lengthy report issued in 1990, followed by a number of scholarly papers prepared for medical, economic, and statistical journals. A distillation of our findings and their implications will appear in a forthcoming law review article that I wrote with Dr. Troy Brennan, of Harvard University, the only doctor-lawyer on the study team. At numerous points in this book I refer to the Harvard study's empirical findings when they are relevant to my policy judgments and proposals, together with the results of the rapidly growing body of excellent scientific research now being done on this complex and contentious subject.

Although I originally suggested and sketched the idea for a full-scale empirical study of this problem, its success depended on the participation of Harvard colleagues with the scientific background and skills to mount and carry it out. My primary responsibility on the study team was to serve, in effect, as its "client," specifying what types of empirical data were necessary to make intelligent legal policies for medical injuries. My advice in that regard was strongly influenced by my participation in a parallel research project, the American Law Institute study of compensation and liability for personal injuries.

This project was also initiated in 1986 as a result of discussions among the institute's director, Professor Geoffrey Hazard, of the Yale Law School, Professor Richard Stewart, of Harvard Law School (who served as the project's chief reporter until he left for the U.S. Department of Justice in 1989), and me, who succeeded Professor Stewart as chief reporter. The ALI undertook an in-depth analysis of the performance of the tort system in handling high-stakes litigation in the areas of product liability, environmental and occupational accidents, and medical injuries. One of my responsibilities was reviewing medical injury liability, and this book is an outgrowth of a lengthy background study I first prepared for the ALI project in 1987. Portions of this book appear in chapters that I wrote for the two-volume final report of the ALI study, which was presented to the institute's council in December of 1990, and I gratefully acknowledge the ALI's permission to publish that material here. I owe a special intellectual debt to my scholarly colleagues who served as reporters, contributors, and special advisers to the ALI study, as well as to the many practitioners from the "real" worlds of law, medicine, and insurance who served as ongoing advisors to the project. Our always lively and sometimes heated discussions over the last five years have left an indelible imprint on my understanding of such topics as the sources of the liability insurance crisis, the appropriate design of tort damages, payment of attorney fees, the virtues of common law fault versus administrative no-fault liability, the scope and limits of the market for preventing and compensating medical injuries, and a host of other issues that I tackle in this book.

It is one thing to imagine a set of ideas about malpractice liability and its reform. It is quite another to translate the ideas into a publishable volume. For their indispensable help in that effort over the last several years, I thank my Harvard Law School deans, James Vorenberg and Robert Clark; my secretaries, Joann Beserdetsky and Benjamin Sears; my research assistants, Jonathan Wiener, Gregory Maggs, Clare Sylvia, Robert Howse, Sharona Hoffman, Jennifer Zacks, Arti Rai, Todd Townsley, and Jennifer Radding; and my Harvard University Press editors, Michael Aronson and Elizabeth Hurwit. Probably my greatest debt is owed to my wife, Florrie. Not only does Florrie provide the kind of support that eases the pain of long hours spent writing and revising in the faculty library, but she is the person who reads my work most closely, asks the toughest questions about what I am trying to say, and deserves the major credit for whatever felicity of style this book displays.

Finally, a word about my parents, Bernie and Marcella Weiler, who have been a lifelong source for me of support, inspiration, and love. Dedicating this book to them is particularly apt, for when they married my mother was a nurse and my father was (and still is, over fifty years later) a trial lawyer. So they represent the earliest union in my experience of medicine and the law.

Medical Malpractice on Trial

1

The Malpractice Crisis

As 1987 drew to a close, the *Wall Street Journal* carried a story that provided a vivid metaphor for the crisis atmosphere then enveloping malpractice litigation for medical injuries.[1] A Dallas plastic surgeon who had been sued several years earlier had begun videotaping all his conversations with his patients, as well as his treatment of two thousand or so patients each year. Pleased with this innovation in his own practice, the surgeon had licensed his video system to at least a dozen doctors in the area and confidently predicted that video equipment would be as commonplace as the stethoscope in the doctor's office of the future.

This story epitomizes both the similarities and the differences between medical malpractice and other forms of tort liability. Medical malpractice shares with product liability, for example, the economic dislocation of soaring claims rates, damage awards, and insurance premiums. But there is a personal, emotional cast to a lawsuit between patient and doctor that gives medical claims an edge that is not present in suits filed against large, remote corporate manufacturers of defective products. The therapeutic relationship between sick person and physician should not require the kind of unimpeachable documentation that might seem desirable in the adversarial situation of a police officer interrogating a prisoner in custody.

This combination of financial and psychological factors led physician organizations to press strongly for reform of the tort doctrines governing malpractice claims. Doctors enjoyed considerable political success in their efforts in the mid-seventies at the time of the first malpractice "crisis"; they returned to the state legislatures for even broader and deeper reforms as the problem dramatically resurged in the mid-eighties.

One result of these efforts is that medical malpractice has served as a testing ground for most of the legal changes sought by those (most notably in the Reagan administration)[2] who deplored the way that contemporary tort litigation was operating generally. Understanding the arguments and the experience in the medical context is indispensable, then, for developing sound policy for dealing with all disabling injuries, not simply those caused by medical treatment. Such understanding is especially important now, when some of the protagonists in the medical malpractice debates have become skeptical about whether legal reform of the tort regime will be a sufficient cure for its ailments. More fundamental changes are being proposed—in particular, dismantling the tort/fault system and replacing it with something quite different. Whether and how such radical surgery should be performed are matters I shall take up only after I have recounted the evolution of medical malpractice law over the last two decades.

Sources and Dimensions of the Contemporary Crisis

The most immediate, most obvious source of the perceived crisis in medical malpractice[3] is the increase in total expenditures on medical liability insurance in the United States from about $60 million in 1960 to more than $7 billion in 1988.[4] These national expenditures reached a plateau in 1988, and in many states even dropped in 1989, evoking newspaper headlines that heralded the end of the "malpractice nightmare."[5] But doctors understandably feared that the malpractice system was experiencing no more than a remission in its critical condition, already at an expenditure level that was more than a hundred times higher than it had been little more than a quarter-century earlier.

The costs of legal liability are a function of two variables: the frequency of initiating successful claims and the amount ("severity") of damages collected in successful claims. Both the frequency and the severity of medical malpractice claims have soared over the last two decades.

Frequency. The conventional measure of frequency in the medical context is the number of tort claims filed per 100 doctors. This ratio rose from about 1 per 100 doctors around 1960 to an estimated high of 17 per 100 doctors by the mid-eighties before settling back to around 13 per 100 at the end of the eighties.[6] These higher claims rates do not simply represent a host of additional, largely spurious claims that doctors' insurers can successfully fend off. Nearly half of all medical practice claims generate some payment,[7] and this proportion has not dropped as the absolute number of claims has risen. According to even conservative estimates of claims frequency, roughly 1 in 25 doctors in the United States is now successfully sued for malpractice every year.

Severity. It is plausible to surmise that the large number of additional claims are a function of less severe and costly cases entering the tort system. Yet the evidence is again to the contrary. Amounts paid on successful claims rose sharply from the sixties into the eighties, making an even bigger contribution to the increase in premiums. The most eye-catching numbers are those reported by the RAND Civil Justice Project on jury verdicts in malpractice litigation in Chicago and San Francisco. The respective average jury verdicts (in constant 1984 dollars) in the two cities rose from $50,000 and $125,000 in the early sixties, to $600,000 and $450,000 in the early seventies, to $1.2 million in each city in the early eighties.[8] Admittedly, the absolute amounts paid in these two cities as a result of jury verdicts are not representative of settlements nationally, and even in these jurisdictions jury verdicts are often cut back by trial judges and appellate courts.[9] Nationally, however, the average malpractice settlement more than doubled from under $12,000 in 1970 to over $26,000 in 1975, then jumped to $45,000 by 1978, nearly doubled again to $80,000 by 1984, and topped $100,000 by 1986—an aggregate increase far in excess of inflation.[10] Moreover, in states like New York and Florida that had among the highest claims frequency levels, the average settlement on paid claims was well over the national average.[11] And there is, of course, a direct relationship between currently rising jury verdicts and the amounts that will be required to settle cases in the future, and consequently the likelihood of attracting even more patients to file claims in a system that promises them more generous recoveries.

Another disturbing feature of the trend in claims severity is epitomized by the fact that in 1988 and 1989 malpractice litigation produced among the very highest personal injury awards in those years—$52 million from a hospital in Houston, Texas, and $54 million from a hospital in Los Angeles.[12] In the eighties, aggregate liability expenditures were driven up by a relatively small number of extremely high damage awards (which included large sums for pain and suffering or punitive damages), rather than by payments awarded in more typical cases, in which the focus was on tangible financial losses.[13] The effect of this divergence between the median and the far higher mean award is that the premiums charged *ex ante* by insurers to bear the relatively unpredictable risk of a huge award are likely to be considerably higher than the amount eventually necessary to pay for total expenditures calculated after the fact.

Considered by themselves, these figures and trends appear terribly alarming; placed in the context of the overall health care system, they seem much less so. Although malpractice premiums are initially paid by the insured doctors and hospitals, these practice expenditures are incorporated into fees charged to patients, who are in turn typically covered against such charges by health care insurance. At the same time that total malpractice expenditures soared from $60 million to $7 billion, health care expenditures spiraled as well—from around $25 billion (or 5 percent of the GNP) in 1960 to $540 billion (more than 11 percent of the GNP) in 1988.[14] In other words, malpractice insurance as a share of the nation's total health care bill actually rose from just under 0.5 percent to a little over 1.0 percent during that period (though the $5 billion in doctors' malpractice premiums was a much higher proportion of the $105 billion paid to physicians for their services). Indeed, because one of the key items of economic loss in malpractice cases is the medical expense incurred in treating the injury, awards (and consequently claims) have had to rise substantially simply to accommodate the much higher cost of doctors' fees and hospital charges.

In that broader perspective, current malpractice insurance premiums—which in 1988 averaged about $16,000 per doctor (up from $8,000 in 1984), or 6 percent of the average practitioner's gross revenues[15]—might appear affordable, at least as a general matter. This optimistic judgment is subject, however, to three qualifications.

Specialty and location. The costs of malpractice premiums differ sharply, depending on the specialty and the location of the practitioner. For example, while a general practitioner in Arkansas or an allergist in Indiana spends less than $2,000 in annual malpractice premiums, the total malpractice insurance bill for a neurosurgeon in Dade County, Florida, or an obstetrician on Long Island, New York, is approaching $200,000 a year, a differential that is not necessarily matched by a comparable cushion in doctors' revenues.[16] Because these insurance costs are typically fixed, rather than variable according to the level or the quality of individual practice, every doctor who wishes to open an office must pay the premiums or risk facing serious personal exposure to liability.

Revenue lag. Studies of the experience in the seventies show that doctors recover most, if not all, the increased costs of malpractice insurance (now running as high as 25 percent of their gross revenues) by charging higher fees to their patients.[17] However, the time lag that is inevitable in the process of adjusting medical fees to costs has been a special problem given the pattern of change in malpractice premiums. From the early sixties to the early seventies, premiums rose steadily and substantially, then suddenly doubled from $500 million to $1 billion between 1974 and 1976. After leveling off in real terms in the late seventies and early eighties, total premiums skyrocketed again, from $2.5 billion in 1983 to $7 billion in 1988. Physicians forced to absorb such erratic and unpredictable increases in what for many had become a substantial cost of practice took little consolation from macrostatistics that showed malpractice insurance premiums to be a comparatively insignificant component of the nation's total health care bill.[18]

Program constraints. An additional element of the problem emerged in the eighties in the form of a variety of cost-containment programs adopted to stem the growth in the nation's health care budget. One consequence of these programs is that doctors faced with sudden, huge malpractice premium increases (which are often retroactive for a year or more because of delays in the insurance regulatory process) are prevented from unilaterally increasing the fees billed to patients to cover this additional cost of practice by regulations adopted by Medicare, Blue Cross, and other modes of patient insurance. Their frustration at being caught between two bureaucratic regimes helped motivate doctors to adopt vigorous collective action, which in turn prompted state governments to respond with tort reforms. This happened, for example, in New York in 1985, in Massachusetts in 1986, and in Florida in 1987.

It would be a mistake, however, to assume that these financial trends are the only important source of the current crisis atmosphere. In fact, for most physicians malpractice premiums are still only a minor component of their expenses, and an even smaller fraction of their gross revenues. Even though the startling percentage increase in malpractice costs has been disturbing, the absolute dollar amounts have been smaller than the increases in other office expenses (except for doctors practicing in the highest-risk specialties and locations).[19] In reviewing the eighties, the National Academy of Science's Institute of Medicine found that doctors, on average—including surgeons and obstetricians—had preserved their real net income position by the end of the premium spiral.[20]

As a further basis of comparison, consider the statistics for workplace injuries. Workers' compensation premiums rose from $2 billion in 1960 to over $34 billion in 1986, including a huge $9 billion jump from 1984.[21] Over the last decade the business community has expressed serious concern about these trends, and many state legislatures have been moved to reform their workers' compensation system. But little sense of crisis emerged about the basic structure of the workers' compensation program. Most of the debates took place at a fairly low level of political visibility; equally important, most of the legislative packages contained measures that also addressed special concerns of injured workers. This is in stark contrast to the atmosphere and the tone of debates about medical malpractice in both the mid-seventies and the mid-eighties.

One major difference is that a workers' compensation claim is made on a no-fault basis against an employer—typically a large corporate firm—while the vast majority of malpractice claims are filed against individual doctors and others who are charged with personal negligence.[22] From the doctor's point of view, such a claim arises out of a relationship in which he or she was trying to care for the patient, something happened to go wrong, and the patient decided to blame the doctor for the unfortunate event that was simply a risk endemic to modern medical treatment. Even an innocent doctor is forced to spend considerable time and emotion in defending his or her judgment in the unfamiliar formal surroundings of a courtroom dominated by lawyers, in front of what the doctor perceives to be a lay jury that will be naturally sympathetic to the plight of the injured patient and inclined, if at all possible, to reach into the deep pocket of the doctor's insurer to provide relief to the victim. Even if hindsight suggests that a mistake was made in the treatment provided, the morality play of the tort/fault system reacts to what was in most cases the momentary lapse of a doctor acting under the pressure of a busy practice—occasionally in a life-threatening emergency—by legally condemning the professional character and reputation of the unlucky doctor whose mistake happened to cause a serious injury to a patient who was prepared to sue him.

Not surprisingly, then, physicians who are sued feel deeply resentful about the way they are treated by the legal system. They sense that their relations with patients must be less trusting and more guarded, and they experience greater stress, even demoralization in their professional career.[23] To physicians generally, the looming presence of a tort regime in which lawyers and juries in the courtroom purport to second-guess the judgments of doctors in their offices or hospitals, constitutes an offense to the medical profession's sense of its own independence, status, and self-respect. The tort system may well be a lightning rod for broader discontent felt by many doctors about a world in which government bureaucrats and corporate employers wield increasingly more authority over medical decisions.[24] As the dean of the Yale School of Medicine put it:

> The quality of medical care today is threatened by the pervasive, unwelcome, crushing embrace of the law. Every participant in the health care system . . . is beset by an onslaught of new laws and regulations . . . Worst of all, because it is the most personal, physicians are forced to live with the spectre of malpractice litigation constantly in their mind's eye. This legal assault has occurred so swiftly and has been implemented so harshly that it has begun to erase some of the very attractions long associated with pursuing a medical career—autonomy, independence, approbation, inquiry.[25]

In sum, it is this peculiar combination of financial cost and psychological stress that has generated the passionate resentment that so many doctors feel toward the malpractice regime.[26] Physicians are not the only ones with a vital stake in malpractice law, however. Even considering the burden of tort litigation alone, it is regularly observed that the broader community must pay for unnecessary modes of "defensive medicine" that cost two to three times the amount paid by doctors and hospitals for malpractice premiums.[27] Equally if not more important are the legitimate concerns of patients, the people who eventually become plaintiffs in the tort system. Some of these patients seek compensation for losses suffered on account of medical negligence in the past, others need the protection of tort incentives trained on doctors to practice more careful medicine in the future. The real issue, then, is not whether doctors are upset about malpractice suits and premiums—we know they are—but whether the present tort system, a revised tort system, or an alternative liability system can actually produce sufficient savings in patient losses, in patient anguish and suffering, and even in patient lives to warrant the substantial direct and indirect expenditures that American law now imposes on American health care. This crucial question is the major theme of this book.

The Interplay of Medical, Legal, and Insurance Institutions

Changes in liability premiums alone are only a barometer of innumerable actions taking place in one or more of the key spheres that operate in the malpractice universe: the health care system, in which medical injuries occur; the legal system, which transforms patient injuries into tort claims and payments; and the insurance system, which translates legal expenditures into liability premiums. If it is true that something disturbing has been happening to malpractice premiums—their sudden lurching, if not their absolute increase in size—then in order to respond intelligently to the problem, it is important to have a clear idea of what precisely are the trouble spots within these overlapping spheres.

Liability Insurance and Tort Litigation

Many observers consider the insurance industry, the immediate source of premium increases, to be the major culprit. Patient attorneys and consumer advocates, in particular, are wont to blame insurer ineptitude, even insurer exploitation, for the current ills of medical malpractice—indeed, for undesirable trends in tort litigation and liability insurance generally. That analysis, if true, would make the quest for changes in tort law, rather than in insurance practices, misguided as well as retrograde. As Gerry Spence, one of the country's most prominent and colorful personal injury lawyers, lamented in his 1987 testimony against tort reform in Florida, "The insurance industry in this country has a gun to the head of doctors and the doctors, in turn, have a gun to the head of legislatures." [28]

Several deficiencies are commonly attributed to the liability insurance system, one of which appears in the pattern of premium increases depicted in the previous section. Recall that malpractice premiums crept up slowly but steadily for fifteen years, before suddenly doubling from 1974 through 1976; then they plateaued in real terms for the next half-dozen years before doubling again in the mideighties; they have now paused once again, even retreated. It seems implausible that anything happening in tort litigation during the same period could match that extremely erratic pattern of premium hikes.

The charitable interpretation of this development is that premiums are subject to a natural cycle that is endemic to the insurance system. [29] Lines of insurance such as medical malpractice have a "long tail," that is, an interval of perhaps ten years or more between the period for which coverage is purchased and premiums paid and the time at which all the tort claims for that year are eventually settled. In the interim the carrier is able to invest and earn a sizable return on the funds initially collected as premiums. As a result, an apparent "loss" experienced by the insurer in its underwriting account (the account that simply matches premiums received and expenditures made on claims) will be balanced by gains in the investment account, with the difference used to pay for the carrier's general cost of doing business and earning a target profit rate. Given these features of long-tail casualty insurance, a standard diagnosis of what happened in the eighties is that premiums were artificially low at the beginning of the decade because interest rates (and consequently investment earnings) were so high; but when interest rates dropped in the mid-eighties, premiums had to increase sharply to make up the difference on the insurers' balance sheets.

To the extent the foregoing account is valid, there is of course little that should or even can be done to the tort system to smooth over uncomfortable lurches in the premium charges borne by the insured. Yet I believe that although the insurance cycle may be part of this story, it fails to explain the huge swings that occurred in malpractice premiums in the eighties.

It is a mistake to focus on changes in *nominal* interest rates. Although it is true that the higher these rates are, the greater the carriers' investment earnings are, the major component of the high interest rates is a premium designed to offset the inflation expected to occur during the life of the investment. However, inflation equally affects the projected awards that insurers will have to pay out for tort victims' medical costs and lost earnings. So upward or downward inflation-driven trends in insurer interest earnings are largely matched by the same trends in underwriting expenditures. Only changes in net *real* interest rates can cause the difference in the insurance premium cycle described above. But even though real interest rates moderated somewhat in the mid-eighties, one cannot focus on that factor in isolation. Insurers are not limited to investing in interest-bearing assets: they can and do invest in equity stocks, for example. And although interest rates dropped in the mid-eighties, the phenomenon was associated with (indeed, helped to produce) a steadily rising stock market, which served to sustain the insurers' overall yield on their investment portfolios.

If the insurance cycle theory cannot explain the magnitude of the premium increases experienced by doctors and others in the eighties, let us consider an alternative hypothesis—that carriers have been exploiting their allegedly quasi-monopoly power to charge exorbitant prices for their essential service.

This argument can be stated quite simply. Medical malpractice insurance is a comparatively concentrated industry. Although through-out the country there are a large number of carriers, none of which dominates the industry (Saint Paul's, the largest, has only 20 percent of the national market), malpractice insurance is actually bought and sold in more segmented state or regional markets, in each of which only a few carriers operate. At the same time, on the other side of the relationship are doctors who must practice medicine in order to live and who must have liability insurance in order to practice (because of the requirements of either state law, hospital regulation, or simple fi-nancial self-preservation). In this context, it would seem easy for a small group of insurers offering this indispensable product to collude in charging inflated prices in order to earn excessive profits. To the extent this alternative explanation for soaring premiums is valid, the remedy can hardly be found in diluting the tort rights of patients. A more appropriate measure would be better enforcement of antitrust protections for doctors, the purchasers of malpractice insurance, whether by lodging an antitrust suit against the insurance industry or by repealing the McCarran-Ferguson exemption of certain insurance rate-making practices from antitrust scrutiny.[30]

In an industry like casualty insurance, in which revenues and costs are heavily dependent on projections of future trends, it is always difficult to determine with certainty whether carriers are earning above-market returns that warrant suspicion of anticompetitive be-havior. Extensive investigation and analysis of the crisis of the eighties, however, indicates that insurer monopoly is an unlikely cul-prit in the premium explosion, for the following reasons.

Comparative premiums. The increases in malpractice premiums in the eighties were paralleled by comparable hikes in product, environ-mental, governmental, and other modes of casualty insurance. Yet documented findings of very low levels of industry concentration in these nonmalpractice lines mean there is little potential monopoly power over insurance prices in these sectors.[31]

Competition. Even in the medical malpractice realm, the observed level of insurer concentration is only a static phenomenon. Nationally there are a large number of carriers; moreover, because relatively little start-up cost is required to enter the malpractice line in any one state, firms regularly enter and leave these markets.[32] As a result, if premi-ums were raised to unwarranted levels by the incumbent insurers in any region, other carriers would likely appear to compete for that business with lower prices at which reasonable profits could still be made.

Self-insurers. The monopoly-exploitation thesis is undermined by a phenomenon peculiar to the malpractice area. Unlike the situation in the seventies in which malpractice coverage was provided largely by for-profit commercial carriers, by the eighties a sizable share of the market was held by not-for-profit carriers owned and operated by the doctors and hospitals themselves. By one count more than 40 such "bedpan mutuals" were operating in 33 states, covering half the physicians in the country; such "captive" insurers are an even more prominent feature of the hospital liability insurance field.[33] So even if the incumbent malpractice carrier in a particular area enjoys some market leverage in the short run—before competitors appear to lure away some of the carrier's customers—why would a bedpan mutual use that market power to charge excessive prices to the very parties who own and control it?

Empirical evidence. In any event, it is unnecessary to rely solely on analytic refutations of the plausibility of the monopoly theory, because in-depth empirical investigations have been carried out under government auspices in Florida and New York, two of the highest-premium states.[34] Using different methodologies, each of the studies concluded that, viewed over the longer run, major premium hikes in the eighties were warranted by the trends in tort claim frequency and severity that had occurred in the previous couple of decades. Stating the proposition from the other point of view, casualty insurers have not earned a higher rate of return than carriers in other insurance lines that did not experience the same kinds of premium hikes; moreover, insurer returns are in line with the earnings of American business generally.[35]

Tort Litigation and Medical Care

Just as it should, then, the malpractice insurance system has been absorbing and passing on the steadily rising costs of more numerous tort claims and higher awards for each successful claim. To say this is not to deny the dislocation created by the extremely erratic pattern through which insurers and their actuaries incorporate higher tort costs in the malpractice premiums they charge. But in the longer run it would be a mistake for policymakers to assume that they can solve the problem of higher premiums with measures designed only to prevent excess profits in a supposedly noncompetitive insurance industry.

Doctors, in turn, have their own favorite culprit: the American tort system. Their familiar refrain, echoed by many pundits and politicians, is that tort costs have soared because patient attorneys seeking hefty contingent fees are filing far too many spurious allegations of medical negligence, and because unsophisticated juries, moved by the plight of often seriously disabled plaintiffs, too often give in to the temptation to use the doctor's insurer to award huge damage sums as redress for the patient's needs, irrespective of whether there is any tangible evidence of fault on the part of the doctor.

This indictment of the tort system, however ingrained the list of its vices may be in the popular mind, is based largely on myth rather than fact. Two major studies of medical malpractice claims have documented rates of patient injury caused by negligent treatment that are far in excess of tort claims made by the patients, let alone claims eventually paid.

Each of these studies used essentially the same methodology, a careful review of the medical records of hospitalized patients (who make up the vast majority of patients with any kind of significant injury). The first study, done in California in the mid-seventies,[36] examined the records of roughly 20,000 patients. It was discovered that 1 in 22 of these patients suffered a disabling iatrogenic (treatment-generated) injury from hospitalization; of these injuries, 1 in 6 was caused by careless treatment as judged by the reviewing doctors. When these injury estimates were compared with another data set of closed malpractice claims reported to the National Association of Insurance Commissioners (NAIC), rough calculations indicated that only 1 tort claim was actually filed for 10 such events, and only 1 in 25 was actually paid.[37]

The California study was replicated in New York State in the late eighties by my colleagues and me in the Harvard Medical Practice Study Group.[38] We reviewed more than 31,000 hospitalizations in New York in 1984, a carefully stratified sample of patients and hospitals that permitted extrapolation of our findings to the population at large. Our results showed a somewhat lower rate of patient injuries than in California (roughly 1 in 27 hospitalizations) but a much higher proportion of injuries due to negligence (slightly more than 1 in 4) and a bottom line estimate that 1 negligent adverse event (1 "tort") occurred for every 100 patients hospitalized. Extrapolating our New York population estimates to the nation as a whole implies that every year there are more than 150,000 fatalities and 30,000 serious disabilities precipitated by medical treatment in this country.

But when a comprehensive effort was made to locate every tort suit arising out of medical treatment in New York in 1984, we concluded that for every 8 potentially valid claims, only 1 claim was actually filed; of the claims filed, we estimated that no more than 1 in 2 would eventually result in money paid to the plaintiff. Of course, much of that shortfall is due to the fact that our group's (and California's) definition of adverse event was deliberately broad: a prolongation of the hospital stay by at least one day. Our figures included, then, a large number of moderately disabling injuries, as well as injuries to people who suffered little in the way of compensable losses. However, even when we narrowed our focus to the more serious and "valuable" tort claims—iatrogenic injuries to patients under seventy that produced disabilities (including death) lasting six months or more—we still found that for every 3 such events there was only 1 tort payment. And this situation exists in the context of the malpractice insurance regime in the state of New York, under which, after the surge of the mid-eighties, doctors pay among the highest premiums in the entire nation.

The immediate implication of these two systematic and mutually corroborative studies is that it is wrong to charge the tort system with inflating the true incidence of medical negligence. In fact the contrary is true: a large gap obtains between the number of tort events taking place inside hospitals and those that eventually filter into the court system. William Ira Bennett, editor of the Harvard Medical School Health Letter, recently observed that

> [t]here are, for the doctor, two kinds of malpractice claims to be feared: the valid and the false. The valid claim is a public, painful and expensive declaration of failure or bad faith. The false claim may be equally public, painful, expensive to defend, and may or may not lead to vindication. Less discussed, no doubt less feared, *and certainly most common,* is a third possibility: lack of any claim at all when malpractice has in fact occurred.[39]

Indeed, the extent of this litigation gap makes it easier to understand the malpractice litigation spiral that has occurred over the last two decades. It is difficult for a patient to discern negligence in and to lodge a tort claim about his medical treatment; it is also difficult for a lawyer to prove even a meritorious malpractice case. But what seems to have happened over the last twenty years is that injured patients, especially in urbanized areas,[40] have become much more willing to sue their doctors when they perceive that something has gone wrong; in addition, the personal injury bar has displayed a much stronger technical capacity for documenting such claims in court.

Nor should we assume that these trends are peculiar to doctor-patient or lawyer-patient relationships in the United States. Although they started from much lower absolute levels, both Canada and the United Kingdom experienced the same steep increases in malpractice claims, payments, and premiums in the seventies and the eighties. Unlike the United States, however, both countries have comprehensive medical insurance, and neither uses juries or contingent fees in tort cases (in fact in both countries legal fees for unsuccessful claims are assessed against the patient).[41]

It would be a mistake for policy makers to leap from these empirical findings to the confident judgment that a culprit has been found: the doctors. As I discuss in detail below, the reason so many "torts" occur in the hospital is that modern medical treatment is an inherently risky enterprise.[42] Recall that for every negligent medical injury there are three non-negligent patient injuries. Most of these failures consist simply in momentary mishaps caused by inadvertent inattention, but when doctors make these all-too-human mistakes, the consequences can be severe and irreversible, unlike the mistakes made by lawyers or law professors. Even within the realm of medicine the rates of suits and premiums are much higher among obstetricians than among pediatricians, higher among surgeons than among internists. The explanation is not that surgeons or obstetricians are characteristically more careless or accident-prone, but rather that the types of conditions these specialists must treat and the kinds of procedures they must use entail a level of risk that is significantly above what their medical counterparts normally experience.

It is important also to recognize the significant imperfections in the tort and liability insurance systems. In New York State, for example, when we attempted to match the tort claims we found recorded in the insurers' files against the treatments we appraised in the hospital records, we discovered that a substantial proportion of the claims actually filed were for cases in which we had concluded on the basis of hospital records that no medical injury at all had occurred, much less one caused by medical negligence. (This finding, by the way, enlarged even further the gap between the total of torts that occurred in the hospital and claims that were filed for *those* torts.) Because our sample of claims arising from 1984 hospitalizations is still far from fully disposed of, we are unable to say whether the tort litigation/settlement process will successfully winnow out the spurious from the valid claims. But a recent study of a large sample of anesthesia claims that were closed in the last two decades found considerable imprecision in the tort system.[43] While only a fairly small percentage (10 percent) of the claims appraised as negligent were not paid, a larger percentage (42 percent) of the cases that were paid were judged not to be the result of negligence (though the amounts actually paid by the insurer to settle these non-negligent disabilities appear to have been heavily discounted because the patient's case was weak on the liability side). The tort system, then, just like the medical system, inevitably falls somewhat short of the ideal standards that it sets for itself.

Finally, although I defended the insurance industry earlier against the charge of extracting excessive premiums and profits, it is true that the industry's price adjustments have taken an extremely erratic course. Even if malpractice premiums were roughly at the appropriate level by the end of the eighties, the path they took to get to that point is hardly justifiable. An endemic problem for the insurance industry is the unpredictable expansion and contraction of capital available for its use, with corresponding sharp swings in price from periods of surplus to periods of shortage. In addition, liability insurance is a peculiar product in that the bulk of its costs of production—the payments made on tort claims—will be incurred long after the product is priced and sold. Actuaries must try to project from past trends what will likely be the incidence and costs of future claims. The last decade has thoroughly demonstrated how imperfect is "actuarial science." However, the consequence of such insurer misjudgments about tort trends—first an underreaction, then an overreaction—is especially troublesome for a doctor who must rely on his professional income to support himself and his family, but who, in the short run at least, is deprived of fully effective insurance protection against swings in the tort system when he is charged steep hikes in premiums for which he cannot immediately adjust his medical fees. (And recall that this burden is imposed equally on doctors who have *not* been the target of a meritorious tort suit.)

To a considerable extent, these imperfections in liability insurance have been aggravated by uncertainties in contemporary tort law, especially on the damages side.[44] Both in medical malpractice and tort litigation generally, insurers have rightfully been concerned about wild card factors such as pain and suffering and punitive damages. Because these items are not tied to tangible and reasonably predictable lost earnings or treatment costs, they are intrinsically more susceptible to swings in the popular (and consequently a jury's) mood. Whether it is possible to rationalize these elements of damages while preserving whatever legitimate value they have in malpractice law is a challenge I will have to confront later.

For the moment, however, let us consider some sobering implications from the empirical material sketched in this chapter. Reflecting on the history of the last two decades, and considering this history in tandem with the malpractice gap disclosed in the New York and California studies, suggests that it is a gamble to assume that our troubles are behind us.[45] A safer bet is that we are now in the midst of a period of uneasy calm and are likely to face yet a third malpractice crisis in the nineties. It behooves us, then, to have a sounder legal structure in place before the next storm hits. Unfortunately, there are no obvious culprits nor easy measures to call on for that effort. Medical care is a hazardous enterprise, the injuries inflicted on patients are real and painful, and careful analysis and design is required before we tackle the network of health, legal, and insurance institutions that have evolved to address these problems.

2

The Tort/Fault Model:
Malpractice Law in Transition

Alternative Models for Disability Policy

Before embarking on a detailed review of various efforts to reform
medical malpractice law, I shall briefly sketch four basic models from
among which a community might select in designing its policy for
disabling injuries, medical or other. These models will then serve as a
framework for analyzing the current malpractice system and the multitude of proposals that have been made for changing it.

Contractual agreement. The first option would have the law itself do
nothing about the problem, or at least not impose mandatory obligations upon the parties. The rationale is that unlike motor vehicle col-
lisions between strangers, for example, medical injuries take place
within a direct contractual relationship between doctor and patient. It
is perfectly feasible in that context for the parties themselves to bar-
gain over how they will allocate the risks of injury from the medical
treatment, though many would feel qualms about the likely substantive outcome of such dealings—the doctor extracting a liability waiver
from the patient as a condition of treatment. The only role for the law
would be to enforce such *consensual* arrangements as and when they
were arrived at. In the medical context, this contract model was emphatically rejected in a series of decisions in the sixties and seventies
but returned to favor, at least theoretically, in the eighties.[1]

Tort liability. The second model allows the community to establish
its ideal allocation of the responsibility for injuries and obligates individual actors to adhere to this norm in their relationships. The standard tort solution, clearly illustrated by medical malpractice law, is to
hold a party (such as the doctor) responsible for all the harms attributable to his *fault* but to assign no responsibility for the victim's injury
in the absence of fault.[2] Once they had decided that this quasi-moral
allocation of the risk of injury was too important to leave to the parties

to devise on their own, lawmakers (in this case, judges) naturally deemed unconscionable and treated as legally invalid any attempt by the parties to use the contract model to secure waiver of such tort rights and obligations.[3]

Administrative no-fault compensation. An alternative model for disability policy, which emerged first in the workplace context, replaces the tort/fault regime with an administrative program of compensation paid on a no-fault basis.[4] This scheme would still constitute a form of legal liability for medical injuries, because the health care provider—doctor, clinic, health maintenance organization (HMO), or hospital—would be financially responsible for all injuries suffered by the patient as a result of its medical treatment, whether or not the provider was at fault and regardless of any fault on the part of the victim. But such an administrative compensation scheme would provide redress for only a defined proportion of the financial injuries suffered, leaving the patient to absorb the remainder, in particular, the pain and suffering and loss of enjoyment of life from the injury. Moreover, this obligation of the health care system would extend only to patient injuries *caused* by medical treatment—adverse consequences "arising out of and in the course of" medical treatment, to borrow the workers' compensation phrase—and not to disabilities attributable to the patient's original unhealthy condition and the treatment that the condition required.

Social insurance. Even though the concept of "cause" is more expansive and easier to apply than the concept of "fault," the no-fault model makes compensation available only for a limited category of injuries. In addition, the problem of establishing the boundary line of causation is often particularly troublesome in the medical context. In light of these problems, it is easy to see the appeal of a final model for disability policy, social insurance, which conditions entitlement to benefits not on the cause of the injury but rather on the kind of *loss* the injury inflicted—temporary or permanent, partial or total, disability. From the point of view of the injured victim, compensation provided by social insurance is broadest in reach and requires the fewest arbitrary distinctions among needy victims whose disabilities are the same whether their injuries were suffered in the hospital, at work, or elsewhere. The disadvantage of the social insurance model, however, is that it relieves the individual doctor or hospital of any special responsibility for paying for injuries produced by their own course of treatment.

Changing Medical Malpractice Law

The Common Law

The four basic models for disability policy permit us to understand and evaluate the developments and proposals of the last two decades for handling medical injuries. The four alternative bases for compensation—consent, fault, cause, and loss—correspond to the institutions of contract, tort, no-fault, and social insurance, respectively.

Some observers might object to the assertion that contemporary tort law can aptly be characterized in terms of fault. They would retort that in fact the modern history of tort law is characterized by the *erosion* of the fault principle—perhaps in the form of the gradual trend toward negligence without fault epitomized by the treatment of railroad workers' injuries under the Federal Employers' Liability Act (FELA),[5] perhaps in the guise of the dramatic adoption in the mid-sixties of strict liability for hazardous products. Yet, even in these contexts tort law retains strong overtones of moral responsibility. The nub of the legal inquiry is whether some deficiency or fault in the product or operation gave rise to the mishap, a preoccupation that is almost entirely absent in no-fault workers' compensation. In any event, however valid the claim that fault is disappearing as a feature of tort law generally, in the medical context tort doctrine continues to place a strong premium on a finding of personal blameworthiness on the part of a doctor before affixing liability for a particular injury.

Medical custom. The most important manifestation of the fault requirement in malpractice cases is the well-entrenched principle that the legal standard of care required of doctors is the standard of practice established by their own profession.[6] As a rule, a plaintiff can succeed in a malpractice action only if expert testimony supports a finding that the defendant doctor failed to follow the customary or accepted practice then prevailing in the relevant specialty or discipline. Absent such evidence and such a finding, juries are not legally entitled to impose on the doctor the stigma of a negligence verdict merely on the basis of their after-the-fact second-guessing of the "reasonableness" of the medical practice followed by the doctor.

Several arguments have been offered to support the predominance of custom in medical malpractice cases. Perhaps the most obvious is the inability of a lay jury to understand the complex medical problems that doctors must deal with and to evaluate the feasibility and desirability of alternative forms of treatment.[7] Yet while this argument appears applicable to a host of technical problems in modern tort litigation, such as the best way to design a safe car or airplane, in other tort contexts juries, instructed by expert testimony, are authorized to decide whether or not the prevailing industry practice is negligent. Courts realize that business practice is influenced not only by expertise, but also by financial self-interest in a setting in which the firm must bear the cost of safety precautions and users of its products bear the risk of injuries. Recognizing that even "an entire calling" may have lagged unduly in the adoption of safe practices, the standard tort doctrine is that custom is relevant but not decisive in a negligence action.[8]

The justification for the exceptional treatment that tort law reserves for doctors must consist, then, not simply in the technical difficulty of presenting and understanding medical issues in the courtroom, but also in the tacit assumption that the medical profession can generally be trusted to adopt on its own the appropriate level of care for its patients. Doctors do not, continues this argument, need additional legal incentives to comply with their ethical obligation to provide every sensible precaution in the course of medical treatment, an objective that is usually in the doctor's economic interest as well.

Whatever its rationale, and however persuasive the arguments for it may be, this central doctrine of malpractice law has remained largely intact in spite of the many changes that have taken place in the last quarter-century. In the early seventies there was a brief flirtation with the position that the usual standard employed in negligence law—"business custom"—should be applied to medical practice as well. In its widely known decision in the case of *Helling v. Carey*,[9] the Supreme Court of Washington found that a doctor who had acted in accordance with what the court understood to be standard ophthalmological practice (not to give routine pressure tests for patients under forty) had nonetheless failed to display reasonable prudence because the test was apparently simple, harmless, and relatively inexpensive, and it would have detected the patient's glaucoma condition early enough to avoid his subsequent blindness. Later analysis of *Helling* demonstrated that the decision itself is a textbook illustration of the dangers of a court's taking upon itself the responsibility for deciding which medical practices are reasonable and which are not. As it turned out, the test in question was neither entirely harmless nor reliable;[10] in any event, it was *not* the uniform practice of all Washington ophthalmologists to refrain from routine pressure testing of their younger patients.[11] Be that as it may, other state courts have not followed Washington's lead in authorizing judicial scrutiny of accepted medical practice.

In spite of its long-standing primacy, the central doctrine of the medical standard of care spawned a number of corollaries that placed severe obstacles in the way of the patient's ability to mount viable malpractice claims even when the profession's own standard of treatment had been violated by the doctor in question. These legal hurdles were significantly lowered in the sixties and the early seventies by a number of judicial revisions to the common law.

Perhaps the most prominent hurdle was the "locality rule," which defined the relevant group whose standard of practice would govern as the *local* medical community in which the defendant doctor practiced. In principle this rule had a plausible basis. Assuming that there were significant differences between the methods used and the competence displayed in isolated rural communities on the one hand and sophisticated urban teaching hospitals on the other, a patient electing to be treated by a local rural doctor should not be entitled to hold that doctor to the highest standard of care practiced in an urban setting, any more than a patient who consulted a chiropractor for a back condition should expect to receive from the chiropractor the methods and skills of an orthopedic specialist.

The practical problem in applying the locality rule was that the expert testimony necessary for the plaintiff's case would have to come from a doctor familiar with the local standards, yet it was terribly difficult to find a local doctor who would testify against his colleagues and friends from the same community.[12] Recognizing these evidentiary problems and reasoning that developments in medical education, communication, and transportation had eroded much of the basis for significant variations in standards of treatment, most state courts either relaxed the locality rule (by permitting reference to "similar" communities or to the state as a whole) or dispensed with the rule entirely, especially for specialties that required practitioners to pass national board examinations. If particular tangible limits on local facilities or capacities existed, such as the absence of CAT scan equipment, evidence of such deficiencies could be offered by the defendant doctor if it was pertinent to his case.[13] But in spite of such judicial whittling at the edges of medical custom, it is still the basic principle that medical standards are set and judged not by juries but by the medical discipline to which the defendant belongs.[14]

Res ipsa loquitur. Courts were sensitive to the more general and frequently expressed concern that a medical "conspiracy of silence" prevented many deserving plaintiffs from establishing meritorious malpractice claims. Even if an available expert witness were willing to testify as to the appropriate general standard of care that the defendant doctor should have complied with, neither the patient nor his expert would be in a position to know precisely what had occurred in the course of the treatment; indeed, the patient might have been under anesthesia during the operation. Moreover, even if they could, the various doctors, nurses, and other personnel who had observed the treatment would not likely disclose voluntarily what had transpired.[15]

The device used increasingly by courts to finesse this obstacle was the doctrine of *res ipsa loquitur* (loosely translated, "the facts speak for themselves"). Originally the doctrine was simply a commonsense inference from circumstantial evidence: if something happened that would normally be attributable to an individual's carelessness—such as a barrel's falling out of a warehouse and hitting a pedestrian on the sidewalk below—it was deemed fair to conclude that the defendant in control of the particular situation at issue had been negligent. Once this notion was expressed and invoked repeatedly in Latin, it assumed sufficient legal veneer for courts to presume automatically that a *res ipsa* case should survive a motion for dismissal and reach the jury, perhaps even with a rebuttable presumption of negligence requiring an explanation from the defendant, and occasionally even shifting the ultimate burden of proof to the defendant.

Traditionally *res ipsa* had not been considered an appropriate doctrine to invoke in medical malpractice litigation. The same esoteric characteristics that produced the standard of medical custom implied that there was no commonsense basis on which a jury could infer negligence merely from the adverse event. However, *res ipsa* could be employed in cases in which the circumstances seemed more amenable to a lay judgment than to a purely professional one: sponges left in the patient after an operation, a fall from a bed, table, or wheelchair, injuries or burns to healthy, nontreated parts of the patient's body, and so on. Once courts became accustomed to using *res ipsa* in this subset of malpractice claims, the ground was cleared for a significant extension of the principle by the California Supreme Court. That court permitted use of *res ipsa* if an expert witness testified that the injury in question, even if it involved complex medical issues (brain damage during an operation under an anesthetic, for example), would not likely have occurred without negligence on the part of the physician.[16]

On the one hand, these developments did much to relieve plaintiffs of their difficulties in proving violations of the professional standard of care. On the other, the significant relaxation of the kinds of specific evidence needed to get a case to the jury also raised the specter that juries would be prone to find legal negligence on the mere basis that an exceptional but unfortunate incident had occurred. *Res ipsa* gave sympathetic juries a way to avoid requiring tangible proof that the doctor was to blame, if such "negligence without fault" was the only way of giving the disabled patient access to the deep pocket of the doctor's insurer to satisfy the patient's need for financial help.[17]

Informed consent. A third significant development in substantive malpractice doctrine is the notion of informed consent. The roots of this doctrine are in the tort of battery; its principle is that anyone (including a doctor) is prohibited from inflicting a harmful or offensive contact on another individual without the latter's consent. The value underlying the doctrine—one should have the right to determine whether and how his or her body will be treated—is not satisfied if the touched individual misunderstands the circumstances of the contact. So the general law of battery holds that misrepresentations about the nature and quality of the contact will vitiate the validity of an apparent consent. In the medical context the law has gone even further,[18] imposing on doctors a positive obligation to disclose all the relevant risks and benefits of the proposed treatment so that patients can make fully informed, and therefore truly free, choices about their medical care.

This obligation is now considered to be part of the law of medical negligence rather than battery. In fact, a doctor's failure to disclose the risks of *not* undergoing the treatment—of not being touched—now also exposes the doctor to a tort suit for a lack of informed *refusal*.[19] But the crucial practical implication of this legal development is that even if the actual care of the patient was entirely reasonable, a doctor is still exposed to a tort action if something went wrong, an injury occurred, and the patient is able to show insufficient disclosure of the risks of the treatment. The justification for liability is that had the patient received this information there would have been no patient consent; with no consent there would have been no medical treatment, and without the treatment there would have been no disabling injury, whether or not the injury was purely accidental.[20]

The advent of the legal requirement that doctors obtain informed consent from patients did not in and of itself mark a major change in the doctor-patient relationship. The ethical canons of the medical profession already imposed on physicians the duty to disclose the important features of proposed treatment plans. However, when the law reinforced this ethical obligation by permitting a tort action for any and all adverse consequences of uninformed treatment, a major tactical difference occurred in the relationship. What would be crucial was the standard of disclosure to which tort law would subject doctors.

The initial reaction of the state courts was simply to require individual doctors to meet the normal standard of professional practice regarding the kinds and probabilities of risks that are significant enough for discussion with the patient, or the kind of situation in which disclosure need not be made because the patient might become unduly alarmed, perhaps even refuse treatment that seemed medically necessary. This position regarding disclosure fit quite comfortably with the general judicial inclination to defer to medical expertise in appraising the behavior of individual doctors. It was also fair to the doctors, for it required no more than that they comply with the customary behavior of their colleagues, a pattern that they should and could be familiar with.

A notable and controversial change of direction was taken by a number of courts in the early seventies.[21] Instead of asking what the reasonable *doctor* believed should sensibly be disclosed, these jurisdictions substituted the norm of what the reasonable *patient* believed would be important to learn. Given this new conception, the jury would naturally be allowed to decide what risks patients—people like themselves—would want to know about before accepting a doctor's proposed treatment. In principle, the new standard seemed to accord better with the policies of patient autonomy and self-determination that this branch of tort law was supposed to serve.[22] But since claims of uninformed consent were lodged almost invariably in the context of treatment that had ended in a serious disabling injury, the new doctrinal development simply added to the odds that the patient's lawyer would be able to get a claim through to a jury presumably anxious to do something for the unfortunate patient if it legally could.

These were the important changes in substantive malpractice law occurring in the seventies. At the same time, significant alterations were made in other parts of the law to make it easier for injured patients to launch claims that the new legal standards had been violated. Many courts interpreted their statutes of limitation as not running against the patient during the period when a negligently inflicted harm had not been and could not reasonably have been discovered by the patient. This development was important because of the late manifestation of many adverse consequences of medical care and the inability of many patients to learn what had actually transpired during their treatment. Expansive concepts of tort damages were deployed in so-called wrongful life cases in which, following a botched sterilization procedure, patients unexpectedly conceived and gave birth to children, sometimes healthy, sometimes not. Moreover, hospitals became more inviting targets for malpractice suits because of erosion of the principles of governmental and charitable immunity and the development of direct legal responsibility on the part of the hospital for the quality of care in the institution.[23] As a consequence, injured patients could find an institution with assets and insurance substantial enough to satisfy readily any judgments plaintiffs won as a result of the carelessness of individual providers.

However numerous and significant these changes in specific features of medical liability doctrine may have been, the core of the legal regime remained the same. The fundamental predicate for tort recovery by the injured patient was proof of faulty treatment by the physician or other health care provider—some deviation by the provider from the standard of care that his peers considered appropriate in the situation under review.

In the eyes of a great many doctors, though, changes in the law in action were far more influential in malpractice litigation than were any of the changes in the law on the books. Although formal doctrine makes professional medical practice legally decisive and requires expert testimony about deviations from the standard, it is ultimately the black box of the lay jury that produces the governing decisions. Popular lore has it that Americans now have a far greater propensity to sue when they are injured, that judges are ready to accept newfangled legal theories in support of these claims, and that juries are eager to find in favor of injured victims and award them large sums of money—all in the service of what contemporary tort theorists applaud as spreading the costs of injuries across the broader community.[24] Yet however plausible that account may be with respect to tort litigation against business enterprises (as in the area of products liability litigation), it seems to me that this pattern does not describe what has been happening in medical malpractice. Even now injured patients recover in less than half of their tort claims, and much less so in cases tried to a jury verdict.[25] Lawyers to whom I have spoken on both sides of the malpractice fence do not believe that juries systematically bend over backward to uphold patient claims against individual doctors, irrespective of the presence or absence of actual lack of care (as juries seem to do, for example, in suits brought by injured workers against railroads under the Federal Employers' Liability Act).[26]

It appears that the dramatic rise in malpractice claims, even in a system that has remained fault-based, stems from a number of external trends in the medical and legal professions. Empirical research demonstrates that medical practice is highly risky, regularly producing a large number of patient injuries and potential tort claims that never see the light of day. Through medical research and education, explicit standards of appropriate treatment are constantly developed and refined, then communicated to doctors in the field, who are expected to be familiar with and comply with the elevated standards. An increasingly sophisticated personal injury bar stays abreast of the evolving accomplishments of medical care and has become more astute at searching out and documenting deviation from these standards in situations in which a patient has suffered a significant injury. As a result of the conjunction of these and other factors, the tort system now responds to a much higher proportion of the potential caseload that was always available. It may be troubling when a legal regime makes an individual doctor liable for all the injuries of the victim in any case in which there is the slightest doctor fault. But even if our response to this concern is an attempt to revise the system of tort liability, we should begin the undertaking with no illusion that the current fault-based program is sharply different in practice from what it professes to be in principle.

Statutory Reform

For whatever complex of reasons, malpractice claims and premiums rose steadily and substantially during the sixties—reaching $370 million in 1970, or six times what they had been just a decade earlier.[27] Concern in the medical profession about this trend was sufficiently acute to impel the secretary of health, education, and welfare to appoint a commission that sponsored the first serious research and analysis of the problem. The commission's report, issued in early 1973, was decidedly nonalarmist in tone. Interestingly, rather than calling on state legislatures to roll back the doctrinal developments in the common law described above, the commission advocated as its basic principle for law reform that doctors should not be treated significantly differently than other tort defendants.[28]

The ink was still drying on the commission's report when the first big malpractice crisis broke out.[29] In the mid-seventies malpractice claims spiraled, a number of insurers suddenly pulled out of that line of business, and doctors who could obtain insurance found that their premiums had skyrocketed. As a result, physician groups organized in protest, some even taking strike action (in California, for example). The state legislatures responded by enacting substantial changes in tort law specifically for the doctors' benefit. As these legislative changes were assimilated and their constitutionality tested in the late seventies and early eighties, claims and premiums appeared to level off.

However, the problem reemerged in the mid-eighties in even greater proportions. Doctors returned in protest to the state legislatures for additional statutory reform and were again successful in obtaining new legislation. This time the doctors were accompanied by municipalities, by operators of day-care and recreational facilities and of clubs and bars, and by other groups hit with huge liability premium increases. In some states only the doctors were successful in obtaining legal relief for their second malpractice crisis. Often, though, legislatures extended the new reforms to cover the physicians' fellow petitioners for statutory help.[30]

During both periods of crisis the aim of the state legislatures was to contain malpractice premiums, and thereby to relieve the pressure felt by the doctors who had to pay the premiums and the health care system that ultimately had to bear the cost of malpractice litigation. The legislation focused on each of the pressure points of malpractice law: access to the courts, standards of liability, and damages.

Limiting Access to the Courts

One way to affect the volume of malpractice litigation is to alter the rules that influence the original entry of patient claims into the system. By erecting obstacles to litigation, legislatures can lower the likelihood of injured patients' launching legal proceedings, and increase the likelihood of their agreeing to drop "nonmeritorious" claims. Malpractice reform legislation has introduced a variety of barriers, the most common of which are revising judicially fashioned openings in statutory limitation periods, imposing restrictions on plaintiff attorney fees, and creating professional screening panels for malpractice claims.

Statutes of limitation. Under a judge-made doctrine known as the "discovery rule," most state courts began to adopt the interpretation that their statutes of limitation were not "tolled"—that is, did not begin to run—until the victim had discovered or reasonably should have discovered his medical (or other) injuries.[31] This innovation responded to the unfairness of a rule that could strip an injury victim of a tort claim before the victim ever knew that one existed, but it also created a problem for health care providers. A doctor could be faced with a tort action brought a decade or more after the occurrence of the event on which the action was based. During this period evidence may either have disappeared or become stale, and the medical/legal standards for judging the doctor's behavior may have changed substantially in the interim. These factors increased the risk of a doctor's mistakenly being found legally negligent even when no medical fault existed as of the time of the injury. Physician insurers also faced the problem of having to reserve funds to pay for potential claims long after the period of original coverage and premium payments.

To improve the situation, a few states simply repealed the discovery rule and required that all tort claims be launched within a specified period—two years, three years, or more—from the time of the negligent behavior.[32] However, about forty states, recognizing that such an approach would simply recreate the original problem for the patient, developed instead a concept that they embodied in so-called statutes of repose. Like statutes of limitation as they were interpreted before the discovery rule, statutes of repose are tolled at the time of injury; but they run longer than the standard limitation period, perhaps as long as ten years. After the statute of repose has run, all claims are cut off whether or not they have been discovered. State courts have upheld as constitutional almost every medical malpractice statute of repose.[33] In at least one case, however, a court held that such statutes must contain exceptions for minor children.[34] Many of the later statutes contain such a provision, as well as an exception for harms that a doctor has concealed.[35]

Attorney fees. A lawyer's willingness to develop and present a malpractice case is linked to his expectation of payment for his services. Plaintiff attorneys in malpractice cases usually receive a contingent fee: if the plaintiff wins, the lawyer receives a percentage of the award; if the plaintiff loses, the lawyer collects nothing.[36] In effect, the lawyer finances and insures the plaintiff's claims. Strangely, doctors and other tort defendants argue that such contingent fee arrangements promote meritless law suits, thereby increasing the frequency of malpractice claims. In addition, those who oppose contingent fees contend that such arrangements may allow undeserving lawyers to reap windfalls. In order to reduce the number of patient claims against doctors and to prevent lawyers from exploiting clients, physician associations have lobbied for limits on attorney fees.

In response, many jurisdictions have statutorily restricted contingent fee arrangements. Reflecting the reasoning of critics of the current fee system who fear that lawyers may gouge their clients, a half-dozen or so states explicitly empowered judges to review the reasonableness of lawyers' fees.[37] More jurisdictions, however, directly regulate contingent fees, either by imposing a flat percentage ceiling[38] or, more typically, by constructing a sliding scale that allows lawyers to collect a diminishing proportion of the recovery as the size of the award increases.[39] Florida was the only state to adopt the Anglo-Canadian rule of awarding fees to the prevailing party in order to deter nonmeritorious claims and defenses,[40] a law that was recently replaced by a sliding scale based on the timing of the settlement and the size of the award.[41]

Screening panels. Screening panels are typically composed of doctors and lawyers who review a case and evaluate its merit before a claim is filed. Such panels filter access to the legal system by influencing the parties' evaluation of their probability of success in the courts. The assumption is that if the panel finds a claim invalid, the plaintiff will not file suit, whereas if the panel judges the claim to have merit, the defendant will settle. If the dispute were not voluntarily resolved in this manner, the parties would still retain their right to a jury trial, though in a number of jurisdictions the panel's verdict is admissible at trial.[42] Because the screening panel, an early experiment in alternative dispute resolution, was expected to avoid in many cases the expense and trauma of legal proceedings and to reduce the incidence of nonmeritorious suits, many states adopted such a screening mechanism during the first wave of medical malpractice reform in the mid-seventies. However, states relied on screening panels less frequently in the eighties as courts and commentators questioned the mechanics, the effectiveness, and the constitutionality of these boards.[43]

Liability Rules

A second line of defense is to make the tort claims that do get lodged more difficult to win by altering the content of the rules that courts apply in evaluating malpractice cases. The most significant means for doing so is adopting doctrines that define the standards of behavior for doctors and other health care providers and the manner of proving negligent treatment. Interestingly, although tort scholars are often preoccupied by common law rules that define appropriate standards of behavior and liability, these rules were of only peripheral interest to the proponents and authors of statutory reform.

Locality doctrine. About a dozen states attempted to restate the standard of care by reference to local practice.[44] Some states adopted the standard of care prevailing in the "same or similar community,"[45] "neighborhood,"[46] or "state,"[47] while others permitted only experts familiar with local standards to testify about the standard of care.[48] The effect of these statutory revisions was limited, however. State courts have interpreted the revised standards expansively, refusing to limit their inquiry to the standards prevailing in a given locality.[49] The only state law purporting to reinstate the strict locality rule was struck down as unconstitutional.[50]

Res ipsa loquitur. Over a dozen states have laws designed to limit the operation of the doctrine of *res ipsa loquitur*. But a half-dozen of these laws merely require that the plaintiff bear the burden of proof in malpractice cases,[51] a proposition consistent with the normal conception of *res ipsa* as specifying the inference that may be drawn from circumstantial evidence, not altering the burden of proof.[52] Although a few states restrict the doctrine to specific types of injury, the injuries listed constitute the principal uses of *res ipsa*.[53] The only two states that purported to abolish *res ipsa* entirely had their malpractice reform legislation struck down as unconstitutional.[54]

Informed consent. Perhaps because of the recent and controversial character of judicial innovations in the area of informed consent, revision of these standards was the feature of substantive malpractice law most commonly addressed by state legislatures.[55] Many states enacted the reasonable practitioner standard,[56] several legislatures established the patient need standard,[57] and a few gave more explicit directions about the timing and content of the required disclosures.[58] Although most states that considered the issue adopted the physician practice rather than the patient need standard, this trend did not constitute a statutory reversal of judicial consensus. In fact, a majority of state courts have rejected the reasonable patient standard of disclosure established in *Canterbury v. Spence*,[59] requiring only the reasonable practitioner standard of disclosure.[60]

Restrictions on Damages

Last, but certainly not least, state legislatures have devoted a great deal of attention to the principles governing damage assessment. The size and the unpredictability of only a few large tort awards can have a major effect on liability insurance premiums. A standard feature of almost every legislative package for malpractice reform has, consequently, been the revision and restriction of the types and amounts of damages recoverable after the patient has succeeded in getting to court and proving the doctor liable. By limiting the expected size of malpractice damages recoverable, legislatures have hoped to reduce directly the impact of large awards on insurance costs as well as to inhibit the filing of marginally meritorious claims. The states have altered damage laws with three important measures: requiring periodic payments, deducting benefits from collateral sources, and capping total damages, especially damages for pain and suffering.

Periodic payments. The standard tort award is a lump sum that compensates future losses by discounting to its present value the estimated stream of later payments. A problem inherent in such lump sum awards is that they offer no means for revising incorrect damage assessments. If the patient recovers or dies earlier than predicted, the amount paid for subsequent loss-years becomes a windfall for the victim or his heirs.[61] The error might also occur in the opposite direction: the patient might live longer than anticipated or the disability might worsen, making the award insufficient to cover the actual losses. An open-ended periodic payment provision could provide both sides with some protection against such future contingencies.[62] In any event, the principle of periodic payments of large medical malpractice awards had been adopted in eleven states by the end of 1985.[63] Nine additional states adopted the practice in 1986, some of them expanding their existing medical malpractice example to all other tort actions.

Collateral source rule. Tort law traditionally stated that the damages payable by a culpable defendant would not be reduced even if other sources, such as health or disability insurance, compensated the tort victim's losses.[64] The application of this principle did not depend on who had paid for the loss coverage; collateral sources were ignored even when the government or the claimant's employer financed the insurance. Doctors, of course, are well aware of the significance of these collateral sources: a considerable share of the economic losses from medical malpractice are the expenses of additional medical treatment, and most of the population has health insurance. Physicians' organizations contended that tort awards for losses already covered by insurance significantly overcompensate the victim.

About twenty states have responded by revising the collateral source rule for medical malpractice cases. In the mid-seventies, many states merely permitted introduction of evidence about outside insurance.[65] The jury retained discretion as to whether or how to take such insurance into account. More recently, legislatures have mandated that courts deduct collateral insurance payments from the award.[66] The popularity of this collateral source option is reflected in the fact that in 1986 ten states enacted some version of such legislation.[67]

Damage caps. The single most important and controversial issue in tort reform is the legislative creation of ceilings on damages. As a rule, a relatively small number of large awards account for a substantial share of the total amount of money paid in tort claims.[68] In the seventies a number of state legislatures instituted a variety of caps on the permissible amounts of damages. Some states put a ceiling on personal liability for physicians but placed no limits on recoveries from state-established Patient Compensation Funds financed by annual surcharges on health care providers.[69] Other states imposed monetary limitations only on awards for pain and suffering.[70] Still other jurisdictions placed a ceiling on both economic and noneconomic losses,[71] capping both the awards paid personally by the physician and those financed through a Patient Compensation Fund.[72] After the effectiveness and constitutionality of these provisions were tested in the late seventies and early eighties,[73] in 1986 and 1987 thirteen additional states put some cap or other on noneconomic damages, many applying the cap to all tort claims, not simply malpractice.[74] Only a few jurisdictions (including Texas, Kansas, and Washington) contemplate regular adjustment of their ceilings to reflect changes in wage and price levels.[75]

The Impact of Malpractice Legislation

Having summarized the basic thrust of conventional tort reform of malpractice law in the seventies and of tort law generally in the eighties, I shall address the constitutional controversy over whether such reforms exacted too high a price in the legitimate interests of injured patients. But before I do, let us consider whether these reforms did effectively satisfy the concerns of their doctor proponents. In particular, let us see whether the legislative revision of malpractice law actually reduced the frequency and severity of malpractice claims, consequently containing liability premiums as well as the costs of litigation that must be borne by the health care system.

At first blush it appears self-evident that statutory packages composed only of rules restricting plaintiffs' rights and remedies would restrain to some extent malpractice litigation and premiums. The more important questions for policymakers are, how great is this effect? Insignificant, enormous, or somewhere in between? And which of the various proposed measures is responsible for it?

To answer those questions one cannot adopt the approach of the Justice Department's Tort Policy Working Group[76] and simply compare one state (such as California, with comparatively severe restrictions) with another (such as New York, with comparatively modest restrictions), then infer that the recent lower rate of premium increase in the more restrictive state is due to differences in state laws. Legislation is only one of the ingredients shaping tort litigation and insurance rate making. Malpractice doctrines interact in complicated ways with changes in medicine, legal practice, the general economy, and social and cultural values and relationships. These nondoctrinal factors exert considerable influence on the likelihood that patients will be injured in treatment, that they will then sue their doctor, that either side will be willing to settle the claim, that juries will favor one party or the other in liability verdicts and amounts of damages awarded, and that these trends in litigation will be translated into higher insurance premiums. How effectively the legislature is able to alter these patterns and trends by rewriting the legal rules can be determined only through carefully designed econometric research that controls for a host of variables.

Medical malpractice has served as the major testing ground not only for new tort doctrines but also for empirical research about the real-world impact of new laws. Although most of the common law changes in the sixties occurred in a fairly short time, as did the legislative changes in the mid-seventies, various states acted at different times and in different ways—some not acting at all. That divergence among jurisdictions has enabled scholars to compare the impact of different laws in states with similar background conditions, and of similar laws in states with different conditions, so as to isolate the specific contribution of legal reform. Because this issue is important for medical malpractice, and because the research in this domain represents almost all the reliable existing empirical analysis of the impact of any area of tort law, it is worth taking a brief look at the nature and results of the half-dozen studies on the subject.

The early research dealt with the effect of developments in common law doctrine. The major items of legal interest were isolated by the staff of the Health, Education, and Welfare Commission:[77] the abolition of the locality doctrine, the development of informed consent, the use of *res ipsa loquitur,* the expansion of vicarious liability, the abolition of charitable and government immunity, the discovery rule, and so on. Three studies tried to discern the consequence of a state's adopting pro-plaintiff positions on some or all of these doctrines.

M. W. Reder developed the initial methodology for this kind of research and investigated the net effect of common law changes upon interstate variations in hospital and surgeon premiums in 1970 and 1972.[78] He found a correlation between a state's receiving a pro-plaintiff score on an unweighted index of the entire set of legal doctrines and higher premiums being paid by the surgeons in that state.[79]

Roger Feldman examined interstate differences in the rate of malpractice claims in 1970.[80] He too found that a pro-plaintiff legal index accompanied an increase in the number of claims per capita in the state. When he attempted to trace the effect of individual doctrines, however, he was much less successful at isolating any particular impact. A statistically significant effect was discernible only from a broad discovery rule and from the abolition of governmental immunity.[81]

Patricia Danzon considered the effect on the frequency and the severity of claims in 1970, and then from 1975 to 1978, of a state's position on the locality rule, charitable immunity, informed consent, and vicarious liability.[82] She found that a pro-plaintiff position in 1970 on all these doctrines had a pronounced impact, producing 53 percent greater claims frequency, 28 percent higher severity, and 86 percent larger total costs over the period 1975–1978, by comparison with states that were pro-defendant along all these dimensions.[83] Disaggregating the effect of each of these doctrines revealed that informed consent had the largest individual impact.

Just as the common law innovations of the sixties were succeeded by the legislation of the seventies, the focus of empirical research turned to the impact of statutory revisions. Three studies dealt with the effect of such legislation upon claims and premiums in the immediate aftermath of enactment.

Kathleen Adams and Stephen Zuckerman analyzed the average annual incidence of claims per physician in the years 1976 through 1981.[84] They tried to estimate the effect of seven legal doctrines, some still in their common law version, some altered by statute. Only informed consent had a statistically significant effect in the anticipated direction: the maximum estimate was that a strong version of the doctrine would increase the claims rate by 12 percent.[85] Adams and Zuckerman did not try to develop and estimate the significance of a general index summing up a state's cumulative position on all these legal issues.

Frank Sloan studied the factors influencing changes in premiums paid from 1974 through 1978 by general practitioners, ophthalmologists, and orthopedic surgeons.[86] He looked in particular for the effect of twelve statutory changes (taken individually, not cumulatively), including caps on damages, collateral source offsets, informed consent, *res ipsa*, contingency fees, screening panels, and the statute of limitations. The only legal change that had a negative and statistically significant effect on either the level or the rate of change in premiums was the mandatory screening panel.[87]

Danzon also explored the influence of statutory rules on the frequency, severity, and total cost of claims closed by insurers from 1975 through 1978.[88] Of the various legislative changes she analyzed, the most effective were the collateral source rule, for which a mandatory offset reduced the severity of awards by 50 percent (though the discretionary use of evidence of such sources had no apparent impact), and a cap on the damage award, which reduced severity by 19 percent.[89] The apparent effect of limits on contingent fees on claims severity and claims cost was not statistically significant. Changes in neither the statute of limitations nor such substantive doctrines as the locality rule, *res ipsa*, or informed consent had any visible impact.

The research projects described above studied the possible effect of legislation in the years just after the laws were enacted. Such a limited time frame might not give a fair picture of the longer-term impact once the parties and the courts had adjusted to the statutes. Two studies, however, have traced the mid-seventies legislation over a more extended period of time.

The first was conducted by Danzon, who updated her research to look at claims closed through 1984,[90] and who discovered some interesting revisions of her earlier findings.[91] In the later study the reduction in the limitations period showed a statistically significant effect on claims frequency, reducing claims by 8 percent for every year by which the limitation period was reduced. While there is no longer a discernible difference between the mandatory and the discretionary versions of the collateral source offset, adopting such a rule reduces claims severity by between 11 and 19 percent and claims frequency by around 14 percent—presumably, the prospect of lower recoveries was reducing the incentive to file a claim. Although the cumulative result of caps on damage awards was to reduce the claim severity factor by 23 percent, the device had no such effect on the plaintiff's propensity to initiate claims. Danzon's verdict about the screening panel procedure was that it had no significant impact on either the frequency or the severity of awards.

Sloan and colleagues combined data from one survey of claims closed in the years 1975–1978 and from a later survey of claims closed in 1984 in order to test the longer-term effectiveness of the mid-seventies' legislative reforms.[92] Because their analysis assumed that a claim had been filed, these investigators were able to test only the likelihood and the amount that a given claim would be paid, not the frequency of claims made relative to some independent index of injuries. Nevertheless, their research involved a closer look at the details of each statute and the timing of each malpractice claim—differentiating, for example, between caps on total damages and caps on noneconomic damages—and included a determination for each claim of whether a particular law was in effect at the time it was filed or resolved. Their findings about the impact of statutory changes, controlling for a number of other variables, can be summarized as follows. Legislative alterations in common law liability rules such as *res ipsa* or informed consent had no discernible effect; alterations in access rules such as statutes of repose or limits on attorney fees had only a modest effect on both the likelihood and the amount of recovery; but alterations to damage rules had a powerful effect. In particular a mandatory collateral source offset reduced insurer costs (both plaintiff indemnity and defendant adjustment expenses) by 21 percent on average; a cap on noneconomic damages reduced insurer costs by 23 percent; and a cap on total damages produced a reduction of fully 39 percent.[93]

Looking back, then, at what is now a substantial body of research employing quite disparate data sets and methodologies, a general convergence about the impact of tort reform emerges from the various findings.

Standards of liability. Variations in the standards of liability make little difference in aggregate outcome, a result that should not be particularly surprising. As long as juries are still asked to apply the basic common law paradigm of physician fault, tinkering with doctrines such as informed consent or *res ipsa* is unlikely to have a pronounced effect on claims or premium levels, even though the new rules will make some difference in the disposition of particular cases.

Access rules. Variation in access rules—limitation periods, screening procedures, and attorney fees—had an overall impact of modest proportions. Such rules are more likely to affect the timing and tactics employed by the parties in tort litigation, thereby influencing the types of medical accidents that will be channeled into the tort process; but they will not generally have a large impact on the amount of litigation doctors have to face or the premiums they have to pay.

Limits on damages. More striking results ensue from legislation that limits the amount of damages to be awarded, through either offsets of collateral sources or caps on damages. Imposing a blunt, mandatory ceiling on possible tort verdicts is far more difficult for attorneys or juries to finesse; moreover, it has both a direct effect on the average payment in those claims that are made and a further dampening effect on the readiness of patients and their attorneys to file claims in the first place, given the limit on the potential return from a litigation investment. It is also unsurprising that the impact of damage caps has become more powerful over time. When they were first enacted, the ceilings tended to be set at levels that would accommodate the vast bulk of settlements then being reached in the tort process; as a result, they constrained only a few outlying jury verdicts. However, because few of these dollar caps were made adjustable to subsequent inflation, they became significantly more binding in the eighties, and consequently more helpful to their intended beneficiaries.

The payoff from conventional tort reform, then, is more likely to be realized in the damages area, perhaps with some help from limits on attorney fees (a topic that should itself be seen as part of the broader damages question). Even so, it is important to underline two qualifications to this empirical conclusion.

First, even within its own cost containment frame of reference, statutory reform has served only to slow down the spiral in medical malpractice litigation. The untapped pool of malpractice events taking place in hospitals has provided ample room for absolute growth in common law tort claims and liability insurance premiums, even in states like California with substantial reform packages. Second, the empirical findings cannot be decisive because they assume the value judgment implicit in such legislation: that the malpractice problem consists of too many claims and damage awards that are too high. For understandable reasons that assumption does not always appeal to judges, who themselves fashioned the original common law doctrines in the context of lawsuits filed by the severely injured victims of apparent doctor negligence, and who, in that same setting, have had to decide how to treat the new statutes when the problem reappeared before them.

Constitutional Review

Once a state legislature has enacted a package of reforms of its medical malpractice law, the legal dialogue is by no means concluded. At a minimum, the state courts must provide authoritative interpretations for all the new legislation. These decisions usually have little effect on bright-line rules such as those that set damage caps or schedule lawyers' fees, although even in these areas judges must determine such issues as whether punitive damages should be included in a damage cap. However, it is judges who make the critical decisions about the content of broader statutory standards, including those that address the substantive behavior of doctors.[94] Whenever possible, state courts have typically read these legislative reforms as hewing closely to the common law rules and practices that the judges themselves had developed in light of their own views about sound public policy for medical accidents.[95]

In addition, courts must consider challenges to the validity of legislative reform under both the federal and state constitutions. This response has been important because through it the courts have established the parameters not only for malpractice legislation, but also for judging the constitutionality of tort reform in general,[96] although the potential long-term effect of constitutional review is difficult to assess.

After an initial series of cases calling numerous statutes into question, judicial attitudes seemed to relax. For a while it appeared that malpractice reforms in most of the urbanized and industrialized states, especially states that had experienced rising claims and insurance rates, would pass constitutional muster.[97] Then, in the eighties, by broadening statutory restraints to apply across the board to all tort claims, many legislatures eliminated a crucial argument about the unfairness of treating injured patients differently from other accident victims. One might also have thought that the judges themselves would have felt the same popular discomfiture about excess litigation and liability costs in American society. Yet the growing number of re-

cent cases indicates that there remain substantial constitutional obstacles to the types of tort restrictions (especially damage caps) that
empirical research shows make a significant difference.[98] Since it
would take another book of this length to survey in depth all the constitutional issues raised by malpractice legislation, I will simply sum-
marize the jurisprudence that addresses them.[99]

U.S. Constitution. The federal Constitution provides little or no relief for plaintiffs dissatisfied with a state's malpractice legislation.
Courts are highly unlikely to invalidate reforms under either the
equal protection or the due process clause. Moreover, although some
exceptions may exist, courts generally have not found other provisions in the federal Constitution to stand in the way of reform.

In dismissing equal protection challenges, courts have held that
malpractice legislation does not interfere with any fundamental right,
and that in differentiating between malpractice claimants and other
kinds of tort claimants the statutes do not use suspect or quasi-
suspect classifications.[100] Accordingly courts have treated such legislation as just another form of socioeconomic legislation, reviewing it
with only minimum scrutiny and upholding it on the basis that it
might rationally serve some legitimate state purpose.

Judicial rejection of federal due process objections has been similarly emphatic. In accordance with long-established constitutional
principles, courts have refused to judge the wisdom or fairness of
malpractice legislation.[101] In addition, they have rejected on three
grounds the so-called due process "quid pro quo" argument: that
malpractice restrictions such as damage caps limit the potential recovery of claimants without providing them with an adequate benefit in
return.[102] First, some courts have held that plaintiffs do not have a
vested right in any particular measure of damages, and that the legislation consequently does not take anything from them.[103] Second,
some have suggested that preservation of the medical malpractice insurance system provides a benefit sufficient to justify any losses that
individual plaintiffs might incur.[104] Third, other courts have simply
dismissed the issue on the ground that the United States Supreme
Court has never established any such quid pro quo requirement.[105]

Other federal constitutional impediments to reform may exist, but
they have gained little recognition. A federal district court invalidated
Virginia's dollar limitation on total tort damages as violative of the
Seventh Amendment right to trial by jury, but that decision was subsequently overturned by the Fourth Circuit Court of Appeals,[106] in
line with the general posture of federal judicial restraint toward state

legislative reform of the tort system. This hands-off attitude on the part of the federal courts has not, however, been emulated by their state court counterparts.

State constitutions. In the last decade state courts have taken seriously their responsibility for scrutinizing the validity of malpractice legislation under the provisions of their own constitutions.[107] Because state constitutions contain protections similar to those of the Fourteenth Amendment, state judges have been able to consider for themselves due process and equal protection arguments that the federal courts have rejected. Moreover, because state constitutions often contain guarantees of rights that extend beyond those found in the federal Constitution, state court judges have been able to entertain arguments that plaintiffs could not make to the federal courts.

State courts have struck down malpractice legislation in three discernibly separate waves. The first courts to invalidate malpractice reforms were in Idaho, Illinois, North Dakota, and Ohio; they were followed in the early eighties by courts in Arizona, Colorado, Florida, Georgia, Michigan, Missouri, Montana, New Hampshire, New Mexico, Pennsylvania, and Rhode Island, and most recently by courts in Florida (for a second time in response to another round of reform), Kansas, Oklahoma, Texas, Washington, and Wyoming.[108] Although the history of this judicial action is easy to document, drawing lessons from it requires careful attention. One must recognize both the courts' nondoctrinal motivations and the doctrinal grounds in which they rooted their decisions.

State courts have had strong reasons for disliking medical malpractice legislation, reasons that have undoubtedly influenced the content of the constitutional restraints the courts have imposed. In most instances the new legislation sought to undo, in the name of reform, tort law doctrines that the courts had themselves fashioned and that they presumably considered sound. Moreover, the courts perceived that powerful physician organizations were lobbying for the reforms, aware that they would cut back on the rights of injured patients without offering them anything like the quid pro quo of limited but guaranteed no-fault benefits that had been a part of almost all prior tort reform legislation, from early workers' compensation[109] to contemporary limits on nuclear facility liability.[110] Although courts have seldom explicitly offered reasons for their distaste for tort reform legislation, their sentiments have not escaped the attention of commentators and others.[111]

State treatment of equal protection challenges has differed from federal treatment in that some state courts have not limited themselves to reviewing the legislation on a "rational relationship" basis. Courts in Arizona and Montana, for example, characterized the right to bring a tort action for personal injuries as fundamental and consequently required that the legislature demonstrate a compelling justification for impairing that right.[112] The New Hampshire Supreme Court utilized an intermediate standard of review, asking both whether the legislation had a substantial relation to an important legislative aim and whether the benefit to the general public would outweigh the restrictions that would be imposed on the rights of individual victims.[113] Judges in Rhode Island, along with vigorous dissenters in California and elsewhere, deemed a rational basis test sufficient but looked for actual evidence that a malpractice crisis existed in order to determine whether particular restrictions on tort claims would make an appreciable difference.[114]

In some instances state concepts of due process accord with federal concepts, in others they do not. Like the federal courts, most state courts refuse to scrutinize the efficacy and fairness of legislative enactments. What might be called substantive due process still prevails in only a few states, such as North Dakota.[115] Ironically, a resounding victory for judicial restraint was won in the same California courts that had done so much to develop modern malpractice and general tort law. Confronted with one of the earliest and most sweeping pieces of reform legislation, the Medical Injury Compensation Reform Act of 1975 (MICRA),[116] a sharply divided California Supreme Court reversed its initial course and successively upheld statutes establishing the periodic payment of sizable malpractice awards,[117] a sliding scale ceiling on contingent fees chargeable by the patient's lawyer,[118] a monetary cap on noneconomic damages,[119] and a method for reducing tort awards by the amount payable from collateral sources.[120]

State courts have had mixed reactions to the due process quid pro quo argument rejected by the federal courts.[121] Siding with the federal judiciary, courts in California, Indiana, Nebraska, New Mexico, and Wisconsin rejected challenges to legislation that allegedly took rights from plaintiffs without providing them with sufficient compensation.[122] Courts in Illinois, New Hampshire, North Dakota, and Ohio, however, used quid pro quo arguments to strike down malpractice reform statutes under their state constitutions.[123] In addition, recent decisions by the Florida and Texas Supreme Courts to invalidate their damage caps, although not phrased in due process terms, amounted to the same thing: these courts held that the legislature could not, in the name of malpractice reform, impinge the right to a jury trial without providing a reasonable alternative remedy or commensurate benefit.[124] Encouragingly, however, almost all state courts that have spoken on the matter have indicated that tort reform would be possible if the state legislature truly balanced detriments to tort plaintiffs with meaningful gains to injury victims.[125] It is likely, then, that no-fault compensation schemes, such as the ones recently enacted in Virginia and Florida for neurologically impaired infants, are likely to withstand due process challenges.

Interestingly, in the eighties the favored approach for overturning malpractice reform legislation was to appeal to a state constitutional right to a jury trial or to analogous provisions guaranteeing access to the courts or separation of powers. This tack initially provided plaintiffs with a means of challenging mandatory certificates of merit or screening panel procedures. Whatever may be the theoretical benefits of alternative dispute resolution, such mandatory prescreening of all claims is fraught with difficulty. Some injured patients are unable to get the certificate from a doctor that would permit them to launch and begin discovery in what might have ultimately turned out to be a meritorious tort claim against another doctor. Mediation panels typically confront the parties with long scheduling delays, even to the point that expiration of the statutory limitation period may extinguish their claims. Moreover, in states in which tangible consequences ride on the panel's appraisal of the case—in which the appraisal is admissible in evidence, for example—the parties must put together a costly presentation for what is, in effect, only a dress rehearsal for the real trial. At the same time, although the panels consume a great deal of time and money, empirical evidence has not indicated that they produce any serious benefit in additional and faster voluntary settlement of cases beyond what would presumably happen in the tort claims process alone. So although most states have upheld such legislation,[126] and although states such as Illinois and Missouri struck down the mandatory screening procedures early on, finding that they violated the citizen's abstract right of access to the court, without regard to their actual effects,[127] other states, most notably Pennsylvania and Florida, rejected such legislation only after reviewing the serious procedural deficiencies that actually occurred.[128]

It is not surprising that judges would take seriously their state constitutional guarantee of a right of access to a court and a jury, and accordingly strike down statutory provisions that establish unwarranted barriers or obstacles in the way of injured patients trying to pursue their tort claims. What is remarkable, though, is that in the last several years this type of constitutional provision has developed into the favored argument against laws that merely constrain what juries can do when a malpractice case does reach them; in particular, legislation that cuts back on the amount of damages that a jury can award. In the nine recent cases in which this position was advanced, it was embraced by at least some of the judges in all but one proceeding and was adopted by the majority as often as not.[129]

On the surface, this legal theory would seem rather forced: the argument is not that a legislature is precluded from denying malpractice victims their day in court, but rather that the legislature cannot establish substantive criteria that will shape and define the potential outcome of the jury proceeding. Thus there is a message in the growing willingness of state court judges to stretch constitutional provisions and shed the broader judicial reluctance to second-guess legislative judgments about issues of social and economic policy. Judges see before them seriously injured victims of medical negligence or other mishaps, people whose common law rights to meaningful redress have been cut back sharply in the pursuit of cheaper malpractice insurance and cheaper health insurance, but without any effort by the polity to set up an alternative regime that would respond to the victims' needs—a regime such as a no-fault program on the model of those that won judicial approval in the context of earlier legislative retrenchments on tort law governing workplace or motor vehicle accidents. The significance of the judicial reaction to this apparent inequity is that many state legislatures can no longer be confident that they will have the final word on this hotly contested issue.

Ironically, neither can the state courts. If the political pressures are strong enough, state legislatures will try in a variety of ways to circumvent judicial rulings. In states like North Dakota and Florida, for example, where the state supreme courts have struck down early damage caps, new—albeit somewhat modified—versions of this idea have been reenacted, with an as yet uncertain fate. The need that is perceived for such changes in malpractice law seems to be as great as the apparent inequity such changes produce.

3

Serious Reform of the Tort/Fault Model

Frames of Reference

The last two decades have witnessed constant lawmaking activity in the area of medical malpractice, undertaken from a common law, a statutory, or a constitutional standpoint. Feeding the related political and judicial debates were countless documents issued by the supporters and opponents of the changes.[1] This chapter will focus on those components of the tort system through which the greatest leverage might be exerted on the future evolution of malpractice litigation, detailing the arguments for a program that would make the tort process more sensible and more equitable for both patient-victims and doctor-defendants.

It is important to note at the outset that a major source of controversy in any revision of tort law is the two competing conceptions of the tort system lurking behind the policy debate. These are the "corrective justice" and the "efficient insurance" models, each of which is consistent with certain crucial features of the malpractice system. Therefore, as a prelude to my defense of specific policy proposals, I will first set out my own assumptions about the important background philosophical themes.

Historically the value of corrective justice has been more prominent in shaping the evolving structure of tort law.[2] Under the corrective justice model, the tort suit is pictured as a contest between two individual parties, reflecting the same bipolar relationship in the outside world, in which the defendant caused the plaintiff to suffer an injury. Viewing the situation simply as a contest between the two parties, and the legal challenge as determining a mechanism for producing the fairest adjustment to their relationship after the loss has occurred, the tort system's basic inquiry has been whether the victim's loss was caused by the fault of the defendant. Expressed another way, did the defendant's actions display an unreasonable preference for his own interests and insufficient regard to the risks his actions generated for the plaintiff's rights? If the answer to that question is yes, the law judges it only fair to require the defendant to make the plaintiff whole for the injuries suffered, with the defendant forced to shoulder the burden of the losses engendered by his own misconduct.

This mode of private ordering has public advantages as well. It provides victims and their families with compensation for the losses that have occurred in the past; it also supplies potential defendants with incentives not to engage in such unduly risky behavior in the future. But these are fortuitous by-products of the tort regime, not its central justification. In fact, from a compensation point of view there is no reason to confine redress for accidents only to victims "fortunate" enough to be injured by another's fault. Likewise, the goal of prevention provides no reason either to confine imposition of the tort sanction to defendants unlucky enough to have their fault accidentally materialize in injuries to someone else, or to set the level of the sanction at whatever happens to be the cost of a particular victim's injuries, rather than in accordance with the level of fault inherent in the defendant's actions. In short, the crucial limiting features of the tort regime—causality, fault, and quantum of damages—can be understood only as implications of a legal effort to restore the preexisting real-world relationship between the immediate parties, a relationship that was unjustly disturbed by the misconduct of one and the resulting injury to the other.

Even though corrective justice has historically provided the most accurate and coherent explanation of the core features of tort law, the assumptions of the model have become increasingly less salient to the modern world of tort litigation.

Corrective justice has its immediate intuitive appeal in the kinds of situations that produced such classic tort cases as *Brown v. Kendall*,[3] in which the victim was accidentally struck in the eye by a stick wielded by another in an effort to break up a fight between the parties' dogs, and *Summers v. Tice*,[4] in which the victim was shot in the eye by a fellow hunter who mistook him for a bird in the woods. In each of these cases the law defined the ground rules under which the actors themselves might or might not have had to pay for the injuries suffered by their victims. Yet it is common knowledge that in the contemporary world it is rarely the person actually at fault who ends up paying the tort award. If a plane crashes because of the inattention of a pilot or the mistake of a mechanic, it is the airline, not the careless employee, that will foot the bill for the consequent huge tort damages. It is likely that the airline will discipline or fire the employee for whose tort it is vicariously liable (although doing so is just an extrinsic response to, not an integral part of, the tort system). Yet in the case of many present-day tort claims, the responsible parties are no longer available to offer restitution. For example, many of the scientists and executives who put the drug diethylstilbestrol (DES) on the market in the late forties and early fifties had left the pharmaceutical company for which they then worked long before the latent effect of the drug manifested itself and generated massive tort litigation in the late seventies and early eighties. The people who actually absorb the cost of the decades-old misconduct of the guilty individuals are the present-day shareholders, employees, and customers of the firms that are held legally responsible; the financial burden is distributed among the three groups according to the interaction of the capital, labor, and product markets in which the firms function.

On the surface medical malpractice appears to be a conspicuous exception to the trend toward enterprise liability. Recall that roughly three-quarters of all malpractice suits are still brought against individual doctors as an outgrowth of their personal relationships with patients.[5] Is malpractice law, then, still a viable enclave for the values and assumptions of corrective justice?

Even in that context the legal image is much more myth than reality. The doctor may be the nominal defendant in the injured patient's lawsuit, but the doctor's insurer is the major presence in the background. The insurer selects and pays for the defense attorney, decides whether to settle or fight the claim, and pays the bill for the settlement or trial verdict if the doctor appears to have been negligent.[6] The insurance company in turn collects the funds for its tort expenditures in the form of liability premiums charged to the collectivity of doctors within the relevant specialty and region. In medical malpractice as well it is not the individual careless doctor who pays the tort bill, but all his fellow doctors in the same insurance pool, whether or not the other doctors themselves have been negligent.[7]

The tort-insurance circle is actually wider than the foregoing description implies. Doctors and patients are in a financial as well as a therapeutic relationship; the patient is contractually obligated to pay the doctor's fees. Thus, in the medical fees charged to their patients doctors predictably collect the revenues needed to pay their malpractice insurance carriers for their liability insurance overhead. In turn, the vast majority of medical fees are paid for by private or public health insurers to whom patients pay premiums directly or through their employer or government.[8]

In sum, the malpractice doctrines that our judges have created and our legislatures have modified do much more than define the moral features of a relationship between careless doctor and injured patient. Malpractice law operates within an elaborate set of insurance arrangements which require that healthy future patients purchase a form of disability insurance against the risk of negligent iatrogenic injuries. The latent function of contemporary tort litigation is to serve as a port of entry into this disability insurance fund, determining how much money is to be distributed to which set of candidates from the larger pool of injured patients.

Looking at tort law through this modernized lens gives rise to a more utilitarian mode of analysis: how should tort law be designed to make it the most efficient form of disability insurance?[9] This question, in turn, may be subdivided into three related lines of inquiry. How sensibly does the entire system distribute *compensation* to injured patients out of funds accumulated from the broader community of health care users? More important, how effective is such a program in the *prevention* of substandard medical treatment and consequently the protection of all patients from injury before the fact? Finally, how economical is the *administration* of this disability insurance program in terms of the money, time, and emotional outlay required of the parties?

Tort Damages for Economic Losses

Having observed this tension between corrective justice and efficient insurance as frames of reference for tort reform, let us now turn to the policy merits of a number of substantive proposals. This deeper examination will probe points in the system that significantly influence the operation and effects of the system as a whole. The proposals I shall endorse are those that not only respond to the legitimate concerns of doctors about their growing exposure to the legal risk of tort liability, but that also serve the needs of patients facing the physical risk of medical injury.

In present-day tort litigation the most important topic is the choice of legal principles governing damage awards. There is a consensus among serious investigators of the subject that the main factor driving up the cost of malpractice insurance has been the escalation of award levels, which imposes a direct cost on malpractice insurers and entails additional indirect costs in the form of more claims being attracted into the tort system by the prospect of greater financial rewards.

The most striking manifestation of this inflationary tendency is spiraling jury verdicts, epitomized by the $50 million awards referred to earlier.[10] Although these Houston and Los Angeles verdicts are the highest won so far by any malpractice claimants, jury verdicts in the eight-figure range are no longer considered remarkable, especially in obstetric malpractice cases.[11] Plaintiff attorneys have become extremely sophisticated at presenting both economic evidence of the projected long-term financial losses of their clients and graphic depictions (often using video techniques) of typical unhappy days in the lives of severely injured victims. At the same time jurors have become accustomed to huge award requests, and they are more willing to reach into the deep pockets of malpractice insurers to compensate the victims generously—more willing than when they encounter the victims of automobile accidents, for in these cases the insurance premiums at risk are paid directly by jurors themselves.[12]

Of course the jury does not necessarily have the final word on damages. Using the *remittitur* procedure at the trial or appellate level, judges have considerable power to force plaintiffs to accept a lower damage award figure as the price of retaining a favorable jury verdict. In aggregate, the process of judicial review, including voluntary settlement by the parties themselves under the shadow of appellate reversal, produces overall reductions in initial jury verdicts of roughly 30 percent, with a somewhat higher proportion when the largest awards are involved[13] (leaving little doubt that the aforementioned $50 million awards will not survive unscathed). But the jury's open-ended *first* word about the appropriate level of damages is still the crucial driving force in the system, because the jury verdict sets the parameters for any judicial second look. As a result, even substantial cuts in a jury verdict will produce a final outcome that appears moderate only by comparison with what the jury gave the judge to work with.[14]

The fact that million-dollar malpractice verdicts have become rather commonplace, and that 5 percent of successful claimants with the largest awards receive well over half the total dollars disbursed in such suits,[15] is not by itself evidence of a malfunctioning litigation system. It is equally plausible to infer that this tiny minority of accident victims actually suffers an equally disproportionate share of aggregate compensable losses.[16] But recall that the unpredictable risk of a huge damage award poses significant difficulties to the smooth and economical operation of a liability insurance system, especially one with a thin pool of insureds, as in the case of obstetricians.[17] In any event, given the strong political pressures on state legislators to do something in response to physicians' discontent about the malpractice system, the understandable legislative reaction has been to focus on the pressure point at which the bulk of the money is being spent.

The strongest legislative reactions to this perceived problem have taken the form of a statutory cap on the tort damages permitted in malpractice cases. In the eighties, states generally followed the lead of California's 1975 legislation and focused their ceilings on damages for pain and suffering and other nonfinancial injuries (a policy whose merits will be addressed in the next section). But in the seventies Indiana was the pacesetter for several states (Nebraska, North and South Dakota, Kansas, Virginia, Louisiana, and Texas) that imposed caps on the total damages of any kind that could be levied on health care providers. Typically such a policy would be accompanied by the creation of a new insurance entity, a Patient Compensation Fund (PCF), that shared legal liability with the doctor involved in a medical accident. The doctor bore the risk of (and purchased insurance for) the first $100,000 in damages and the PCF for the next $400,000; beyond $500,000 any further patient recovery was simply cut off by legislation. Although I have just attempted to explain why state legislatures were tempted to act in this fashion, I must quickly point out that the Indiana model is entirely unjustifiable as a matter of policy, from the point of view of either corrective justice or efficient insurance.

The fundamental assumption of the current tort system is that in the absence of demonstrated fault there is no more justification for making an innocent doctor responsible for his patients' medical injuries than there is for seeking compensation from any other deep pocket in the community. But the flip side of the corrective justice rationale for this tort principle is that if it was the doctor's careless treatment that caused the injuries, then the innocent plaintiff is entitled to have the resulting financial burden shifted from him to the doctor (or the doctor's insurer, if that is what the doctor has arranged). Therefore, any legal policy that simply terminates the financial liability of the culpable doctor at a certain point constitutes unfair and unconscionable treatment of the patient-victim.

From an insurance perspective, statutory limits on the scope of common law tort liability are *not* anathema if they serve to smooth out the operation and reduce the costs of the litigation-insurance system.

But viewed from the insurance/risk distribution vantage point, essentially the same negative verdict must be given about the real-life design of such caps.

The first problem is that legislatures (with the exception of Texas) used nominal dollar figures to express the statutory limit. At the time the legislation was enacted, figures such as $500,000 may have seemed reasonably generous because they were at the outer bounds of malpractice awards then being won by plaintiffs;[18] the law could, therefore, be justified as a sensible fail-safe protection against outlandish verdicts rendered by maverick juries. But in the last fifteen years general price inflation has cut the real value of such caps to 45 percent of the original 1975 levels, and the even faster pace of medical cost inflation has reduced to only one-third the original real value of this crucial component of a tort award.[19] So even if it were considered defensible for the legislature to use caps to define economic parameters for the judge-made malpractice system, there can be no justification for allowing the original policy to be steadily undermined by inflation, eventually to an unconscionably low level.

However, even a statutory cap that is indexed or occasionally adjusted to subsequent inflation (as in Texas and Virginia, respectively) does not address a more fundamental objection to this device. The problem is that society's objective of containing the cost of malpractice insurance (for which capping is highly effective, as Indiana's experience demonstrates) is pursued through a policy whose entire burden is imposed on a small number of relatively young, seriously injured victims of medical negligence. If a senior citizen suffers a moderately disabling injury, even a fixed nominal dollar cap of $500,000 will likely not have any effect on his tort claim. But if a baby is born with permanent brain damage as a result of something that went wrong in the delivery, even an inflation-adjusted cap cannot begin to cover the huge cost of treating that victim in the same health care system whose malfunctioning produced the injury in the first place. Unsurprisingly, then, when such "bad baby" cases appeared in the courtrooms in the eighties, judges increasingly looked with favor at the constitutional challenges lodged against a statutory rule that arbitrarily and unfairly cut off necessary redress for this small category of helpless malpractice victims.

An alternative policy tack could accomplish much of the legislative goal of malpractice cost containment without falling prey to the objection of unfair treatment of the small number of malpractice victims who would be deprived of appropriate awards under a cap regime.

The preceding discussion has tacitly assumed that if an injured patient cannot shift his losses to the negligent doctor and the doctor's liability insurer, then the innocent plaintiff must bear all the losses himself. In fact, we know that this is not the case. Most people have insurance coverage for the bulk of their hospital and doctor bills, as well as some protection against lost earnings through sick leave or disability insurance programs. In the case of malpractice claimants, Patricia Danzon has estimated that 60 percent of all tort payments are for economic losses, and about 60 percent of these costs are already covered by a host of public and private insurance programs such as Blue Cross, Medicare, Medicaid, sick leave, disability insurance, workers' compensation, and Social Security Disability Insurance.[20] It would be a simple policy step, then, to deduct from the tort award the amount of any payments made by external insurance sources for injuries that are the subject of a tort claim. In the seventies this kind of collateral source offset was adopted by a number of jurisdictions, typically in a discretionary form; in the eighties the collateral source was adopted by other states, in most instances as a mandatory procedure. Empirical research has shown that this policy, especially when it is mandatory and automatic, will successfully hold back rising malpractice costs by around 15 to 20 percent.[21]

The collateral source offset also addresses the several objections to the statutory cap that were noted earlier. Because the injured person does secure compensation for the particular losses suffered, any claim of unfair denial of redress is eliminated, at least from the point of view of the rights of the innocent victim. There is a natural economic equilibrium to the operation of this legal policy. As the value of the social safety net expands or contracts as a result of community choice or inaction—in the face of inflation, for example—so also will the payment burden imposed on malpractice insurance.[22] Because the collateral source offset policy serves as a floor rather than a ceiling on tort recovery, the funds from malpractice insurance will be channeled toward the small number of especially needy victims of catastrophic medical injuries. Finally, the elimination of duplicate recovery reduces the risk of "moral hazard" on the part of patient-victims: otherwise the prospect of a tort windfall for losses already compensated would aggravate rather than reduce the overall risk of medical injuries.[23]

There are two alternative methods for avoiding this tort windfall and insurance hazard. One is to offset the disability benefit against the tort award. The other is to allow the disability insurer to recoup its past and future payments from the tort award, using the procedures of indemnity or subrogation. State legislatures have typically employed the second approach in the design of their workers' compensation systems for cases in which an injured employee who has received workers' compensation benefits is also able to mount a successful tort action against an outside party, usually a product manufacturer.[24] When the legislatures decided to take the opposite tack with respect to malpractice liability, they also had to eliminate by statute any contractual right of the disability insurer against a patient's tort award. Although such an option does help contain the cost of malpractice insurance for doctors, it necessarily increases the cost of disability insurance for patients and other potential victims. Granted that there can be no free lunch in personal injury policy, there remains the question of finding a basis for defending selection of the collateral source offset option.

Focusing on the objective of providing medical accident victims with the most sensible compensation arrangements makes this quest simple. The fundamental problem of liability insurance from this point of view is that it requires proof of fault on the part of the doctor as the precondition for paying insurance benefits to the injured patient. The economic justification, if there is one, for this central feature of tort law is the contribution the tort regime may make to the prevention of future patient injuries, an argument I shall take up in the next chapter. But given the substantial administrative costs—in time, money, and equity—of having to litigate the fault requirement in individual cases, one can readily justify relegating malpractice law to a secondary insurance role as a backstop source of compensation.

Take the time variable first. According to the General Accounting Office (GAO) survey of malpractice claims closed in 1984, the median time from medical injury to tort claim was thirteen months, and the time from claim to payment was another twenty-three months, or a total of three years before the typical patient received any financial redress for an injury.[25] Such a delay is a serious drawback in any compensation scheme. The personal trauma of having to deal with a major disabling injury cannot be alleviated simply by receiving a benefit check in the mail years after the injured party and family had to adjust to the disaster. Under standard disability insurance arrangements, medical bills are paid and earnings are either continued or replaced without any significant hiatus. Even in a tort liability system like workers' compensation, which hinges recovery on proof that the workplace was the *cause* of the accident (though not necessarily at *fault* in bringing it about), benefits are paid in a median time of only three weeks for uncontested claims and four months if the claim is contested.[26]

Litigation over doctors' fault is as expensive in dollars as it is in delay. To determine the dollar amount it is necessary to abstract from the expenses of raising the insurance funds—brokerage and sales commissions, taxes and fees, profits and dividends—which are the overhead costs of the community decision to use voluntary insurance through private business rather than mandatory insurance through government agency.[27] If one focuses instead on the administrative costs of distributing the insurance to victims and of resolving disputes about entitlements or amounts, the relevant expenditures are the insurer's nonallocated costs of claims adjustment personnel and overhead, the fees and expenses of lawyers for both doctor and patient, the time spent on the case by the parties themselves, and a proportionate share of the costs of running a public court system. Having reviewed a number of such breakdowns, I estimate that malpractice insurance now expends approximately 55 to 60 cents to deliver 40 to 45 cents of the claims dollar into the hands of injured patients.[28] This ratio is several times greater than the proportion of the claims dollar spent for administration by first-party disability insurance or third-party, no-fault workers' compensation insurance.[29]

There is an additional reason for preferring first-party to third-party insurance as a mode of compensation. Not only does tort litigation require substantial expenditures of the parties' time and money, but the administrative burden of the system sharply alters the substantive compensation policy that emerges in practice.

This is so because nine out of ten malpractice claims are resolved by negotiated settlements rather than tort verdicts.[30] Usually both sides find it sensible to save time and money by voluntary compromise rather than by insisting upon having their day in court. The terms of these negotiated settlements are influenced not only by the formal legal rules of liability and damages that would be applied by a jury if the case were to go as far as a verdict, but also by the relative ability of each side to bear the costs of *not* settling, of waiting years for a trial. Unfortunately, the delay following an injury is not a neutral factor. The more seriously a patient is injured, the greater is his immediate need for compensation and the consequent pressure on him to "sell" the tort claim back to the defendant for a fraction of the amount the claim might be worth if it were appraised on its merits by a jury.

This tilt in tort litigation is strikingly documented in the GAO's review of malpractice claims in 1984.[31] The two injury categories that produced the most sizable economic losses were "major" and "grave" permanent total disabilities. Comprising less than 10 percent of the entire group of paid claims, these cases had economic losses that averaged about $1.7 million apiece; yet the total awards received by the victims for all their injuries averaged only about $400,000. By contrast, the injury categories that the GAO labeled "emotional" or "insignificant," which together included about 20 percent of paid claimants, received indemnities that averaged about four times the amount of the victims' losses. These findings graphically convey how far the tort system diverges in practice from the compensation principle implied by either the corrective justice or the efficient insurance perspective—the principle that priority should be given to compensating the tangible economic losses of the few people who are the most severely disabled. So, returning to my earlier assertion, if a legislature decides to stem the rising cost of malpractice insurance, the preferred policy instrument must be the floor of a collateral source offset rather than the ceiling of a cap on total economic damages.

Damages for Pain and Suffering

Even though the collateral source offset is more equitable and sensible than a damage cap for containing the aggregate cost of malpractice liability, such a measure does not come to grips with the problem of predicting and insuring against occasional huge malpractice awards. In my opinion, that concern should take second place to the need to provide compensation for the catastrophic financial losses of the most severely injured victims of medical negligence. Fortunately this conflict is not acute, because the most troublesome feature of large tort verdicts is the amount of damages awarded for pain and suffering, not for direct medical costs.

"Pain and suffering" is a term that covers several categories of non-pecuniary loss, the most important of which are the following:

· The physiological pain felt by the victim at the time of the injury and during recuperation, a period that can be lengthy but is often brief.[32]

· The anguish and terror the victim felt in the face of impending injury or death, before as well as after an accident. This kind of claim has now become staple fare in suits arising from airline crashes.[33]

- The immediate emotional distress and long-term loss of love and companionship that is the result of an injury to or death of a close family member.[34]

- Most important is the accident victim's enduring loss of enjoyment of life when a permanent physical impairment precludes the pleasures of normal personal and social activities. (Such a loss may or may not be appreciated by victims who suffer brain damage.)[35]

In a serious malpractice action the jury will typically be asked to make separate awards for a number of such distinct nonpecuniary categories. Juries are likely to respond with substantial amounts of money under each heading, with the cumulative result that damages for pain and suffering, broadly defined, now make up nearly 50 percent of total tort damages paid for medical cases, with the largest awards taking the lion's share of this money.[36]

The perceived problem of pain and suffering awards is not simply the amount of money expended, but also the erratic nature of the process by which the size of the awards is determined.[37] To arrive at the economic component of a tort award, the jury begins with medical bills and wage statements, then expresses the projected total losses in the same monetary terminology as the tort award itself. For pain and suffering, by contrast, while the jury will have evidence, frequently dramatized on videotape, of the difficulties and distress experienced by the victim in his daily life, no legal criteria exist for assessing the degree of harm that has been done and then translating that harm into a dollar figure. Indeed, the jury, which sees only this one case, cannot even be apprised of the pattern of awards in comparable cases. Jurors are simply told to apply their "enlightened conscience" in selecting a monetary figure they consider to be fair. Judicial review offers little help: in most jurisdictions judges will overturn only damage awards that are so excessive that they "shock the judicial conscience," or that indicate that the jury was moved by "passion and prejudice."[38] Even when a judge decides to intervene, his point of departure is the base established by the jury's original award, so any reduction he imposes will appear moderate only by comparison.[39]

Widespread sentiment that pain and suffering awards were out of control inspired many states in the eighties to establish caps solely on this type of damages. These more recent caps often applied to tort litigation generally, not simply malpractice claims.[40] As we shall see later, material improvements can be made in the design of such statutory provisions that at the moment adversely affect only the most seriously injured victims. But in many quarters caps on pain and suffering damages have not been considered troubling because of long-standing doubts,[41] recently reinforced by sophisticated law and economic analysis, about whether any substantial money should be awarded for the pain and suffering of even the most severely injured victims.

The Uneasy Case for Pain and Suffering

The argument for compensating pain and suffering fits quite comfortably with the traditional corrective justice perspective on tort law. Injured victims in many cases suffer not only substantial financial losses but also a traumatic experience—real pain, an inability to engage in and enjoy the normal activities of life, or the emotional distress of having a loved one crippled or killed. Though these kinds of losses are not expressible in precise pecuniary terms, it is intuitively evident that they are extremely harmful. In fact, the market puts a substantial economic value on avoiding these very risks.[42] On the other side of the coin is a defendant, such as a doctor whose careless behavior caused the serious injury to the victim. The same rationale that requires the negligent doctor to bear the burden of the injured patient's financial losses also demands that the doctor shoulder the cost of the equally harmful—albeit not as easily quantifiable—psychological injuries.

Yet, as I pointed out earlier, the principle of corrective justice has not so much been refuted as it has receded from view in a world in which tort awards are paid not by the guilty doctor but by his insurer. In fact, the awards are ultimately not even paid by the liability insurer, but rather by people who buy health insurance against the risk that they will become sick, need medical treatment, and perhaps suffer a negligent iatrogenic injury in the course of that treatment. From this insurance perspective, the claim of pain and suffering to *any*, let alone *full*, compensation is difficult to justify.[43]

It is plausible, at least, that people who enter a hospital for treatment or who use a pharmaceutical product would pay an additional premium for insurance against the financial losses they might suffer if a mishap occurred in connection with the treatment or the drug. Such insurance is designed to reduce an individual's current income by a small amount when he is in able-bodied condition in order to provide him with a cushion against a possible drastic reduction in income in a future unhealthy state. This trade-off stabilizes the ongoing marginal utility of his income, no matter what misfortune might occur to him. However, no such rationale justifies insurance against the losses that fall under the rubric of pain and suffering. If an injury is temporary, the actual pain is over long before any money is collected; if it is a permanent injury, the eventual payment will not directly undo the ongoing harm from the loss of a limb, for example, or of a child. All the tort-insurance regime can do is reduce the money a victim has available to spend *before* he is hurt in order to provide him with more money to spend *after* he is hurt. The problem is that, unlike the exigencies of medical bills that must be paid or lost earnings that must be replaced, infliction of a painful injury does not increase the need for and valuation of money, and a sizable share of the funds set aside for this purpose will be spent on the cost of using the litigation system to transfer income from one state to the other. Since strong corroborative evidence indicates that people do not voluntarily purchase first-party loss insurance against such types of harm,[44] it is reasonable to conclude that the tort system should not mandate expensive third-party coverage through awards of pain and suffering.

The preceding analysis provides a powerful argument against compensating many of the harms that are now included in the category of pain and suffering: temporary pain during the period of recuperation from an injury that eventually ends in full recovery, the total loss of ability in a brain-damaged and comatose victim to experience, let alone enjoy, life, or the anguish felt by those who have lost a close family member in a fatal accident. Each of these examples unquestionably represents severe human losses. But what is the point of paying money now to repair a harm that cannot be affected by the payment? It is lamentable but true that the parent who loses a child has less, not more, need of family income after the fatal accident. A good illustration of such dubious expenditures by the tort system is the growing tendency to award large sums to airline passengers for the momentary terror they experienced when they faced an imminent crash, from which they might or might not have survived—especially given that the money to make these payments ultimately comes from the ticket prices charged to everyone who flies on these airlines.

However, perhaps a different conclusion about pain and suffering damages is appropriate in cases like the following. A person suffers a severe physical impairment such as the loss of a limb or of a sense (sight or hearing), or the capacity for bodily movement on account of quadriplegia. Individuals who suffer such harms cannot afterward enjoy many of the activities to which they were previously attached, but they do retain the capacity to substitute other activities and pleasures in their lives. Awarding pain and suffering damages would provide the financial wherewithal for such victims to purchase the equipment, training, assistance, and services necessary for them to lead the best life possible after the tragic injury. In a sense, this kind of damage award is really designed for rehabilitation and support in the broader sense of the term, helping the accident victim to adjust socially and psychologically, rather than just medically and vocationally, to the new disabled state. The role of tort insurance in such instances is to distribute the financial cost of injury adjustment among the many users of a product or service, who therefore currently pay a modest premium for protection against the chance that they might one day be among those unfortunate enough to suffer a severe injury.

From the Cap to the Scale

This "functional" rationale for pain and suffering damages, which has been adopted in Canada, for example,[45] justifies a carefully tailored distribution of such awards. The questions the court should ask are whether a particular injured victim, as opposed to his family or his heirs, will really be able to use the financial compensation for rehabilitative purposes, and what level of annual income flow would be appropriate for such substitute expenditures. When the problem is posed in such pragmatic terms, the resulting lump sum awards that would be paid to even the most severely injured victims would likely fall well within the range of the statutory damage caps recently adopted by the state legislatures.

Significant flaws remain, however, in the design of this statutory policy. Some were noted earlier in connection with the caps that a few states have imposed on all malpractice damages, economic and noneconomic, but some revealing differences emerge when the focus is on pain and suffering alone.

The most important variation is that where pain and suffering damages are concerned, the principle of a legal ceiling is generally quite attractive. The basic objection to a legal ceiling on economic damages is that it is the external health care and employment systems that determine the actual medical and earnings losses suffered by the victim, financial harm which the tort award is supposed to redress. By contrast, it is the tort system itself that makes the value judgment about how to translate into monetary terms the inherently nonmonetary loss of enjoyment of life. In the common law litigation system, the upper level of such damages is the *de facto* product of countless jury reactions to the facts and advocacy in individual cases, limited only by a vague outer boundary of acceptability imposed by judges whose conscience may have been shaken by certain jury verdicts. It is hard to imagine why that process is preferable to a state legislature's or a state supreme court's consciously adopting a damages ceiling to be applied across the board in all tort cases in a jurisdiction.[46] At least an explicit ceiling would give insurance adjusters and actuaries some legal guidance for the decisions they must make on the liability insurance side of the tort system.

However, if a legislature is going to create a damages ceiling expressed in dollar terms, it must not allow its initial policy judgment to be undermined by subsequent inflation. The purpose of the award is to give severely injured victims a flow of additional income to purchase amenities that will soften the hardship of disabled life. So the dollar ceiling must be indexed to an appropriate measure of inflation in order to preserve the real value of the public policy level that was originally agreed upon.

Yet even an inflation-proof cap is inherently discriminatory against one kind of victim: those who have been most severely injured, especially the youngest, who are expected to live the longest with their disability. The way that damage caps operate in practice is that the jury is first invited to make its own appraisal of the case while left in the dark about the legislative policy. Only if the jury verdict comes in at a point above the statutory cap will the excess amount be deducted. Consequently, if a jurisdiction has a $500,000 ceiling on pain and suffering damages, and a jury awards close to that amount to a plaintiff with an injured finger or toe,[47] the verdict will stand at exactly the same financial level as a maximum award granted to an accident victim who is left quadriplegic or totally blinded by a negligent injury. In effect, the entire burden of containing malpractice costs is imposed on the small number of the most catastrophically injured victims. And such a legal policy is entirely unappealing from the point of view of both corrective justice and efficient insurance.

A perfectly viable method does exist for implementing the ceiling objective. The legislature should use a *scale* rather than a *cap*. The statute would first specify that the ceiling is applicable to cases of the most severe disability (such as quadriplegia or blindness) and the longest life expectancies (say, fifty years or more). Ideally, the law would also establish a floor or threshold that would remove from the malpractice system most of the less significant temporary pain and suffering claims, claims for which there is little compensation justification under an insurance system but which now tend to be overpaid because it costs the insurer more to defend them than to pay them off. As an example of such a floor, Michigan's automobile accident law now allows pain and suffering damages only for victims who suffer significant disfigurement or impairment of a bodily function. Such a qualitative threshold would free up enough insurance funds to permit a more generous ceiling for the most seriously injured victims, who are already under great pressure to settle their claims for much less than would adequately compensate their economic losses alone. The jury would be explicitly instructed about the meaning and the level of both the statutory ceiling and the floor, and directed to place the immediate case with its degree of impairment and life expectancy at the appropriate point on the scale. The objective of the scale approach is to secure a more equitable distribution of pain and suffering awards to all victims with reference to the relative severity of their losses, rather than merely establish an arbitrary cut-off point beyond which the losses of the most severely injured are deemed legally noncompensable.

Some scholars go even farther to advocate use of a *schedule* that would fix the precise damage price for each type of injury.[48] The problem that remains in the rather amorphous scale sketched above is that there would still be ample (albeit somewhat compressed) room for subjective and erratic treatment of individual cases, depending on how the jury reacts to the immediate facts and presentation.[49] Worse, the unpredictability of such jury awards requires substantial expenditures of time and resources to resolve disputes over this component of tort claims. One way of addressing this problem would be to employ the schedule developed by the American Medical Association to help doctors make comparatively objective and reliable estimates of the degree of purely physical impairment. This schedule is now widely used for calculating workers' compensation.[50]

Unquestionably, the schedule approach to pain and suffering awards has significant advantages. It would be easier, more impersonal, and less contentious than ad hoc jury appraisal even within a floor and ceiling. The vice of an impairment schedule based strictly on the physical nature of the injury is that it does not permit a more individualized assessment of the important features of each victim's life and personal interests, and of how the impairment specifically affects him or her. Consider, for example, the tremendous difference that the loss of a hand would make in the future enjoyment of life for someone whose main avocation was playing the piano rather than for someone whose passion was playing chess.

There is an intermediate solution that retains many of the benefits of both the pure schedule and the pure scale models. In the scale model there would be a specified threshold beneath which no pain and suffering would be awarded—such as cases of temporary pain that did not produce a serious or permanent impairment—and a ceiling that would define the maximum award for the most severe disability, such as blindness inflicted on a child at birth. Added to these would be a number of standardized profiles developed for cases deemed to be of intermediate severity (such as permanent limp in a mature adult or a disfiguring scar on a young person), with appropriate inflation-adjusted dollar values attached to each injury type in line with the floor and ceiling.[51] Once that index was established as the general tort policy of a jurisdiction, future idiosyncratic cases would be resolved by juries invited to appraise the specific facts in light of considerably more precise and meaningful legal guidelines. In turn, appeal judges would have a sounder footing from which to review jury verdicts and decide whether the award materially deviated from what would be reasonable compensation in the particular case (New York's recently adopted standard for such judicial review). Finally, private settlement negotiations between the parties would operate more smoothly in light of the shared parameters for the appropriate monetary values for recurrent cases.

Thus, it would be relatively easy to construct a different response to the problem of excessive tort damages expended on dubious candidates. Whereas the standard legislative approach is just as inequitable and irrational as the abuses for which it is prescribed, the alternative, the scale of injury profiles running from a floor to a ceiling, would channel the appropriate amount of money to those victims who were in a position to use the award to ameliorate their present loss of enjoyment of life.

The Contingent Attorney Fee

Considered in isolation, my proposals for a mandatory collateral source offset and a prescribed scale for pain and suffering damages would markedly rationalize and restrain expenditures in our malpractice liability regime, yet still satisfy the legitimate needs of tort victims for compensatory damages. But before passing final judgment on such measures, we must situate them in the tort system as a whole and consider how they would affect the capacity of malpractice litigation to achieve its objectives of compensating and preventing injuries to patients.

When the two proposals are viewed in this broader strategic perspective, a practical problem becomes apparent in both of them. My analysis up to this point has assumed the tacit premise of tort reformers that the common law collateral source doctrine and the pain and suffering award provide unduly generous compensation to tort victims beyond their actual financial losses. Yet in the real world of tort litigation, that assumption is largely mythical, for the money provided by these so-called luxury damage items is typically used by successful plaintiffs to pay for another significant financial cost of the injury: legal fees.

Under the standard attorney fee arrangement in personal injury litigation, the plaintiff is required to pay for his or her attorney's services only if the lawyer succeeds in winning something from the action. If the plaintiff wins, then the lawyer takes a substantial percentage of the award as his share. Typically that percentage is fixed at one-third, though sometimes it is more (often, if the case must go to trial) and sometimes less (such as in airline crash litigation, in which liability is assumed *de facto* and the only issue in dispute is the size of the plaintiff's damages).[52] Given the one-third figure as the norm, the significance of this arrangement is that the successful plaintiff must actually recover at least one-third more than his tangible financial losses merely in order to obtain full economic recovery. Assuming the victim has suffered severe financial losses, as in the case of the huge medical bills of a brain-damaged baby with long life expectancy, a large margin will be needed in pain and suffering damages or in payments covered by collateral sources to amass the funds needed to pay the attorney's share.[53] Consequently, eliminating collateral source payments and sharply scaling down pain and suffering awards in an effort to rationalize these two damage items in their own right results in cutting sharply into the plaintiff's net recovery for financial losses caused by the defendant's negligence.

Some recognition has been given to this problem by the malpractice reform movement. Comprehensive statutory packages such as California's Medical Injury Compensation Reform Act of 1975 typically impose legal ceilings on the permissible contingent fee percentage— in California, 40 percent of the first $50,000, one-third of the next $50,000, one-fourth of the next $100,000, and 10 percent of everything above $200,000.[54] The immediate effect of the legislation is to entitle successful malpractice claimants to keep a larger share of their tort award, thereby providing some redress for cuts in pain and suffering damages and collateral source benefits enacted in the same legislation.

Of course, since the primary advocates of this measure tend to be doctors rather than patients, one should expect to find a rather different political motivation behind its enactment. The typical refrain of physicians and their representatives is that the contingent fee is a major culprit in the malpractice crisis. Because this fee arrangement promises plaintiff attorneys huge rewards, it is assumed that the lawyers have a great financial incentive to foment unnecessary, even frivolous, litigation and thereby impose unjustified economic and emotional costs on doctors. The virtue of a statutory cap on the contingent fee, argue the doctors, is that by sharply reducing the potential bonanza for the attorney, it will ameliorate the malpractice problem for health care providers, with the happy by-product that more money is left in the hands of the deserving patients who do succeed with their claims.

Unfortunately, in an adversarial setting such as malpractice, in which a patient may have been hurt by the carelessness of a doctor, it is unlikely that measures which help one side will also be advantageous to the other. It might appear at first that injured patients do reap the benefit of higher tort recovery by statutory cutbacks on the allowable contingent fee; however, the fallacy in that argument is its reliance on *ex post facto* calculations. Most injury victims (especially injured patients, in contrast to injured pedestrians, for example) will not likely win *any* tort payments, let alone an award that approaches the full cost of their injuries, unless they have the services of a lawyer prepared to invest substantial effort and resources on the victim's behalf. From the patient's point of view, then, the real question is how such fee regulation will affect the *ex ante* incentives of the parties and their attorneys as they pursue claims for which there has not yet been a verdict.

Under the contingent fee arrangement the plaintiff pays the lawyer only if he wins; he pays nothing if he loses. In that context, looking only at the fees paid to a lawyer by any one client makes the fee appear excessive. In medical malpractice, for example, if the patient has a lawyer the claim will succeed roughly 60 percent of the time.[55] As a result, the lawyer must bill his successful clients about two-thirds more than the fee he would charge if he were paid the same rate, win or lose, by all his clients (as defense counsel are paid by insurance carriers). A higher contingency fee therefore covers the time and expense consumed by the other 40 percent of the cases, in which the patient loses and the lawyer receives nothing for his efforts. So the implication of the contingent fee system is that victorious plaintiffs end up paying for the legal services of the losing plaintiffs. Of course, when the arrangement is entered into, none of the clients know who will be the winners and who will be the losers. The personal injury lawyer assumes *de facto* the role of financier-insurer of the legal costs of his entire portfolio of clients, guaranteeing each of them the opportunity to pursue his malpractice case on its merits without having to worry about the risk of an enormous legal bill if he should lose. At the same time, the underlying incentive structure of the arrangement is actually more conducive to an efficiently operating litigation process. The attorney, who is the best judge of whether a malpractice case has a fair chance of success, has a direct personal financial stake in weeding out spurious claims and avoiding unproductive motions or discovery, because it is his time and money, not the clients', that are wasted if a case is a loser.[56]

This is not to take a purely sanguine view of all the fees that are charged by personal injury lawyers, nor to imply that simply because a patient voluntarily entered into a contingent fee contract, the terms of the arrangement are necessarily ideal. Considerable evidence indicates that some plaintiff attorneys earn large economic rents in the imperfect market for legal services, and that this situation has worsened rather than improved in recent years.[57] In my opinion, however, the standard contingent fee cap is an even cruder and more inequitable policy than the problem it is intended to cure.

First, it is a mistake to target such regulation only at the percentage that is applied to awards of different magnitudes. At a minimum, one should emulate Florida's recent legislation and focus as well on the *stage* in the litigation process at which the case is actually disposed of. For example, a legislature might adopt a sliding scale that ranges from a 15 percent fee if the case is settled at the pre-suit screening stage to 35 percent if the case must go to a trial verdict.[58] Not only does this kind of fee scale bear a more rational relationship to the actual amount of work, expenditures, and risk undertaken by the patient's attorney, but it encourages defendants to make early settlement offers because a potential 20 percent discount on the attorney fee is waiting to be shared with the victim. Such settlements also reduce how much the insurer itself must pay in hourly fees to its lawyer.

Next, medical malpractice is far from the most urgent target for a legislative effort to reduce excessive attorney fees, compared, say, to airline crash litigation, in which the smaller standard percentage (20 percent) generates much more lucrative absolute lawyers' fees in cases that are actually easier to win.[59] Given the structure of malpractice liability law sketched in Chapter 2, it is a rather difficult and chancy undertaking for the patient's attorney to analyze complex medical records, to secure and pay for expensive expert testimony, and then to contend with a defendant doctor who has an emotional as well as a financial stake in resisting malpractice claims. These obstacles help explain why malpractice attorneys, especially the better ones, turn away several times as many patient clients as they eventually accept,[60] and why there is consequently a huge gap between the number of serious injuries negligently inflicted on patients in the health care system and the number of successful tort claims eventually compensated by the legal system.

Finally, there is no evidence that imperfections in the market for legal services generate excessive earnings for plaintiff attorneys, at least in comparison to the earnings of defense attorneys practicing in the same personal injury setting. Two systematic studies of medical malpractice found that when the time spent by the patient attorneys in their losing cases as well as in their victories was counted, the overall return per hour of legal services was roughly the same for plaintiff as for defense lawyers.[61] Indeed, if a legislature were serious about reducing the cost of malpractice litigation and insurance, the simplest, most direct way to do so would be to cap *defense* attorney fees, which have been the fastest-rising component of liability insurance costs in recent years.[62] Of course, doctors and their insurers would object vigorously to having such a statutory "benefit" conferred on them. Evidently they feel that there is an advantageous net return in this rising legal expenditure insofar as it has helped contain the number and the cost of the more expensive patient claims that they would otherwise have to pay. But given such a free legal hand for the defendant, a law that prevents an injured patient from promising to pay the money needed to induce a lawyer to take his case can only be judged an unfair and one-sided intrusion into our adversarial system of civil justice. Moreover, such a law is especially likely to hamper access to good legal services by younger, seriously injured victims in difficult and complicated medical settings, the circumstances in which the typical statutory fee scale binds most painfully.

Rejecting the conventional reform of a statutory cap on the plaintiff's attorney fee, however, means that another way must be found to solve the problem that is a side-effect of such other measures as a collateral source offset or a pain and suffering scale. Where is the injured victim to get the extra money to pay his attorney fees without having to cut into the award of supposedly full compensation for medical bills and lost earnings?[63] The solution that I favor is direct and simple. As part of any package of tort damage reform, the reasonable attorney fees incurred by successful plaintiffs in pursuing their claims should be treated merely as another type of economic loss for which the culpable defendant should be required to pay damages.

The positive argument for this measure is quite straightforward.[64] Victims of medical injuries suffer a variety of harmful consequences: extra medical bills, lost earnings, and possible interference with the future enjoyment of their lives. The tort system formally promises the victim full redress for all such losses at the expense of the health care provider whose negligence caused the accident, the rationale being either corrective justice or efficient compensation and prevention. For a variety of dubious historical reasons, American tort law has consistently turned a blind eye on an additional harmful consequence of the negligent injury, the fact that legal services are obligatory in order to secure the tort award necessary to pay medical bills and make up lost earnings, and it is the victim who must pay for the legal services. There is no legal policy justification for treating an injured patient's decision to consult a lawyer to repair his legal and economic harm any differently from the patient's decision to consult a doctor to repair his physical harm. A good time to adopt this measure would be when the legislature undertakes reform of other features of damages law, in order to tailor the tort damages to the net financial losses of the victim, of which attorney fees are generally a significant component.

This is *not* a proposal for adopting the Anglo-Canadian litigation rule that the loser pays the winner's attorney fees, a practice that was briefly tried in Florida malpractice law in the early eighties.[65] Although a two-way fee-shifting rule might appear superficially to be a more equitable and efficient means of allocating the cost of tort litigation, brief reflection on the vast differences in the real-life situations of the contending parties reveals that such equality is only formal.

My proposal rests squarely on the tort principles that govern risk-taking behavior in the outside world, not on procedural principles that perhaps should govern civil litigation. These tort principles dictate that an injured plaintiff who wins his case is the innocent victim of the negligent behavior of the defendant and is therefore entitled to full redress for his injuries—which, for the reasons just stated, include the expenses of enforcing his tort rights. By contrast, when a plaintiff loses his case, even though the defendant has suffered admitted losses as a result of the plaintiff's suit, the suit itself was not a wrong to the defendant. Patient lawyers, motivated by the contingent fee arrangement, screen out almost all obviously groundless claims. Nevertheless, it is inevitable that some claims that looked reasonably promising at the outset will turn out to be ill-founded when all the evidence is in and the jury has spoken. Yet the mere fact that a plaintiff's reasonable litigation mistake caused another party a loss is not grounds for treating the decision to litigate as a tort (just as it is inappropriate to treat as torts those initially reasonable medical decisions of doctors that ultimately leave patients worse rather than better off).[66]

In addition, the typical plaintiff and defendant are in disparate positions with respect to the costs of litigation. Most defendants are large organizations such as hospitals, which are regular players in the tort system and consequently able to make rational economic judgments about whether the chance of success from a particular legal position is worth the expense. Even doctor-defendants are personally insured for the legal expenses of malpractice litigation, so they need not worry about the financial consequences of resisting a claim, even unsuccessfully. An injured plaintiff, by contrast, is a lone individual, already in relatively straitened financial circumstances and entirely uninsured against the legal expenses of a malpractice suit. Changing the law to make unsuccessful tort claimants automatically liable for the legal bills of the malpractice insurer is likely to make such accident victims unduly risk averse about even launching a tort claim, let alone rejecting a low settlement offer from the defendant because of a reasonable expectation that more adequate redress will be secured at trial.[67] Because there are now far fewer malpractice suits than malpractice incidents, and because the most seriously injured patients already receive damages far smaller than their real financial losses, a full-fledged, two-way fee shift would be a regressive rather than a progressive malpractice reform.

As a matter of both legal principle and practical politics, imposition on defendants of the legal responsibility for the successful plaintiff's legal expenses must be accompanied by measures that deal with the financial and psychological costs inflicted on doctors by the not insignificant number of spurious malpractice claims, claims that should never have been filed. Tackling this issue can also be achieved quite simply.

In a case in which it appears that a malpractice suit was not simply unsuccessful *ex post,* but should clearly have been withheld *ex ante,* the defendant should be entitled to reimbursement of its legal costs as redress for its legal injury. Furthermore, this obligation should be imposed on the plaintiff's *attorney* rather than on the patient himself. The attorney is in a much better position to judge whether a malpractice claim is baseless before signing his professional name to the suit; moreover, the attorney is more likely to have the funds (or the insurance) to be able to satisfy the defendant's claim. But any such change in the legal responsibility and incentives of plaintiff lawyers should be paralleled by similar measures for defense lawyers. In particular, a defense attorney who files a frivolous (as opposed to a merely unsuccessful) defense or motion should be personally responsible for all the additional costs thereby imposed on the plaintiff, with a legal bar to any reimbursement by the defendant's insurer.

Although many malpractice claims might appear reasonable at the outset, it may become obvious at later stages in the litigation process that they are groundless. In such cases, further measures are needed to deal with the problem. In particular, defendants should have available to them a procedure for making a formal offer of settlement. If the offer is rejected by the plaintiff after a sufficient period of discovery to permit informed appraisal, but the plaintiff does not receive materially more than this offer at trial, then the defendant should not be responsible for any additional legal costs of the plaintiff arising subsequent to the rejection of the offer. Further, if the rejection was not simply a mistake in judgment but an unscrupulous tactical maneuver by the plaintiff's attorney, then the latter should be held responsible for the additional legal expenses thereby imposed on the defendant.

Obviously, much more detail is necessary to flesh out this barebones framework for changes in the personal injury attorney fee system. In particular, a critical issue is how to calculate the "reasonable" attorney fee. Should we use the standard present-day formula of a specified percentage of the tort award, thereby avoiding the transaction costs of litigating case by case the appropriate size of the attorney fee? Or should we use the civil rights "lodestar" model, in which a reasonable number of hours to be compensated at the prevailing community rates is calculated, then multiplied by a contingency factor that takes account of the actual risks of failure posed by the claim? This approach would permit judges and masters to scrutinize the actual efforts and rewards of personal injury lawyers, ideally with a comparison of the time and money expended by defense attorneys on the same cases. Although, on balance, my inclination is toward the first model, sorting out this issue involves complex considerations of the market for legal services and of the administration of civil justice that are too remote from the immediate subject to explore here.

However, for reasons that should be clear by now, it is crucial to focus on the plaintiff's attorney fee, in particular on the issue of who should pay that fee, as a problem that is inextricably intertwined with the appropriate scope of tort damages for patient injuries. I am convinced that the package of reform measures presented in this chapter—a collateral source offset, a pain and suffering scale, and attorney fees as a separate category of tort damages—would produce a less expensive and more easily insurable malpractice regime for doctors, while at the same time providing a more sensible mode of compensation for patients who suffer substantial unreimbursed financial losses from their injuries.

4

Prevention of Medical Injuries

The Deterrence Debate

The major changes proposed in the last chapter would sharply improve the equity and efficiency of redress through the tort system for the losses of the most seriously injured victims of medical injuries. But even if all these reforms were enacted, tort litigation would remain deficient as a means of compensating past injuries. Conditioning entitlement to tort benefits on establishing the fault of the doctor who caused the harm arbitrarily selects only a fraction of the patients who suffer iatrogenic injuries, with no regard to their relative need for financial support. Even worse, the adversarial contest over the question of whether there was doctor fault generates administrative costs that consume an even larger share of the claims dollar than the portion which eventually ends up in the hands of victims. Unquestionably, first-party loss insurance, public or private, is a much better mechanism than even dramatically reformed tort damages for delivering fair and economic compensation to accident victims.

The proponents of the tort/fault system base their case, as they must, on a very different role for the institution. From an instrumental point of view, the prime function served by tort law is preventing injuries to potential future victims. From this perspective, the flaw in pure loss insurance is that it removes virtually all the financial burden for the victim's harm from the party responsible for the accident. Tort liability, by contrast, legally attributes the cost of injuries to the party who was in a position to but did not take the steps necessary to keep the harm from occurring. The prospect of legal intervention gives actors a financial incentive to do what is reasonable to protect others from the risk of injuries arising from the actor's conduct. In the medical context, then, the strongest argument for malpractice law would be the improvement it secures in the general safety and quality of medical care.

This appears to be an attractive vantage point from which to defend the malpractice regime. We are indisputably better off if we can prevent injuries from happening before they occur rather than simply try to provide what is almost always inadequate monetary compensation after the fact. This need is especially important in the medical context, in which patients face such a high risk of iatrogenic injury. Recall the conclusion from the large-scale New York and California studies:[1] approximately 1 out of every 25 patients who are hospitalized suffers a disabling injury as a result of treatment, and 1 in 100 hospitalizations results in an injury that is due to the carelessness of a doctor or other provider. A 1 percent chance that a tortious harm will occur is a very substantial risk exposure in a nation that has a total of nearly 40 million hospitalizations a year. Even granted that substantially higher administrative costs are generated by using third-party liability insurance rather than first-party loss insurance to compensate those who are hurt, malpractice litigation need exert only a modest preventive effect on the much larger population of potential accident victims to more than pay for itself.

Those scholars who analyze tort law, and in particular malpractice law, from the law and economics perspective are generally comfortable with this prevention rationale.[2] The economic function of tort law is to assure a reasonable standard of care—technically, the *optimal* level of care. The optimality standard implies that resources should be allocated for safety up to the point at which the cost of the precautions equals the injury losses that they prevent. Liability sanctions are needed to elicit such socially rational behavior in order to alter the incentive structure that has the cost of necessary precautions paid for by actors, while the cost of injuries is borne by victims.

The logic of this analysis is most compelling in cases of accidents between strangers, such as motor vehicle drivers and pedestrians. Legal intervention is less obviously necessary in settings in which actors and victims are in a contractual relationship whose terms are set by competitive markets; an example is the relationship between motor vehicle manufacturers and owners. In such cases the market itself tends to shift the cost of reasonable precautions to the consumers (who are also the beneficiaries) in the price they pay for the product or service, while the cost of injuries that seemed excessive to consumers would be shifted back to substandard providers in the form of lower sales and profits. However, in the case of the doctor-patient relationship, even though it is contractual and its terms are influenced by the general health care market, imposing mandatory tort standards on the relationship is defensible if we assume that the patient is typically ignorant of the relative risks and benefits of different forms of treatment and levels of care. An uninformed choice by individual patients, even a choice between the doctors and hospitals that are competing for their patronage, cannot be relied upon to produce the ideal blend of precaution and economy in the course of the patients' medical treatment.[3]

The foregoing is the standard account of how the tort system can be used to induce a more satisfactory level of injury prevention. There is also a standard critique of the potential contribution of tort litigation to prevention.[4] Only a fraction of all potentially litigable claims are resolved by the tort system, by either a verdict or a settlement. The decision to process a claim is heavily influenced by factors other than the culpability of the victim; most important is the level of damages anticipated if the claim is successful. This estimated return dictates whether a personal injury lawyer will invest the time and money first to develop and then to pursue a claim for a share of the damages under the contingent fee arrangement.[5] Even when a tort case gets to trial, a lay jury which is selected ad hoc for each such case must often grapple with highly technical issues before rendering a verdict about what precautions were reasonable. Because the jury is considering with the benefit of hindsight a serious accident that has *already* occurred, jurors are understandably prone to overestimate the risks and to underestimate the benefits of the activity that produced the mishap.[6] So even granting the limitations of nonlegal incentives for reasonably safe behavior, critics of tort litigation believe that the system is unlikely to improve things and may actually leave them worse off.

Plausible *a priori* arguments can be made, then, on both sides of this debate. Moreover, there has been very little empirical investigation to provide useful material for either position, because such research is so difficult to carry out. With respect to the compensation function, tort litigation does transfer money from some insurers to some victims; systematic investigation can document how many victims collect money through the tort process, what proportion and what distribution of total patient losses are reimbursed this way, and how much of the funds allocated for compensation are used up in lawyers' fees or other administrative costs in effecting the transfer. By contrast, the preventive influence of tort law rests on a logical inference that imposing liability on those at fault in prior accidents will induce similarly situated individuals to avoid such culpably risky behavior in the future. Although the assumption is plausible, it is difficult to pin down how much of an incentive is created and whether the behavioral reaction of potential defendants materially reduces the injuries to potential victims. To test that proposition one would ideally compare outcomes in places where there is such a tort risk with outcomes in places where there is no such risk, research that is just now beginning to emerge with regard to jurisdictions that have moved away from tort/fault liability for motor vehicle accidents.[7] But because of the major differences in both the real world and the tort law settings for motor vehicle and medical accidents, it is useful first to look closely at the special features of health care that likely shape any prevention impact of malpractice litigation before reviewing the relevant empirical research that does exist.

Characteristics of Malpractice Law and Insurance

As we saw in Chapter 2, one distinctive feature of conventional malpractice law is that it does not permit courts to define the optimal standard of practice for the medical profession. As long as a doctor has acted in accordance with the customary standard of practice in his professional community, even if the "community" consists only of a "respectable minority" in the profession, a jury is not permitted to accept the testimony of an expert witness that such medical custom is unreasonable and negligent.[8] There is, of course, sufficient play in the joints of medical practice to permit juries some leeway in finding that the defendant-doctor's judgment has no support inside the profession.[9] But formally at least, the role of malpractice law is simply to hold individual doctors to the existing norms of their medical colleagues, not to define new standards for the entire calling.

Even this diluted legal standard for health care providers is remarkably underenforced by tort law. The aggregate numbers of paid malpractice claims are far smaller than the total of even serious negligent injuries. Moreover, there seems to be considerable mismatching of even these claims against the actual negligent injuries. Whereas the Harvard study in New York found that there was roughly one tort claim for every eight negligent injuries (that is, actual "torts"), because the claims that were in fact filed were as likely as not to have *no* negligent injury behind them, the real gap was even greater between true torts occurring in the health care system and tort claims being made in the legal system.[10] By contrast with the situation under motor vehicle law, for example, it is difficult for most patients even to know that they have been harmed by their medical treatment, let alone to be able to detect and prove carelessness on the part of an identifiable doctor or other health care provider.

Empirical research demonstrates, then, how distant is the real world from the analytical models of optimality defined by tort scholars. But the fact that most cases of medical negligence go untouched by tort litigation does not mean that the tort system exercises no meaningful deterrence. Just as is true of traffic law, for example, if it is known that some violations of a legal standard will be punished and it is impossible to predict which ones those will be, there is an incentive to comply with the standard at least most of the time.[11] In addition, research indicates that doctors *overestimate* the true risk of suit by a factor of several times.[12] The publicity that individual suits and trials receive in the reasonably close-knit professional community and the general hue and cry about spiraling malpractice litigation and premiums across the country have apparently made the tort system much more salient in doctors' minds than it is in fact.

The deterrent force of the tort system does not have to be very strong to motivate doctors to take greater precautions. Even abstracting from the professional ethic of caring for one's patient, the standard reimbursement system employed in the medical market puts less weight on the tort incentive than is needed in, say, product liability. In the product context there is reason to worry that profit-oriented manufacturers will scrimp on designing their products safely for fear that the additional costs will cut into sales and revenues. By contrast, in modern health care the doctor has ample economic incentive for investing—even overinvesting—in tests, procedures, and time that might produce better medical outcomes. Even though such elaborate precautions may be expensive—beyond the optimal point—for society as a whole, they are often lucrative sources of income for doctors, and they produce little consumer resistance from patients whose health insurers are picking up the bills in any event.[13]

But if more rather than less care is the physician's natural inclination, why is there evidence of such a high level of negligence in both law reports and empirical studies? Although this is a difficult question to answer, I suggest the following lines of response.[14]

Modern scientific medicine has two faces. There can be no doubt that medicine has steadily and substantially reduced the levels of risk that arise from the interaction of the human body with the natural and cultural environment. For example, a recently heralded development is successfully performing surgery on the fetus while it is still in utero to prevent what would otherwise be severe and untreatable defects after birth. But however sophisticated medical procedures and technologies may become, they ultimately rely on the care and attention of humans for their proper use and safeguards. Human beings, though, are prone to inattention, forgetfulness, and mistakes. We know this is true from our daily experience with another technological mainstay of modern civilization—the automobile. Even reasonably cautious drivers regularly let their minds wander and commit numerous errors on the road.[15] The same is true in medicine, in which trained doctors, nurses, and technicians can never have all their human frailty programmed out of them. Unlike the comparatively safe environment of the highway or the workplace, the hospital, especially the operating room, is a dangerous and unforgiving environment. Even surgeons and obstetricians who exhibit above-average concentration will make occasional and inadvertent slip-ups. Unfortunately, that momentary mistake—which does constitute negligence in the eyes of the law—exposes the patient to serious and irretrievable harm, including the failure to diagnose a condition in a patient who only a decade or two ago would have had no expectation of a medical cure for the ills of nature.

If the foregoing account is valid, it should give us a greater understanding of the phenomenon of human error in modern medicine and enable us to empathize with the physicians' plight. Still, empathy is not reason enough to relax the pressure exerted by litigation for increasing levels of concentration and attention to the standards set for the ever more ambitious and riskier enterprise of medicine. But the question that then arises is whether the enforcement pressures produced by tort law are diluted even further by the institution of malpractice insurance that now covers almost all practicing physicians.[16]

From a compensatory, risk-spreading point of view, insurance is clearly a great benefit. It provides severely injured patients access to a fund from which they can actually receive the money awarded to them in court; at the same time it protects doctors and their families from the crushing impact of a huge penalty for what is typically a momentary, inadvertent mishap. But from the point of view of prevention—the major positive argument for a fault-based system— there is an evident problem. Because it is the malpractice carrier for an entire pool of doctors that actually pays the award and the legal bill when a doctor is found negligent, the prospect of having to face such damages cannot be a meaningful spur to the individual doctor to be more careful and attentive. Liability insurance is the most visible source of tension between the immediate compensation function of tort litigation and the long-term prevention impact that such liability awards are supposed to have.

Fortunately, the incompatibility between the two institutions and the two objectives is not inevitable.[17] It is possible to accommodate the risk distribution role of insurance with the deterrent role of litigation through the careful design of insurance coverage, in particular, by employing an experience-rating formula under which future premiums are surcharged according to the insured's claims experience in a previous time frame.

However attractive this middle ground appears in tort theory, the practice is largely absent from present-day malpractice insurance, although deductibles and surcharges are commonplace features of workplace, product, and even motor vehicle insurance. In a sense this leaves malpractice with the worst of both worlds. Its premiums vary directly with the past and expected future experience of a group of doctors in a particular locality and specialty for which the policy is written. So, for example, a general practitioner in a rural setting pays a far lower premium than does a neurosurgeon in a big city. The vice in such segmentation of doctors into comparatively small insurance pools is that one or two catastrophic injuries or just a few huge pain and suffering awards can sharply drive up the premiums of all the doctors in a particular category. But there is little or no variation in the premium increases charged to the doctors responsible for the mishaps in their own practice.[18] Consequently, there appears to be no financial incentive trained on the individual physician, though it is the cumulative result of such individual behavior that produces the aggregate claims and costs that will be paid in any given insured category.

The absence of this apparently sensible feature from malpractice insurance seems rather surprising. One would assume that doctors with a better safety record would flock to carriers who offered them lower premiums (and consequently higher net income) in recognition of their better malpractice experience. But carriers themselves have traditionally felt that malpractice litigation was too random—in terms of the likelihood and actual costs of individual claims—to give much validity to such actuarial variation in premiums. In any event, any rebate that could be offered to apparently better physicians would be too small to outweigh the predictable consumer resistance from doctors who would be exposed to surcharges from the vagaries of a legal system in which they had little confidence.

Recently, however, mandatory experience rating has been a feature of malpractice reform legislation enacted in New York and Massachusetts, states that saw this feature as an effective prod to greater care for patients, irrespective of whether it was actively sought by the doctor-purchasers of malpractice insurance.[19] The essentials of experience-rating programs are quite simple. The claims record of doctors is tracked over a five-year period, with a certain number of points awarded for each claim and additional points for each paid claim. Surcharges are placed on the future premiums of doctors with more than a minimum point level in this rolling five-year period. Predictably, both states' programs have been mired in controversy since they were first enacted because of thorough disagreement by physician representatives with the design of such programs.

It is useful to look closely at the difficulty of rating individual doctors in this way, because this exercise reveals problematic features of malpractice litigation generally. There are three prerequisites for the experience-rating mechanism to be effective for prevention. The rating formula must produce actuarially credible indications of the true relative risk posed by individual doctors; the premium surcharges must be great enough to give physicians a significant financial incentive to improve their level of care; and the physician behavior in question must be responsive to such economic motivation. Insofar as it applies to doctors, as contrasted with hospitals, experience rating satisfies none of these conditions well.

Let us look at the actuarial point first. If the premiums paid by a particular doctor are to be increased for the future because of a claim or two lodged in the past, one must assume that the past events are a valid index of a greater than average risk posed by the insured doctor for the upcoming coverage period. While that assumption might seem plausible on its face, it must be heavily qualified in practice. Inevitably there is a random quality to an event that is as infrequent in the life of any one doctor as a malpractice suit. So the fact that a doctor's error on one occasion happens to produce both an injury and a lawsuit does not by itself provide credible evidence that the doctor is a poorer risk than his peers who were fortunate enough to have avoided either injury or suit for their own occasional inattention. As illustration, in the experience-rating formula used in workers' compensation, only after a particular employer has a large enough payroll to experience a sizable number of claims per year (perhaps fifteen lost-time injuries annually, depending on the industry) will any significant adjustment be made in the size of the firm's premium.[20] Even though malpractice frequency has risen sharply over the last two decades—now averaging about one paid claim a year for every twenty practicing physicians—these numbers are still far too small for what would be considered necessary for actuarially sound experience rating in, say, workers' compensation.

One might respond that the statistical constraints are appropriate in the case of workplace injuries because workers' compensation is a no-fault program. In medical malpractice, by contrast, liability depends on a specific judgment that a doctor is actually at fault, an evaluation that would appear to provide a direct index of the doctor's regular level of care. Such an inference is dubious, though, because so many factors besides simply the skill and care of individual doctors affect the distribution of malpractice claims. The fact that doctors in New York and Florida pay far higher premiums than those in Indiana and Arkansas, or that neurosurgeons and obstetricians pay far higher premiums than internists or pediatricians, cannot possibly mean that a neurosurgeon in New York is fifty times as careless as an internist in Indiana. It is far more likely that the doctors in the different regions and specialities have, on average, roughly the same disposition to human error.[21] The comparable levels of inattentiveness in the two settings are eventually translated into stark differences in premium levels by the sharp contrast in the risk of injury from the respective treatment procedures, the severity of the injuries when they occur, the likelihood that lawyers can be found to bring suit, and the readiness of jurors to uphold claims against doctors and to assess generous damages. To control for the wide range of such external factors in assessing any one doctor's record of malpractice costs requires a good deal of comparative experience; this is necessary before one can validly judge that the doctor is significantly worse than his peers. It is difficult to develop such a record of experience in the case of an individual doctor, as contrasted with the extensive claims experience of large organizations such as hospitals.

Of course, extending the time frame back far enough may permit us to discern statistically valid indicators of accident-proneness in the claims records of different physicians. Indeed, three studies, one from California in the early seventies, the others from Pennsylvania and from Florida in the late seventies and early eighties,[22] demonstrate that the observed distribution of claims in a specialty or regional pool is considerably different from what would be predicted by chance. To put this in another way, if an insurer were to carve out a separate pool of doctors who had experienced claims in a prior period, the carrier would find that the same pool would also have a larger number of claims in a subsequent period.

Even these statistical findings do not settle all doubts about whether surcharging a "higher-risk" pool is both a good index of the ongoing level of care and an incentive to maintain high standards. First, the statistics show only that the *group* of higher-risk doctors in the earlier period had more claims and costs in the second period. Yet it was also found, in Florida for example, that more than half the individual doctors in the early highest-risk category had no claims at all in the second period, during which time they would be paying a hefty surcharge under a hypothetical experience-rating program.[23] Second, the fact that a doctor has a claim filed against him or her does not itself provide convincing evidence of a problem of performance quality. Most claims are not paid, and even those which are settled with payment may be settled for a variety of tactical reasons.[24] If a particular doctor has a persistently high level of claims, these random factors will even out, and it is fair to consider the doctor to be a special risk. In fact, however, the bad apples are a tiny fraction of the total population of doctors in malpractice cases.[25] Their situation is likely better addressed through a more precisely targeted medical regulatory system than through broad-based, experience-rated malpractice insurance. Indeed, going far enough back down the "long tail" of malpractice claims to gain a sufficiently extensive base of credible experience greatly attenuates the discounted value of any experience-based premium surcharge.[26]

It is possible, though expensive, to respond to the problems inherent in transposing standard actuarial experience rating into the medical malpractice context. Indeed, what the medical societies in both New York and Massachusetts have been pressing for is a type of qualitative peer review of claims experience that is now in vogue with a number of the physician-owned malpractice carriers (the so-called bedpan mutuals).[27] Committees of doctors selected by the insurer or the medical society review the documentation relating to a malpractice claim, evaluate the merit of the claim without regard to what has transpired within the tort system, and then offer the insurer their judgment about the type of risk a particular physician appears to present in his overall practice. The outcome of the process may be some premium surcharge, or possibly even termination of future insurance coverage. Elaborate mechanisms for appealing these decisions are available to the affected physicians.

This peer review process has the virtue of providing a better-informed appraisal of a particular incident of malpractice as well as the broader practice pattern of the physician. Moreover, the review board can select from a wider range of sanctions the one that is precisely tailored to the risk presented by the doctor in question. Such sanctions may include imposing limitations on the doctor's practice as a condition for future insurance coverage. The review process can also be triggered by nontort events, such as complaints to the state medical review board or disturbing information that comes to the attention of the insurer or its committee.

In a sense, then, the peer review system utilized by the bedpan mutuals operates as a parallel process to tort litigation. It complements what now takes place in major hospitals and state regulatory agencies, and it anticipates some of the features of the "administrative fault" program proposed by the American Medical Association (discussed in Chapter 6). Although the tie-in to the current malpractice regime has the advantage of bringing problem cases to light through patient tort claims, its disadvantage is that the internal investigation cannot begin until the claim has finally been resolved, for fear of compromising the carrier's position in defense of the claim. If the outcome of the process is a premium surcharge rather than a termination of coverage,[28] a delay of several years before the charge is imposed greatly weakens the financial incentive for better care that the threat of such a surcharge may provide.

The last point can be viewed from another perspective. Average malpractice premiums across the country are now roughly $15,000 a year. Suppose that an actuarial formula were used that permitted surcharges to average as much as 100 percent of premiums for two paid claims in five years—and I suspect this would be stretching statistical credibility to the breaking point.[29] The maximum potential surcharge would then be on the order of $15,000 per year, discounted by the lapse of roughly ten years between the physician's actions and the disposition of all these tort claims. That financial penalty would not be appreciably larger than the penalty presently inflicted on doctors from the direct, more immediate, and uninsured costs of being sued.

Consider only the tangible financial expenses of being involved in a lawsuit. Doctors lose, on average, up to five days from their practice in order to respond to the typical malpractice claim.[30] Assuming that a doctor can earn about $1,200 a day in gross revenues, the doctor must pay an immediate "deductible" of more than $5,000 in net lost time for each claim, since the expenses of practice are largely fixed and must be paid whether or not the doctor is working and earning revenues from his practice on these days. Beyond these purely financial costs are the reputational damage and the psychological stress that arise from being involved in litigation. Consequently, an experience-rated program that eventually adds a finite surcharge to malpractice premiums is not likely to alter fundamentally the incentives already felt by doctors under the present flat-rate system.

Given that modern malpractice litigation inflicts tangible penalties on individual doctors, can we be confident that the tort system elicits a higher quality of medical care from the profession? Note that the bulk of the uninsured costs of being sued are extracted from doctors irrespective of whether claims against them are found to have merit. That is why so many physicians feel that the legal process has a Kafkaesque quality to it, like a system in which traffic police hand out tickets to drivers who go through green lights as often as they do to drivers who go through red lights. But however accurate or substantial such tort incentives might be, their efficacy ultimately depends on the nature of the behavior the system seeks to influence.

Remember that the focus of malpractice law is not the general standards of practice that are consciously adopted by the medical profession, but rather the momentary slip-ups by doctors, nurses, and others in the execution of medically prescribed procedures. Yet this kind of human fallibility is not the type of behavior for which tort sanctions are best suited.[31] Consider, for example, an anesthetist who is momentarily distracted from indicators of oxygen deprivation to the patient and omits the necessary emergency response. The prospect of a tort suit arising years later as a result of a problem the doctor is too distracted even to be thinking about during the treatment in question will not likely provide him with motivation to adopt the proper precautions. If in that situation the physician *had* been so attentive that he realized he had to take certain measures in order to avoid a lawsuit, simple concern for the needs and safety of his patient would have been sufficient inducement for him to take the steps necessary to prevent irreversible brain damage. By contrast with what occurs in a typical commercial setting, doctors rarely have a serious incentive to economize on necessary precautions for their patients, such that tort incentives must be established to right the safety balance. In fact, doctors are likely to receive even more income by providing their patients with supraoptimal care.

The basic thrust of medical malpractice law, focused as it is on particular incidents in the professional work of usually conscientious individual doctors, is quite different from that of modern product liability law. In product liability law the target is a corporate organization whose products, be they motor vehicles or pharmaceuticals, pose recurring safety problems. These corporations employ people whose job it is to plan the design and the marketing of these products. The firms are well motivated by fully experience-rated liability insurance to invest in safeguards against the ever-present possibility of human error in the use of their products.

Halting steps are being taken in this direction in both hospitals and malpractice doctrine. An illuminating case study is the development by the Harvard teaching hospitals of anesthesia equipment, staffing, and monitoring procedures to provide better precautions against the risk of human failure in the potentially hazardous setting of the operating room.[32] Not only must specified personnel be present during the entire anesthesia period, but oximeter equipment is used that sounds an alarm if oxygen levels drop below the indicated norm. The per-case cost of both the additional personnel and the new equipment turned out to be much lower than the per-case cost of malpractice insurance against anesthesia mishaps. But current malpractice law now largely insulates from court review these more reflective programmatic decisions (or nondecisions) that appear to be most amenable to whatever financial leverage tort litigation wields in tandem with the pricing of malpractice insurance.

Evidence about the Impact of Malpractice Law

My observations in the prior section are largely the product of armchair reflections about the possible preventive impact of malpractice litigation. In that respect they are akin to almost all the analyses we have of this vital tort function. An apt illustration is the work of Patricia Danzon, whose comprehensive and sophisticated writing about the malpractice regime reports a host of empirical findings about the compensation and administrative dimensions of the system, much based on her own research. Yet though Danzon's entire theory (and defense) of fault-based malpractice law rests on its preventive role—

that is, the benign influence of the law on the safety and quality of medical care—her argument on this point consists entirely of abstract theorizing about why this might be so, without any empirical corroboration that in fact it is so.

While my own equally abstract analysis in the prior section leaves me somewhat skeptical about the amount of injury prevention we are likely to procure from the present litigation-insurance system, I expect that there is some such impact. One can find apparent confirmation in research done regarding tort litigation about motor vehicle accidents.

In the motor vehicle setting as well, many tort scholars have expressed doubt that the prospect of a tort suit could exert much independent influence on the individual driver to take greater care to avoid accidents that are typically the result of inattention to a variety of risks encountered on the road. The doubters argue that anyone who adverts to the need to drive more slowly and carefully in order to avoid tort liability to someone else for a collision will surely realize there is an even better reason to be careful: to avoid possibly severe or even fatal injuries to himself. Empirical research data are now beginning to accumulate as a result of recent experimental tests of the tort-deterrence proposition. The research studied the effects of partial (as in the United States) or total (as in Quebec, New Zealand, and the Australian Northern Territory) replacement of third-party, tort-fault liability by first-party, no-fault benefits for motor vehicle accidents, controlling for a host of other relevant variables. The analytic skeptics notwithstanding, the preliminary indications are that these legal changes are associated with an increase in automobile fatalities.[33]

There is still a sharp debate about whether this higher accident rate is a function of the elimination of tort litigation over fault, or of the concomitant adoption of flat-rate pricing of auto insurance that has made it easier for poorer drivers to stay on the road. But whatever the verdict on the precise cause (which will be pertinent to my discussion in Chapter 6 of the pros and cons of no-fault patient compensation as a possible substitute for fault-based malpractice litigation), we do have reason to believe that the combined effect of tort litigation and third-party liability insurance makes a tangible difference in the injury toll on our highways.

I cautioned earlier in this chapter against freely extrapolating conclusions from the motor vehicle situation to the medical field, given the considerable disparities in training and attitudes of the respective actors and in the litigability of accidental injuries when they occur.

Hence the importance of close scrutiny of whatever empirical investigation has been done of the legal influence of malpractice law on physician behavior.

In the legal literature, there are two substantial studies of the same genre—case studies of the effect of widely publicized appellate court decisions on the subsequent accident-prevention efforts by doctors in the specialties at issue in those decisions.[34] One such study investigated the impact on ophthalmologists of the Washington decision in *Helling v. Carey,* to which I referred earlier.[35] The second study examined the impact on psychiatrists, psychologists, and social workers of the *Tarasoff* decision in the state of California.[36] In the latter case, the California Supreme Court had initially held that a therapist whose patient had made a threat of violence against a third party had a duty to warn the potential victim. After reargument, the court softened this holding somewhat to require that the therapist take the "reasonable" precautions needed in the circumstances (a warning or other safeguard).

These studies each followed the same research strategy. A survey questionnaire was administered to a broad sample of doctors, both in the particular state and nationwide. The questionnaire asked the doctors about their behavior in the situations at issue before the court rulings, and the changes, if any, that the decisions had induced in their subsequent practice. Each study found that a significant number of doctors were actually using the prescribed measures before the courts had spoken, and a somewhat greater number of doctors began following the mandated practices after the decisions. Only the second *Tarasoff* study concluded that this behavioral change was mainly attributable to the law as such.[37] These somewhat ambiguous conclusions about the efficacy of malpractice law are noteworthy because these were exceptional and highly publicized appellate court decisions that purported to alter the existing standard of professional practice in settings in which one might expect the legal rules to influence the doctor's conscious judgment and regular routine. Since, as I observed earlier, the vast bulk of malpractice litigation purports simply to enforce attention to and compliance with existing medical custom in a variety of concrete treatment situations, its general influence is likely to be even more elusive.

In any event, even interpreting these studies as supporting the proposition that the legal definition of professional standards makes at least some difference in physician behavior does not necessarily mean that tort law therefore enhances patient safety. For example, in the case of workplace injuries we would hardly agree that the effectiveness of the Occupational Safety and Health Act (OSHA) was demonstrated by a showing that employers are more likely to adopt certain safety standards once they are prescribed by government administrators.[38] What we really need to know is whether such employer compliance in turn produces a net drop in workplace injuries.[39] By analogy, then, to truly test the efficacy of malpractice law what we need to know is whether *Helling* actually reduced the level of glaucoma-induced blindness, or *Tarasoff* the incidence of violent attacks by patients under psychotherapy (controlling for other potential contributors to the same outcomes).

The need for precisely this kind of empirical study is reinforced by the fact that medical research and commentary on this particular topic generally argues that tort litigation has caused doctors to practice "defensive" medicine in order to avoid patient lawsuits, rather than to practice more careful medicine in order to avoid patient injuries.[40]

The claim that defensive medicine is the real product of malpractice litigation has gained wide currency in the broader political debate. Though cost figures ranging from $15 billion to as high as $40 billion were bandied about in the early eighties,[41] a subsequent, more systematic analysis of this phenomenon estimates that in 1984 the price of defensive medical practice was around $9 to $10 billion, dwarfing the $3 billion paid by doctors that year in malpractice premiums.[42] Given this apparently even more costly feature of malpractice litigation, it is no wonder that state legislatures have responded to physician pressures to place restraints (however inequitable) on patients' access to and rewards from the legal system.

But while we now have much more precise quantitative estimates of defensive medicine, we are still far from a consensus about the nature, sources, and even the evaluation of the phenomenon.[43] An initial question is precisely what patterns of behavioral reaction are incorporated in the term "defensive" medicine. One kind of response that has been documented in numerous physician surveys is the decision by certain doctors to stop practicing altogether, or to stop performing certain procedures—most often obstetrics—because of their unhappiness with the malpractice situation.[44] Of course, while such a step may involve a private cost to these doctors, it is not necessarily a social cost as long as there are sufficient doctors remaining to deliver the babies and to perform the other services needed (perhaps doing so at even lower risk if the physicians who remain in active practice in a particular field are those who are the most qualified). However, there do appear to be troubling indications that good and convenient obstetric services are becoming increasingly less available to those who are poor or who live in rural areas and have been dependent on clinics or family practitioners for child delivery.[45]

Interestingly, it appears that this reaction by physicians is due not so much to the experience with malpractice litigation itself,[46] but rather to the crudity of the pricing of liability insurance as this item interacts with health care reimbursement formulas. The problem is that annual malpractice premiums for a coverage year are typically not adjusted to the lower-than-average number of obstetric procedures performed by clinics or family doctors for whom this is a secondary aspect of their practice.[47] The problem is aggravated if much of the doctor's patient load consists of poor people, because in most states the per-delivery cost of malpractice insurance for the full-time obstetrician is nearly as high as or even higher than the total reimbursement paid by Medicaid for such a delivery.[48] A more precisely tailored solution to this access problem, then, would be to alter the pricing of malpractice insurance (such as having it vary directly with the number of deliveries performed each year), in tandem with rationalizing the way that this practice cost is dealt with by Medicaid and other health care programs.[49]

Such changes in insurance pricing and health care reimbursement schedules will not, however, provide relief from the proliferation of costly and unnecessary medical equipment, procedures, tests, X-rays, consultations, and record notations—steps doctors feel compelled to take to reduce the odds that they will be sued, irrespective of whether the patient will be helped by them.

Actually, this last phenomenon appears to be a by-product of the peculiar tilt in both malpractice doctrine and health insurance. I referred earlier to the obstacles posed by the legal standard of customary medical practice to cost containment efforts by the individual doctors, who still make the key treatment decisions on behalf of their patients.[50] The difficulty is that even if it appears to one doctor that a particular procedure—electronic fetal monitoring, for example[51]—is not useful to his patient, he knows that he is taking a serious personal risk in deviating from the current medical consensus that favors the more elaborate and costly procedure. If something happens to go wrong and the baby is born defective, the visible absence of this precaution will be the "smoking gun" that the tort lawyer needs to make his case, whereas if the doctor uses the more expensive consensus procedure there is little or no legal risk from that practice decision.

Tort law alone could not likely produce a pronounced cost effect of that type. So although American doctors regularly assert that the threat of malpractice litigation from any possible complication in a natural childbirth is the major explanation for the burgeoning rate of cesarean sections over the last two decades, physicians' increased use of this more expensive procedure is feasible only because patients typically have health insurance to pay for it. Unlike product manufacturers, doctors have experienced little consumer resistance to the steep bill for allegedly defensive medicine.[52] Still, the contribution of health insurance is not a defense for tort law against the charge that it is responsible for defensive practices. Even if tort litigation is only a necessary, not a sufficient, cause of this phenomenon, the fact is that if patient health insurance is judged a socially valuable institution, the cure for defensive medicine will have to consist in placing constraints upon the tort system that is its accomplice.

What is by no means clear, though, is that tort litigation is even a necessary accomplice. It is easy to understand obstetricians' *saying* that it is fear of malpractice litigation that has produced the sharply increased rate of more expensive, more painful, and occasionally riskier cesarean deliveries.[53] But if greater expense to the patient's insurer also means greater income to doctors who are paid on a fee-for-service basis, perhaps the desire to increase physician income is a sufficient explanation for the trends we observe in practice. The United States has the highest rate of cesareans to total deliveries, but it is also true that in almost all countries cesarean rates have been rising sharply in the last two decades, even though foreign countries may have much lower levels of malpractice litigation (as in Canada or the United Kingdom) or may have dispensed with tort law entirely in favor of no-fault patient compensation (as in New Zealand and Sweden).[54] We can legitimately single out tort law as a significant independent contributor to this medical trend only on the basis of research that relates differences in the incidence of such procedures to variations in the intensity of the tort system, while controlling for such economic factors as the ratio of doctors to patients and the nature of the reimbursement system used in health insurance.

Finally, though, we can adopt a policy position with respect to this phenomenon only after we have resolved a crucial ambiguity in the meaning of "defensive" medicine. In much popular discussion this label is applied to any steps taken by doctors because of their concern about being sued. In other contexts, evidence that this kind of response was occurring would be viewed as a positive compliment to the law. Consider what our reaction would be to a finding that motor vehicle litigation was inducing widespread defensive driving. To merit its intended pejorative connotations, the "defensive" label must be confined to medical practices that, in addition to being costly and even risky, have little therapeutic utility but are undertaken by doctors nonetheless simply because they wish to avoid legal liability. Again our problem is that none of the earlier research on this topic even purports to demonstrate that tort law has been producing higher medical costs without any reduction in patient injuries.[55]

The Harvard study in New York State has attempted to close the gaps in our knowledge of the actual impact (benign or otherwise) of tort law on medical practice.[56] Such research was not feasible up to now because an independent data base displaying the incidence and distribution of medical injuries was lacking. That gap was filled in New York when we undertook an in-depth analysis of patient injuries and provider negligence in a large representative sample of 31,000 hospitalizations. We did not have the luxury of comparing one time frame or geographic region in the state that had a system of tort liability with another one that did not have such a system; if we had, we could have pinpointed the precise effect of the existence of tort liability (as was attempted in the studies referred to earlier that examined the effect in the motor vehicle setting of a shift from tort to first-party no-fault benefits). Still, if the prospect of tort liability exerts any influence on effective precautions and wasteful procedures adopted by doctors, it should follow that the much higher risk of being sued in one part of the state or practice specialty would have correspondingly larger preventive effects than the considerably lower risk of suit in other areas and specialties. What we investigated, then, was whether the real differences in the *intensity* of the tort regime in New York State (differences that are in turn reflected in large interstate variations in premium charges) produced any appreciable increase in the costs of medical care or any reduction in the incidence of doctor negligence and patient injuries in the statewide sample. One thing we certainly discovered was that however laborious a job it was to identify and tabulate the injuries and losses caused by medical treatment, the difficulty of that task paled by comparison with the statistical complexity of trying to isolate a causal effect of the prospect of tort suits on the quality of medical care.

The fivefold variation in hospitals' risk of suit per patient admission did appear to have a pronounced influence on medical practice. One simple measure of that effect was the difference in average hospital cost per patient that was associated with variation in the risk of suit against the hospitals and the doctors practicing in them. Using the most likely statistical approach, it turned out that hospitals facing the lowest tort risk did have lower than statewide average costs, whereas hospitals with the highest tort risk had correspondingly higher per-patient costs (after controlling for a host of other variables that would predictably influence patient length of stay, ancillary services provided, and what the hospital charged for these services).

When we employed other measures, however, this result proved somewhat unstable; consequently I would not rely heavily on any precise estimate of the impact of malpractice litigation on New York State health care expenditures. But considering our econometric analysis together with surveys taken by ourselves and others of how doctors have reacted to increased litigation, and with the AMA's published research about the impact of malpractice on expenditures for physicians' services,[57] I am satisfied that tort law has had a substantial effect on the way physicians now practice in this country.

The somewhat more expensive mode of defensive medicine fortunately appears to have produced some of the hoped-for reduction in doctor negligence and patient injuries. We were not initially able to document a negative relationship between the fivefold divergence in malpractice claims per hospital admission and the tenfold spread in injury rates between the safest and the most hazardous hospitals. We were aware, though, of a significant problem of endogeneity that impeded our research strategy from disclosing a preventive effect. Stated simply, the problem is that the more negligent injuries that occur, the more tort claims there will likely be; at the same time, we hopefully presume that the more claims there are, the fewer the injuries that occur. These two conflicting causal tendencies are likely to offset and mask each other in the observed statistical distribution.

Eventually we decided to control for that factor by recalculating the tort threat as the percentage of claims filed for a given number of negligent injuries. Not only did that step address the endogeneity issue, but it also seemed to be a sounder index of the true deterrent power of the tort system. The highway traffic enforcement model applies here: speeding will be more effectively deterred on a highway on which one ticket is issued for every *two* speeding violations than on a highway on which only one in *ten* violations is ticketed. Likewise, if in Hospital A one malpractice claim is brought for every *two* negligent injuries, the legal sanction is stronger in Hospital A than in Hospital B, in which only one claim is brought for every *ten* injuries.

Using a complex version of the methodology just sketched, we detected a statistically significant effect of variations in the intensity of malpractice litigation on the percentage of adverse events that were judged negligent. Given the size of our sample, this percentage formula was the best index we could use of the rate of negligent injuries that we expected to be most amenable to the influence of tort law.

On its face this finding provides for the first time a strong testimonial for the preventive value of malpractice law. This conclusion should be read with a certain degree of caution, however. Our later methodology posed considerable statistical risk of inflating the estimate of the tort impact. Although we used the standard techniques for adjusting against and testing for that risk, there is some chance we were not fully successful in that regard. These qualms are increased by our inability to detect any effect of the tort threat, measured in the same way, on the overall rate of patient injuries in New York hospitals. Again, there are various possible explanations why our method would isolate a tort-induced reduction in negligent injuries without picking up an observed effect on the sum total of negligent and non-negligent events. But after five years of involvement in this study, my best judgment is that only a fairly modest, though statistically significant, preventive effect of malpractice litigation is discernible in our data.

Concluding Observations

Of course the ideal scientific procedure for allaying concerns about reliability would be to replicate the Harvard study using another data set (preferably from a larger, more widespread sample of hospitals) in order to verify whether the results of the earlier research are real rather than artifactual. But we will not likely have the luxury of such empirical corroboration for some time: it took the Harvard study several years and millions of dollars to compile its limited data base. As I observed above, I have no doubt that doctors and hospitals are reacting to the increased threat of litigation by altering their practice patterns in a variety of expensive ways. In addition, the New York results give us a more informed basis on which to appraise the popular and political debate about whether patient safety is improved when more intense use is made of the malpractice system. Ultimately, though, we must rely on pragmatic analysis of a host of clues, rather than on just a single econometric test, in deciding whether tort law has helped make medical care in this country materially safer.

Unquestionably, the upsurge in malpractice claims and litigation in the last three decades—which raised the insurance bill more than a hundredfold from $60 million in 1960 to more than $7 billion now—has had a pronounced effect on our consciousness of the issue of quality medical care. Doctors, hospitals, health departments, and consumer groups are all far more aware of the phenomenon of iatrogenic injuries. There is widespread acknowledgment of the need for hospital risk management programs as well as for tighter professional and governmental monitoring and disciplining of accident-prone doctors. This level of sensitivity to the issues would not have been reached without the alarming rise in malpractice litigation.

Yet in practice these preventive measures operate at some distance from the generally perceived image of tort doctrine. Recall that malpractice law seeks to enforce compliance with current medical practice standards by threatening doctors with financial penalties if their personal failures produce physical injuries to patients. But most of the effort at risk management has come at the organizational level, from professional associations, government agencies, and especially from hospitals. Hospitals typically are not liable for the negligence of individual doctors, even if the doctors have admitting privileges there. Malpractice law has played a valuable role in stimulating broad-based improvements in the institutional environment and procedures through which medical care is provided: the Harvard study provides revealing (though not impregnable) evidence that increasing the chances that a tort claim will be filed when negligence occurs in a hospital will reduce the danger of negligent injuries occurring in the first place. The study did not show—indeed, was not designed to show—that maintaining the malpractice system in something like its current form may be essential to sustaining the current momentum for quality assurance in the hazardous world of modern medicine.

Yet even the positive role that tort litigation has played is not a sufficient argument for hanging on to the system. We still must balance its net contribution to prevention against the admitted deficiencies of the tort/fault model as a means of compensating injured victims. We know for sure that the malpractice litigation and liability insurance system forces doctors and hospitals to collect $7 billion from their patients to deliver $3 billion into the hands of a selection of injured patients. Even after the Harvard study, there is room for speculation about whether this means of legal compensation also has a pronounced effect on the type of treatment that patients receive in the hospital or the doctor's office (and whether any such net reduction in patient injuries gives us a good enough return on the expenditures it adds to an already burdensome health care system). So it is necessary to consider fundamental alternatives to even a reformed tort system, to see whether better ways can be devised to secure the desired blend of effective prevention and economical compensation for the victims of medical injuries.

5

The Alternative of No-Liability
through Contract

In the last two chapters I analyzed the issues in the debate over medical malpractice within the intellectual parameters of the tort/fault system. Until recently that debate generated much more emotional heat than factual light. Although we are gradually learning how the tort system performs its immediate task of channeling doctors' liability insurance funds into the hands of a select number of injured patients, we still know very little about what influence the prospect of such a monetary transfer might have on the quality of medical care, for better or for worse. It is not enough to respond that we can rely on a commonsense judgment that the prospect of tort liability must be serving *some* injury prevention role. The crucial policy questions are *how much* injury reduction does the system afford, and does that amount provide sufficient justification for the evident inadequacies of malpractice litigation as a compensation program for injured victims.

Suppose that on the basis of the currently available information one were skeptical about the net benefits of malpractice law, even if it were reformed along the lines I advocated earlier for the tort/fault model (especially in the area of damage awards). The proponent of the tort system would immediately ask the skeptic, compared to what? Is there any nontort solution that would do better at preventing and compensating medical accidents?

The answer to that question is that there are two alternative paths one might take. The first would follow the trail originally blazed by workers' compensation and extend protection to the victims of all medical accidents, whether attributable to doctor fault or not. Such a program of patient compensation for all iatrogenic injuries was a natural candidate for legislative consideration in the early seventies, when the problem of medical malpractice first came up for serious scrutiny and when the no-fault model was being debated and partially implemented for motor vehicle accidents. The patient compensation option then faded from serious consideration for reasons that I will discuss in the next chapter. However, no-fault is now beginning to find its way back onto the agenda as several states confront the even starker malpractice crisis of the nineties.

The second and quite different alternative began receiving serious scholarly attention in the eighties: dismantle all tort liability through contractual agreement. For purposes of my analysis, I identify the substantive position of no-liability with the institution of contract, for although there is no inevitable connection between the two concepts, there is a natural affinity. If the law permitted doctors and patients full freedom to contract about the liability issue as they mutually wished, the *de facto* arrangement that would emerge would be wholesale waiver by patients of any tort liability on the part of their doctors. Why that is so, whether that would be a good thing, and whether more limited contract options should be entertained are the issues I will address in this chapter.[1]

Judicial Distrust of Private Contract

There is no question that negotiating such contract waivers is technically feasible. Unlike motor vehicle injuries caused by accidents between strangers, medical injuries are the product of direct dealings between doctors and patients who contract with each other about various features of their relationship, such as the amount and manner of payment of the doctor's fees. In many respects the historic role of tort law has simply been to flesh out the terms of this relationship with regard to the risk of injury by supplying the criteria and the mechanism for enforcing a mutual understanding that the doctor would observe accepted professional standards in providing treatment.

This division of labor between contract and tort was generally acceptable as late as the fifties, when malpractice litigation was an exceptional occurrence, and when there appeared to be no need to develop different terms and arrangements. As the wave of tort claims began to swell in the sixties, certain segments of the medical community responded by proposing contractual revisions to the tort regime. The reported cases seem to indicate that, without exception, these contract terms sought to dispense with all tort liability without substituting any other compensation program in its place. As a result, when injured patients asked judges to scrutinize these contracts, the uniform judicial response was that all such waivers were unenforceable because they conflicted with the judges' view of public policy.

The crucial judicial decision was *Tunkl*,[2] delivered in the mid-sixties by the Supreme Court of California, the same court that was leading the effort to liberalize the more restrictive features of malpractice law. Not surprisingly, these judges would not permit doctors to undercut their judicial achievements by entering into standard-form contracts with hospital patients. This position has been unanimously adopted by every state court that has addressed the issue, even with respect to institutions that offer a lower-priced service in a teaching facility.[3]

There was nothing special or surprising about these legal developments in the health care arena. In the sixties tort law was beginning its upward surge under the impetus of the insurance-risk distribution ethos; the same judicial sentiments had already struck down disclaimer causes in cases of defective products.[4] But the characteristic arguments about medical treatment disclaimers did advert to certain distinctive features of the health care setting. Medical care was a particularly vital human need; special assurances were required concerning the safety and quality of treatment being given to a patient who had placed himself in the care and control of the doctor; because the medical profession enjoyed special privileges in the provision of such care, it should be subject to greater obligations and scrutiny in its performance; and these obligations should not be undercut by a standard form that patients had to sign and accept "as is" in order to secure treatment. In sum, judges deemed it unfair and oppressive for doctors or hospitals to impose on patients a "take it or leave it" decision about medical services that the patients were compelled to obtain.[5]

Given this judicial response to efforts to use contract to secure relief from the tort system, physicians' associations felt compelled to turn to state legislatures in the seventies for statutory help. But by the nineties the promise of legal regulation had faded somewhat, exemplified in the medical malpractice realm by the limited value of one form of law, statutory law, as a source of effective relief from the ills of another, common law. As a result, the virtues of a voluntary contract approach are coming to be more widely appreciated. Perhaps it is time to reexamine judicial hostility to private efforts to tamper with the tort regime.[6]

Wholesale Substitution of Contract for Tort

A state legislature could permit private contract to operate with respect to medical accidents in one of two ways. One approach would be simply to overrule *Tunkl* and its progeny, allowing doctors and patients the same full freedom to negotiate over tort liability that is generally enjoyed in the context of all other terms of personal service agreements. I shall consider that option—the "wholesale approach"—in this section. An alternative approach, generated by a more conservative view of the potential of the contract model, would relax the restraints on private negotiations only with respect to features of the problem for which specific evidence indicates that the new arrangements might be preferable to the old. The second option—the "retail approach"—will be taken up in the next section.

There are forceful arguments to be made for the wholesale approach.[7] The justification has two main strands. First, it is the parties to the doctor-patient relationship who are most likely to know what arrangements will be to their mutual advantage. If the parties did consider all the paraphernalia of tort law, on balance, to be beneficial to them, the tort regime would predictably be preserved. But if voluntary agreements tended to produce different standards and programs, this would be a good index of the comparative inadequacy of contemporary malpractice law.

Second, it is implausible that the perceived mutual interests in the wide variety of patient-doctor relationships are always the same. Tort law, whether it is created by judges or legislators, assumes that there is a single right answer for the many different issues in the design of disability policy. In the malpractice realm the assumption is that patients have a right to collect full damages as assessed and enforced by the ordinary courts, but only if they are injured by the negligent treatment of their doctor or other provider. Under the contractual model a variety of liability arrangements are likely to emerge, differing in choice of forum, nature and level of benefits, standards of entitlement, and so forth. Such diversity is inherently better tailored to the distinctive needs and interests of a variety of parties in particular relationships, taking into account differences in risk aversion and access to alternative modes of disability insurance. Moreover, goes the argument, experimentation with a wide variety of arrangements would eventually demonstrate that some were better than others, worthy of emulation elsewhere.

In my opinion, this argument for private autonomy is largely fanciful in the medical context. If a legislature were to make no-liability a permissible option, no-liability would quickly become the norm. Although it is impossible to prove this assertion, because the legal experiment has not yet been attempted, considerable evidence and analysis and several analogies point strongly in that direction.

Remember that blanket waiver of all tort liability is the uniform pattern in all the cases of contract revision involving patient injuries that have surfaced in the courts. Unlike what has happened in the realm of workplace injuries, for example, where some private employers experimented with alternative no-fault benefits,[8] no positive alternatives to tort liability have been voluntarily developed in the medical context.

The more likely analogy from workplace law is the issue of wrongful dismissal. Even though employer and employee have always enjoyed full legal freedom to adopt any of a variety of modes of contract protection against unjust discharge, the remarkably uniform "voluntary" response in nonunion firms has been to maintain a policy of employment at will for all workers except a few key upper-level employees.[9] This phenomenon can be explained by disparities in the information, inclination, and leverage available to the managers and workers affected by the problem. The same analysis applied to doctors and patients would predict a similar pattern regarding medical malpractice.

Take for example an expectant mother who appears at a doctor's office for consultation and treatment. The obstetrician is likely to have vivid personal knowledge of malpractice litigation, a prospect to which he feels a strong aversion. In the hypothetical new legal environment the doctor would have an artfully drafted release form that would be worded somewhat as follows, though embellished heavily with legal jargon: "Every good faith effort will be made by the doctor to provide quality care; however, obstetric treatment does carry some inevitable risk of error and injury. Because the doctor does not want to become embroiled in tort litigation over any such unfortunate events, as a condition to their relationship the patient agrees to waive any right to sue for possible injury, whether caused by negligence or not." The patient would also be told that since the legislature endorsed such contractual releases, the obstetrician no longer needs to carry highly expensive liability insurance, which has made possible a reduction of several hundred dollars in the doctor's fee for the delivery. The nurse-receptionist asks the patient to read the form carefully and to sign it before the consultation with the doctor begins.

Now consider the situation of the patient presented with this release. The patient knows that she needs medical care, she has already selected this doctor to provide it, and she has now been offered the service at a lower price than she expected to pay. The only condition to proceeding with this doctor is that she give up the right to sue at some distant time in the future if a negligent injury happens to occur. The patient is likely to have little or no information about the incidence of medical accidents due to careless treatment or otherwise.[10] The option to sue could be exercised only if the patient actually suffered a serious injury from the treatment, and suing would put the patient in an adversarial relationship with the doctor from whom she is now seeking personal care. Each of these psychological factors will induce the patient to discount the present value of the tort option which she is being asked to forgo. It seems evident that the initial reaction of the vast majority of patients in this context will be to sign the release and put their trust in their doctor now rather than hold out for the right to consult a lawyer possibly years later.[11] Moreover, any patient who is reluctant to agree to this contractual condition to treatment sends a warning signal to the obstetrician that she is probably a special litigation risk whom it would be better not to accept as a patient, especially given the relatively modest amount of revenue that her delivery would generate.[12]

In sum, when the situation is viewed *ex ante* as of the time when the doctor-patient relationship is being established, the expected value to the doctor, in both financial and emotional terms, of now avoiding the ever-present risk of litigation is likely to outweigh by far the patient's interest in retaining the relatively remote option of being able to sue the doctor years later. The standard outcome of such doctor-patient dealings will be contract waivers of any and all tort liability, certainly in any setting in which malpractice litigation has reached a level that is troublesome to the medical profession.[13]

Yet even if my prediction—that free contractual negotiations over the liability issue would tend strongly to produce the no-liability outcome—is correct, it is *not* a decisive policy argument against contract. Indeed, precisely the opposite conclusion is plausible. Present-day tort law may be locking everyone into an arrangement that is contrary to the perceived mutual advantage of parties generally, given the deeply felt aversion of doctors to being sued and the only moderate inclination of patients to retain the right to bring suits.

Clark Havighurst, in particular, has argued forcefully that *Tunkl* and similar cases rest on certain ideological predilections of judges that have been severely undermined by recent health care developments.[14] Recall that the key component of malpractice law is that the courts must defer to the standards of care developed by doctors themselves. The underlying assumption is that the medical profession offers a special blend of scientific expertise and ethical concern for patients' welfare that is not likely to be found in purely commercial relationships. But if doctors aspire to establish *the* definitive standard of care, and if it is therefore unwise for judges to require a more stringent level of care, then it is only logical that each individual doctor must measure up to that standard, and that judges should tolerate no less. The consequence is that a private contract in which a patient purports to grant the individual doctor immunity if he performs less well than his colleagues would be, *ipso facto*, unfair and unconscionable.

We are now better informed and more cynical about the practice of both medicine and law. As the discussion of defensive medicine intimated, we recognize that the personal interests of the physician influence treatment judgments, whether the doctor's primary motivation is maximizing income, minimizing litigation, or something else. The result is a great disparity in observed patterns of medical treatment that cannot be explained or justified in terms of different patient outcomes. We also realize that many of these standard practices are very costly and have contributed to an upward spiraling, extremely burdensome national health bill. The policy reaction has been a wide variety of public and private programs that seek to contain health care costs by placing restraints on the decisions of individual doctors. The new regulatory theme is that the benefits of additional care must be balanced against the costs, because we will be better off with more affordable health care even if obtaining it entails economizing on some technically feasible forms of treatment.

The same critical analysis is being trained on the tort law component of the health care system.[15] In its own terms, malpractice law is quite costly, now requiring about $7 billion of insurance expenditures in order to deliver approximately $3 billion of benefits to a select group of injured patients, with an indeterminate impact on both the quality and the utility of the treatment provided to patients. Suppose, as I argue above, that patients and doctors would likely contract out of the malpractice system if the law permitted them to do so. This phenomenon would confirm the judgment that the parties would be mutually better off if they were allowed to opt out of the tort system, thereby avoiding the stress of litigation and economizing on patient fees, insurance premiums, and taxes that pay the portion of the national health bill that is consumed by tort claims.

Each of the claims in the foregoing analysis may be valid, including the conclusion that on balance we would be better off with a general norm of no doctor's liability rather than the present rule of liability based on fault. However, if these claims prove to be well founded, it must be primarily on the substantive merits of no-liability, not merely on the ground that no-liability happens to be the outcome of a process of voluntary contract.[16]

This is not to deny the virtues of the expanded choice now being offered to patients with respect to both the organization of physician care and the design of health insurance. In the first instance prospective patients can receive health care through HMO's or preferred provider organizations (PPO's) as well as from the traditional private physician arrangement. In the case of insurance, it is now possible to select among various forms of coverage; for example, one may elect or forgo deductibles or coinsurance. The individual consumer is in the best position to make the appropriate tradeoffs between the visible amenities of medical care and the difference in the fees paid for them. But as a matter of general social policy rather than because of any idiosyncratic tradition in malpractice law, we do not allow people the same freedom to trade the risk of more injuries or less compensation against the dollars they might save in insurance premiums.[17]

To this occasional labor lawyer, the contemporary debate about the possible value of private contract to solve the problems of public malpractice law is strikingly reminiscent of the arguments that have been exchanged for the last century about whether and when the law should intervene in the employment relationship. Should we have mandatory regulation of workplace health and safety? Should we require protection of the income security of workers when they retire? Or should all such issues be left to the private decisions and voluntary agreements of individual firms and employees? Labor scholars have long recognized that dispensing with mandatory employer-provided workers' compensation would add 1 to 2 percent to the wages of the average worker, leaving it to the employee to decide whether to purchase substitute insurance protection on his own. Yet in judging the virtues of this option, the litmus test is not simply whether the outcome happens to be the product of a voluntary arrangement, but whether the community and its workers would be better off with the cumulative product of the pattern of decisions that would predictably emerge from this particular psychological and market setting. Although we begin with a preference for private autonomy over legal intervention with respect to most of the terms of employment, starting with the wage rate, for a variety of reasons we have concluded that a core of mandatory legal entitlements for workers and legal obligations on employers is essential as far as disabling workplace injuries are concerned.[18] Essentially the same policy conclusion has been drawn with respect to injuries inflicted by defective products.

The point of the comparison is evident in these simple analogies. A hospital is not allowed to extract from its employees a waiver of the employer's duty under OSHA to safeguard its workers from avoidable injuries, nor of the employer's obligation under workers' compensation to compensate employees for injuries which do occur. The manufacturer of a defective drug is not permitted to extract from a patient, through a sequence of contracts, a waiver of the protection against injury offered by the federal Food and Drug Administration, nor the consumer's entitlement to compensation under product liability law. Perhaps such infringements on the private autonomy of the worker or the consumer are misguided in both these contexts. But until we are satisfied that such a policy stance is fundamentally wrong, how can we justify malpractice legislation that would give hospitals or doctors the wholesale freedom to extract from their patients full waivers of whatever protection and compensation is offered by malpractice law?

Retail Substitution of Contract for Tort

The foregoing rather jaundiced appraisal of the virtues of untrammeled freedom of contract as a means for dealing with medical injuries does not imply an endorsement of the way present-day malpractice litigation handles such cases.[19] What it does suggest is a different approach to the contract model. A more focused study should be undertaken of specific areas in which the tort system appears to be particularly deficient and where private experimentation might promise a better blend of effective prevention and economical compensation. Rather than give blanket approval to freedom of contract wherever it might lead, the legislature would then loosen step by step the existing constraints on private negotiation, beginning with situations in which it had tangible assurance that contracting would operate to the long-term advantage of all the affected parties.

Private adjudication. The malpractice regime is characterized not simply by the basic legal principle of fault as the prerequisite for tort liability (although liability was the sole focus of the contract provisions dealt with in *Tunkl et al.*). It consists also of an elaborate set of rules for defining and assessing damages, together with the judicial machinery to resolve disputes over both liability and damage issues.

The last component has been the subject of extensive efforts to develop alternative mechanisms for dispute resolution through private arbitration. Fifteen states now explicitly authorize certain forms of pretreatment agreements between doctors and patients, in which the patient agrees to accept binding arbitration in lieu of a jury trial.[20] Most observers consider this mode of contracting out of the standard litigation procedure to be much more equitable than a simple waiver of all liability. Even the California Supreme Court, which rendered the anticontract verdict in *Tunkl*, decided some years later that private arbitration agreements were acceptable and would be enforceable even in the absence of statutory fiat.[21]

The difference in the way courts have treated the two types of contract does not really turn on the relative "voluntariness" of the arbitration agreement.[22] Nor is it the product of a sharp distinction between procedure and substance. Even though arbitration can be cheaper, faster, and more accessible than civil litigation for enforcing legal rights, this change in procedure in turn alters the pattern of substantive results from exercising these rights. The one extensive study comparing the experience of injured patients who had their claims arbitrated with the experience of those who litigated found that the claims of patients who suffered permanent disabilities tended to be upheld more frequently under arbitration then litigation; but the claims in which no physical injury, temporary injury, or fatal injury had occurred were upheld *less* frequently under arbitration.[23] In addition, compared to damage awards in litigated claims, the amount of damages awarded by arbitrators was higher for permanent disabilities but much lower for temporary injuries.[24] Whether or not this pattern of arbitration results seems more attractive as disability policy (as it does to me), it is evident that arbitration can produce gains for both injured patients—more accessible relief—and accused doctors— avoidance of the distressing experience and publicity of the jury trial. These tangible indicia of reciprocity in the new arrangements have made them more attractive to the legislators who permit them and the judges who scrutinize them.[25]

Monetary damages. After experiencing some success with private initiatives in designing adjudicative machinery, a legislature might be inclined to invite further experimentation by the parties with the substantive malpractice rules applicable in either the arbitral or the judicial forum. Take the problem of tort damages, for example. I noted above the special attention that legislatures, courts, and researchers have paid to issues such as periodic awards, pain and suffering, and collateral sources. The fact that tort doctrines are not amendable by private agreement means that change can be secured only by statutory enactment. Ironically, statutory changes to tort law are often attacked in the courts for being too narrow, for applying only to victims of *medical* accidents, thereby denying such victims the equal protection of the law governing other accidents. Yet viewed from the perspective of this chapter, the vice of such legislation is that it may be too broad, because it rigidly requires that the legal treatment of all medical accident cases be the same, no matter what the particular interests and needs of individual patients and doctors may be.

Private contract might well be viewed, then, as a more sensible means for defining the scope and terms of monetary awards once liability has been established. Let us consider the collateral source issue to illustrate the point and the possibilities.

The bulk of malpractice costs are shifted by doctors to health insurers and eventually to subscribers who pay the insurance premiums. A large proportion of these health care premiums are paid by employers who also provide their employees with short-term or long-term disability insurance. It is likely that the workers in question actually pay for these fringe benefits through forgone wages. How does the collateral source rule work in the context of this overall insurance package? A worker who happens to be negligently injured in the hospital will recoup his medical expenses and lost wages under both the tort system and the employer's health and disability coverage. But it is his fellow employees who will have to pay the premiums necessary to fund his double recovery in this exceptional case.

In practice, adjustments are made in the overall insurance arrangements in an attempt to avoid this anomalous result. Many health and disability insurers include a subrogation clause in their agreements with covered employers or workers, a provision that gives the insurer the right to be reimbursed for any funds it expends in connection with losses for which tort awards are received. This avoids the immediate double indemnity for the victim, along with any moral hazard that may entail.

Allocating the loss this way appears attractive because it imposes the financial burden of the injury on the negligent party, who should receive ample incentive to prevent the risk from occurring in the future. But as we saw in Chapter 3, from the point of view of the administration of disability policy, the combination of collateral source and subrogation is a highly wasteful procedure, recycling dollars through very expensive liability insurance back into the much cheaper system of loss insurance.[26]

Given this balancing of different values, some legislatures might conclude that there is no universal correct answer to this problem—neither the traditional common law exclusion of collateral sources, nor contemporary legislation (which I endorsed in Chapter 3) that not only requires offsets of outside insurance, but also prohibits insurers from negotiating any exclusion or subrogation of malpractice events from their coverage. A reasonable intermediate step would be simply to give to the hospital and the worker-patient the same kind of contractual freedom to dispose of the collateral source issue in the direction they prefer as we now typically give the subrogated carrier and its insureds to dispose in the opposite direction.[27]

No-liability versus fault liability. Whatever its uses in particular cases, contractual agreement about tort damages will inevitably tilt toward less liability. This raises anew the question of whether we should seriously consider permitting doctor-patient agreements for no-liability. In reevaluating whether a legislature should overrule the *Tunkl* doctrine completely, the test to be applied is not whether doing so would enhance the autonomy of the parties in the abstract. The issue is whether the no-liability outcome would be attractive in practice, at least when compared with the fault-liability regime. How well does no-liability score when measured along the dimensions of compensation, prevention, and administration?

Not surprisingly, the major gain would arise from administrative savings. More than $4 billion is now expended to raise and distribute less than $3 billion in benefits to injured patients. Medical procedures designed to minimize the risk of litigation rather than to enhance the condition of the patient generate considerable additional expenditures. An example is the routine head X-ray in emergency room treatment after a fall: the X-ray is of little value for detecting complications, but it is prompted by the desire to protect the hospital from liability in cases in which the patient turns out to have complications. The aggregate cost of entirely wasteful defensive medicine is not likely $10 billion (let alone the $40 billion figure occasionally bandied about), but it is plausible that this cost matches the direct expenditures on malpractice insurance. And in our increasingly decentralized, market-oriented health care system, the total savings in administrative costs secured by no-liability would almost surely be passed on in lower premiums to the patient-consumers who are asked to give up their tort rights.

These potential economies are not insignificant, even in a health care system in which total expenditures are now $600 billion annually. The question, though, is whether the administrative savings are great enough to justify what would have to be given up in the trade—the possibility of compensation or prevention from tort litigation.

On the compensation side, the immediate loss is clear—the nearly $3 billion in benefits now paid out to the victims of medical accidents. However inequitable it may seem to distribute those benefits only to victims of negligent medical treatment, the fact is that this kind of tort-mandated disability insurance is targeted primarily at the seriously and permanently disabled, those with cases that are worth the cost of suing, including many who are permanently and partially disabled and who would otherwise tend to slip through the cracks of existing public and private programs for income losses such as sick pay (for temporary disability) or Social Security Disability Insurance (for permanent total disability). It is true that we could devise a much more efficient and more closely targeted mode of disability compensation than the tort system provides. The problem is that the repeal of tort liability, especially if accomplished *sub silentio* through contract waivers, carries little assurance that such other sources of compensation would be made available for a large proportion of the losses.[28]

On the other hand, whatever may be the patient losses on which tort compensation is being expended, the costs are imposed on the providers who are responsible for the accidents and who should be motivated to make stronger efforts to prevent them. But a tort litigation system teamed up with widespread liability insurance is a rather blunt instrument for achieving this end. To the extent that the focal point of medical care litigation and liability insurance is the individual physician, it is only with great difficulty that insurance incentives can be sharpened through experience rating. Yet it is equally true that the huge expansion of malpractice liability has inspired a concentrated effort by many institutions to enhance the safety of the medical and hospital environment, which we now realize is an extremely risky place.[29] Certainly any state legislature would feel great uneasiness about a statutory proposal that would permit a radical change of course toward no-liability and elimination entirely of the prevention role of tort litigation, however crudely the institution may operate.

Market and Regulatory Incentives for Patient Safety

In fairly appraising the contract option, we must not assume that moving from fault liability to no-liability means going from a great deal of accident prevention to no prevention at all. First, as we saw in

Chapter 4, tort litigation provides substantially less safety incentive than is generally assumed. In addition, even a nontort world would contain significant motivation for doctors to adopt precautions for the safety of their patients.

Leaving aside basic ethical concerns, the medical marketplace itself can generate financial incentives for safety. Considerable competition now exists among hospitals to fill their beds and among doctors to fill their appointment books from a somewhat scarcer supply of patients. In principle, a hospital (or doctor) with a worse record of negligent treatment and accidents than its counterparts would lose out in this competition; it might have to lower its price or enhance its amenities. Support for this economic theory can be found in the evidence of compensating wage differentials that must be paid to workers in more dangerous jobs: paying higher wages to induce workers to fill those jobs gives employers a financial incentive to invest in greater safety precautions.[30]

Financial incentives are a much less promising option for patient safety than for employee safety. Workers can readily appreciate the differential risk of working in a coal mine rather than in a bank; and because they may work in a particular coal mine for an extended period of time, employees have the opportunity to evaluate the relative danger of working for one employer rather than another. By contrast, the individual afflicted with an illness who must choose between one doctor and another or one hospital and another is likely to encounter severe difficulty in obtaining and assessing information about the comparative risks.

Of course, government can play the valuable role of generating and publicizing relative risk information that the market is unlikely to provide on its own, and in so doing enhance the quality of consumer choices within the health care system. In fact, the federal government has recently taken the lead in publishing elaborate statistics on relative mortality rates of the elderly when they are treated in the nation's hospitals,[31] and apparently plans to provide the same comparative data about the nation's doctors.

This example actually reinforces the point made earlier. Crude data about in-hospital mortality is highly deceiving to the extent that it does not adequately control for a variety of other factors, most prominently the precise nature of the patient's disease and its life-threatening quality. Ideally, the better hospitals and doctors get the riskier, more difficult cases; assuming that they do, the bare outcomes of such cases provide a poor index of the quality of care offered. Of course, a variety of indexes can be used to control for these other factors that obscure the quality of care, but the efforts made by the federal Health Care Financing Administration to develop such controls have so far been found wanting by the nation's medical researchers.[32]

Eventually, of course, data should emerge that will be sufficiently refined to provide meaningful guidance to health care policymakers about which trouble spots in the system need tackling (though the existing federal data is generally dismissed as of little use, even by the leaders of the top-rated hospitals).[33] It would require a great deal of optimism, though, to believe that such complex material could ever be assimilated and used by ordinary patients with enough cumulative force to generate market pressures of a magnitude that would spur hospitals (or doctors) to provide safer medical care.

The imperfections in the market demand for and supply of medical safety produce the call for government intervention in some form or other. Are any alternatives to the tort liability system enforced by the courts? The natural option would seem to be statutory regulation enforced by an administrative agency, a body like the Occupational Safety and Health Administration, which performs this regulatory role for workplace injuries. In the medical context the prime candidate for that role is the state medical board, which administers the physician licensing and disciplinary process. These boards have the statutory power to enforce appropriate standards of practice for doctors, using measures such as fines, probation (with or without specific limits on practice), temporary suspension from practice, and ultimately revocation of a physician's license.[34]

On its face this regulatory process seems to have major virtues in contrast with tort litigation. The tort case focuses on the doctor's behavior only to decide whether he acted with at least momentary carelessness as the legal predicate for compensating a seriously injured patient. The amount of the tort award depends upon the severity of the patient's injury, not the gravity of the doctor's negligence; in any event, the award is paid not by the individual doctor but by the liability insurer. The sole focus of the licensing board, by contrast, is the nature and gravity of the doctor's substandard practice, manifested not simply in a particular incident but also in a broader pattern of behavior that may indicate a serious risk for future patients. Moreover, the measures the board can employ are tailored to the problem presented by a particular doctor, ranging from probationary restraints to temporary suspension, and culminating in complete termination of his right to practice in the state. The doctor personally "pays" each of these sanctions with substantial reductions in his income. The prospect of such a penalty serves as a powerful deterrent to other physicians' emulating the negligent behavior.

The shortcoming of physician self-regulation inheres not in the theory but in the practice. Medical discipline is notoriously underused.[35] Even after marked increases in state board activism, by the mid-eighties only about 1,000 instances of probation, suspension, and license revocation were recorded across the entire country: only some 400 licenses to practice were revoked from a physician population of about 400,000.[36] More important, the bulk of these "serious" disciplinary measures were meted out for behavior such as improper drug prescription, alcohol or drug abuse, sexual misconduct with patients, and so on. Only a fraction were imposed in connection with substandard medical practice that caused physical injury to patients. To put these figures in a broader malpractice context, recall that there are some 35,000 *paid* tort claims a year, and a much larger number of serious negligent injuries that are never even litigated for one reason or another.[37] The explanation for this disparity illustrates the characteristic deficiencies of the regulatory process, and sheds quite a different light on the contrast between regulation and tort litigation.[38]

Underreporting. Whereas an injured patient's need for compensation will impel him to file a tort claim if he discovers a basis for one, there is notorious underreporting of incompetent practice by the doctor's professional peers.[39] Even if the physicians in charge of a hospital or clinic observe or learn of the danger posed by one of their colleagues, their natural inclination is simply to ease the offending doctor out of the institution rather than go public with complaints to the authorities. Not only does such a complaint not serve the reporting physicians' personal interests, but it may expose them to personal cost and reprisal (such as a civil rights, defamation, or antitrust suit).

Lack of resources. After a particular incident does become known, the tort plaintiff can hire a topflight lawyer, who will have a strong financial incentive to develop the case against the doctor, to do the necessary investigation, and to hire expert witnesses, because the lawyer has a sizable fee contingent on the outcome. By contrast, a state licensing board typically has only modest financial resources and an overworked and underpaid staff at its disposal in order to put together a difficult case of general incompetence against a physician, who likely will have hired a highly skilled lawyer to defend him and protect his future livelihood.[40]

Pro-doctor tilt. Tort cases are heard by a lay jury composed of people who are not representative of either side. Since more than two-thirds of the trial verdicts go in favor of the physician, it is hardly valid to assume that jurors are biased in favor of even seriously injured patients. Traditionally, medical boards have been entirely or at least predominantly staffed by doctors, who appear disinclined to judge their colleagues sufficiently incompetent to lose the right to practice entirely. (Board members, however, are generally less sympathetic toward immoral behavior such as facilitating drug trafficking or sexual exploitation of patients.)

In sum, what physician regulation might seem to gain by comparison with tort litigation in the substantive focus of its judgments and sanctions, it more than loses in the lack of incentive to set the disciplinary process in motion and carry it through effectively. Ironically, the most searching peer scrutiny of errant doctors is probably carried out by physician-owned insurance carriers, whose members are strongly motivated to address the problem in order to limit their own malpractice premiums.[41]

When state legislatures sought to cut back on malpractice litigation but were stung by strong criticism from personal injury lawyers and consumer groups, they typically included measures to improve the performance of the physician licensing and disciplinary tribunals (notable examples are California's legislation in the mid-seventies and New York's in the mid-eighties). Standard legislative provisions include adding more resources and staff to the agency, appointing more lay members to add their perspective and balance to board decisions, imposing a legal obligation on doctors and hospitals to report to the agency any instance of substandard care or adverse event which they may have observed, and requiring that insurance carriers report all claims, payments, and verdicts in connection with individual physicians.[42] In 1986 Congress passed the Health Care Quality Improvement Act (HCQIA), which required that malpractice payments and disciplinary actions in each state be reported to an agency designated by the Department of Health and Human Services so that the data could be made available to other states where an incompetent doctor might want to move and set up practice.[43] A few jurisdictions, including New York, are beginning to require that physicians periodically demonstrate their professional competence as a condition of renewing their license to practice in the state.

All these regulatory reforms are positive and long overdue. They testify further to the "macro" effects of the surge in malpractice claims and premiums in spurring institutions—in this case, legislatures and administrators—into action, whatever the deficiencies of tort liability as a "micro" incentive to individual doctors to adhere to appropriate standards of care. But can the malpractice system now be dismantled (through contract or otherwise) once it has inspired these improvements in the regulatory process, on the assumption that these changes will be self-sustaining? I am somewhat skeptical on that score, if only on account of what I have observed in Massachusetts over the last several years. The state's doctors initially backed a greatly strengthened physician disciplinary regime as part of a legislative package of restraints on malpractice litigation. But since the new tort rules have been in place, the Medical Society has consistently and often effectively challenged the disciplinary agency's regulatory and adjudicative authority. More systematically, the small quantity of empirical research that exists on physician licensing reform found that this effort produced only modest improvement in the vigor of the medical disciplinary agencies;[44] there are no studies at all of whether more action by the state boards in turn leads to fewer injuries to patients. The one substantial existing body of research on the contribution of legal regulation to victim safety concerns the effect of OSHA on worker injuries. The present consensus is that such regulation has had only a small tangible impact on the workplace,[45] a conclusion that provides little basis for hope that the same technique would make a major difference in medical safety.

The perennial problem of government regulation is that the watchdog agency is located on the outside, far removed from the hundreds of hospitals and thousands of doctors' offices in which patients are treated. Consequently, regulation can do little more than establish the minimum precautions suitable for a multitude of treatment settings across the state or nation. Health care providers who satisfy these baseline requirements receive no further incentive from the program to perform as well as they can. Indeed, unlike OSHA, medical boards attempt not to define and enforce appropriate standards of care for the average doctor, but only to restrict or exclude from practice the especially poor doctor.[46] Moreover, agency implementation of even this strictly limited mandate depends on the vagaries of reports and complaints from individuals on the inside in a position to observe what a doctor is doing to his patients.

The most recent innovation in physician regulation begins with acknowledgment of this basic problem and adopts a different tack to deal with it.[47] The power of state regulation is employed to secure more effective *internal* regulation, through such changes as risk management by hospitals and peer scrutiny by medical staff. Again, a forceful precedent in the workplace context—the joint employer-employee safety and health committee[48]—suggests that such internal review and control may be the soundest area in which to invest our regulatory resources. Rather than the agency's devoting scarce time and energies to investigating and adjudicating the relative handful of cases that come to its attention, the medical board would instead develop standards for internal quality control by the institutions, require that these mechanisms be put in place, and then regularly audit the level and quality of such self-policing, relying on these indigenous efforts to influence and improve the behavior of the people who work in the affected institutions.

In theory, this appears to be the most sensible strategy for physician regulation. The question is whether the efforts of a state board to require that such procedures be formally adopted will be sufficient to overcome the natural inertia and reluctance of medical committees and hospital administrators to deal firmly with their accident-prone colleagues. Ironically, one major source of this physician reluctance is the pressure created by another area of law—antitrust law—in which considerable distrust of the practice of self-regulation by the medical profession has recently surfaced.[49]

In the early eighties the Supreme Court encountered several cases that seemed symptomatic of a general tendency of the medical profession to adopt collective practices, supposedly out of concern for the quality and economy of health care, but which too often primarily served the self-interest of doctors themselves.[50] One such target was the restriction historically imposed by physicians on less conventional forms of treatment, including the care offered by chiropractors, osteopaths, podiatrists, and nurse-midwives.[51] But as these precedents began to accumulate, they offered an inviting legal sanctuary to regular doctors whose hospital admitting privileges had been canceled because of apparent substandard care or who had been denied such privileges because of poor care reported from elsewhere. The theory underlying these antitrust suits is that the doctors whom the hospitals must rely on for peer review are in competition with the plaintiff, and the exclusion of the target doctor from the hospital "market" is really designed to serve the committee members' own financial interests rather than the medical needs of the doctor's patients.

Considerable legal obstacles faced any antitrust claims, for example the arguments that the facility or practice in question was not within interstate commerce,[52] or that the hospital in question did not represent a substantial enough share of the patient-admission market,[53] or that the hospital as such could not be found to be in a conspiracy in restraint of trade with its own medical staff.[54] But in *Patrick v. Burget*,[55] a notable decision in the late eighties, the Supreme Court upheld an Oregon jury verdict of $2.3 million in trebled antitrust damages and attorney fees won by a doctor against his peers who were responsible for the loss of his hospital privileges. The Supreme Court rejected the recently popular "state action" defense[56]—which was based on the fact that Oregon law encouraged peer scrutiny of problem doctors— on the ground that antitrust immunity was available only if the state provided full governmental review of the private decisions reached by the hospital committees.

While *Patrick* was wending its way through the appellate courts, Congress was passing the HCQIA, which provided limited immunity for any peer review decision that accorded due process to the affected doctor and that was rendered by the physician committee in the "reasonable belief that it is in furtherance of quality health care, after a reasonable effort to obtain the facts of the matter." It is unlikely that this new statutory provision materially tightened up the existing criteria for antitrust liability, which ultimately require a judgment about whether the committee's real objective is to rid the hospital of a poor doctor or themselves of a good competitor.[57] The problem under both general antitrust law and the HCQIA is that it is difficult for the hospital or doctor to win summary judgment against a carefully drafted claim unless the institution has gone to the trouble and expense of bringing in outside experts to audit the target physician's performance.[58] Consequently, defendants have to lay out substantial resources of their own to defend the case. They may even feel compelled to settle rather than risk the kind of damages awarded by the jury in *Patrick*. Physicians and other health care providers are therefore understandably loath to face these great personal risks in order to serve the public good of protecting patients from the poor quality care of their fellow doctors.

A signal virtue of tort law is that it provides considerable legal and financial incentives to overcome the reluctance of health care providers to get involved in quality assurance efforts. We saw an illustration of that earlier in connection with the meticulous peer review undertaken by physician-owned carriers against their insureds who had experienced one or more disturbing malpractice claims. A major reason why risk management by hospitals has become so prominent in recent years is that the hospital organization itself is increasingly exposed to malpractice liability, either vicarious liability for the negligence of its physician-employees, or direct liability for failure to fulfill its own corporate duty to check adequately the credentials of doctors before giving them admitting privileges, or even for a failure to monitor and deal with an ongoing pattern of substandard care.[59] Unlike the liability of the individual physician, most large hospitals feel the budgetary burden of these tort judgments directly, because the hospital is substantially self-insured. In that vein, the state of Florida recently sought to enforce a recent requirement that hospitals undertake internal risk management by making breach of this statutory obligation itself a basis for a malpractice suit against the hospital. Such a suit could be brought by a patient able to show that he was injured by a careless doctor who should have been detected and dealt with by effective quality control procedures inside the hospital.[60] A logical conclusion from this example as well as the foregoing analysis is that the preferred instruments for enhancing the safety and quality of medical treatment are sophisticated quality assurance programs, run by and in the hospitals or other health care institutions, rather than directives issued by outside medical licensing boards.

The last observation accords with the conclusion I reached at the end of the previous chapter. It is unlikely that even a more informed consumer in the health care market or a more aggressive government regulatory agency will provide sufficient incentive to the hospital and its physician committee structure to commit the resources and energies needed to make the institution less hazardous to the health of its patients. So although I favor some loosening of the legal reins on experimenting with contractual alternatives to malpractice litigation, I am highly dubious about the brave new world of no-liability, which would likely be the denouement of full-scale freedom of contract to determine who will assume the legal and financial responsibility for medical accidents: doctors, hospitals, or patients.

6

Toward No-Fault Patient Compensation

My conclusion in the last chapter that the law performs a necessary and valuable role in imposing on health care providers a nonwaivable responsibility for iatrogenic injuries is not a ringing endorsement of the present-day malpractice litigation system. It would be better if legal incentives to reduce the dangers of medical treatment were generated by a regime that did somewhat less damage to the therapeutic goals of the physician-patient relationship. For this reason, it is worth considering a dramatically different alternative to tort law: moving toward *more* rather than *less* liability, but under a no-fault program that would be far less moralistic and intrusive than the tort-fault version. I shall approach this last major topic by taking a short detour and exploring a recent proposal by the AMA for establishing "administrative fault liability."[1]

Administrative Fault

The core proposal of the AMA Medical Liability Project would remove patient claims for injuries produced by negligent medical treatment from the civil justice system, with its trial by jury, and transfer them to a specialized administrative tribunal. The tribunal would be a reconstituted state medical licensing board with full-time members, a substantial minority of whom would be drawn from the medical profession. The proposed organization and procedures of the tribunal are largely modeled on the National Labor Relations Board (NLRB), which administers federal labor law.

Malpractice cases under the AMA proposal would take the following path from initiation to completion. The patient would file with the agency an informal claim, which would be investigated and appraised by board claims reviewers and peer specialists. Patients whose case was deemed valid would be offered legal representation by staff attorneys working under an independent general counsel to the board; patients who wished to use their own attorney could do so. A hearing examiner would conduct a trial-type hearing and make findings about what had transpired in the treatment. He would determine whether these events amounted to negligent medical care causing an injury, and, if so, what compensable damages had been suffered by the patient. The hearing examiner's decision would be subject to review by the medical board. The board would play the major role in resolving disputed questions about the appropriate standard of physician care and about medical causation in the patient's disability. The board would also have broad rule-making authority to develop guidelines for the practice of medicine and the resolution of malpractice claims. Finally, the medical board would be able to draw upon its experience in handling malpractice compensation claims as it performed its other major role of monitoring and disciplining substandard physician practice within the board's jurisdiction.

Two major virtues are touted for this new administrative process for resolving medical liability cases.

Quality of decision. A civil jury is composed of lay people, selected ad hoc to hear a single case and asked to choose between the views of competing experts who testify about complex issues of medical care and scientific causation. A typical refrain from the medical profession is that juries are likely to be more sympathetic to the injured victim and consequently to grasp for any possible basis for extracting some compensation from the deep pocket of the doctor's insurer. So, for example, doctors assert that jurors tend to ignore the formal legal doctrine that an individual physician is deemed negligent only for deviating from the standard of practice established by the profession. This charge against civil juries has little foundation, at least insofar as the initial liability issue is concerned; there may be some truth to it in regard to the assessment of damages once negligence has been found.[2] What is well founded, however, is the medical profession's sense of grievance about the "black box" of jury decision making. Too often jury verdicts are technically incorrect—that is, they are based on a misunderstanding or misinterpretation of the applicable legal principles—even if the errors are distributed randomly among patient-plaintiffs and doctor-defendants. Moreover, even if they are correct, the decisions are never explained to the parties who are immediately affected; as a result, they provide little sensible guidance to individuals with a major personal and professional stake in the system.

Unlike the jury, the proposed administrative tribunal would be composed of people selected because of their qualifications and aptitudes for the role. Moreover, the decision makers would gradually gain expertise from their ongoing experience with the problems of medical malpractice claims. Detailed written rulings would be issued in particular cases: they would be comprehensible to those immediately affected, and amenable to subsequent scrutiny and criticism, not only by the medical profession, but also by lawyers, the press, and members of the public interested in the medical accident problem. Such a procedure promises a much more sensible and reliable quality of judgment about doctor fault and patient compensation.

Access to the process. Although the ultimate verdict in medical malpractice cases is rendered by a lay jury, the jurors' role is performed in the context of a complex, time-consuming, and costly legal process. Injured patients can hope to navigate through these intricate procedures only with the assistance of well-paid personal injury lawyers. This is one reason why only a small percentage of potentially valid malpractice claims are ever instituted. Cases are selected on the basis of how easy it will be to prove the physician's fault, and how severe the patient's injuries are.[3] From claims which are successful, the attorney extracts a fee that is typically one-third the amount of the jury award which is supposed to provide redress for the harm suffered by the victim.

Under the proposed administrative procedure, by contrast, the injured patient initiates the claim process with a simple informal document. The agency staff takes the initiative in calling for medical records, interviewing the people involved in the incident, and obtaining and paying for expert opinions on the merit of the claim. If the claim appears valid to the agency's own medical experts, the victim is offered (but not required to accept) free legal assistance from a staff attorney for presenting the evidence needed to support the claim in the hearing process. So even though the administrative fault scheme would remove the formal right to a jury trial from the relatively small sample of injured patients who are now able to avail themselves of that right, a much broader array of injured patients would now be able to use the more accessible administrative procedure to have their legal claims adjudicated, to receive compensation if they are entitled to it, and to expose to medical board scrutiny and discipline the careless treatment by their doctors, which otherwise would not likely see the light of day.

Though the AMA's administrative fault proposal has been developed in much greater detail, the preceding description gives the basic idea and its rationale. The personal injury bar and the general legal establishment will certainly react with horror to the notion of tampering in this way with the patient's time-honored right to obtain justice in the ordinary courts, to receive a verdict from a jury of his peers. If administrative screening panels (let alone damage caps) have regularly been struck down as unconstitutional impairments of the right to a trial by jury,[4] total replacement of the jury system for adjudicating tort claims is likely to face stiff resistance in the state courts as well as the state legislatures. My own reaction to the proposal is more positive, however. A serious appraisal of the comparative advantages of the civil jury and the administrative tribunal for handling personal injury claims is long overdue, and the AMA's ingeniously designed proposal would likely fare quite well in any open-minded comparison.

In fact, my major qualm about the proposal is not that it goes too far, but that it does not go far enough. The jury trial is simply one component of a complex network of arrangements through which the tort system attempts to do justice to medical accidents. If we set out to alter that single ingredient of the civil justice system, we start down a path that will likely require reconsideration of the other basic doctrines and practices historically associated with tort litigation before a jury.

Let us compare the basic structure of the malpractice regime for medical accidents with the major existing example of an administrative liability program, workers' compensation for workplace injuries.[5] These two programs differ markedly in four critical respects, only one of which is the choice between the jury trial and administrative adjudication.

Basis of liability. Under malpractice law the fundamental precondition to an injured patient's ability to collect compensation from his doctor is proof that the doctor was negligent in the medical treatment and as a result caused the injuries in question. By contrast, under workers' compensation the injured worker is able to draw upon comprehensive insurance coverage furnished by the employer against any disabling injury that arises out of and in the course of employment. In other words, workers' compensation benefits are payable even though the employer may have been entirely blameless for the occurrence of the injury, and even though the injured worker's own carelessness may actually have caused the accident.

Extent of liability. In the malpractice regime, once the doctor's personal fault and tort liability is established, the patient is entitled to full compensation in order to redress (to the extent that money can do so) all the harms that have been inflicted on him, whether the losses are financial or emotional, and whether or not they have already been compensated by collateral sources. Indeed, fault-based malpractice liability now may extend to the emotional injuries suffered by *other* persons as a result of their relationship with the immediate victim, injuries such as the distress of a mother of the baby born impaired or retarded as a result of the delivery.

By contrast, broader coverage of disabling workplace accidents under workers' compensation carries with it a correspondingly lower level of redress. The primary role of workers' compensation benefits is to pay for medical and rehabilitation expenditures and to replace some proportion of the earnings that have been lost, up to or slightly above the state average wage. Actual pain and suffering is not compensable at all, and any redress for loss of enjoyment of life due to permanent physical impairment is confined to small awards meted out under a general schedule. Finally, workers' compensation benefits are dovetailed to the extent possible with other sources of compensation in order to avoid double payment. This practice often places workers' compensation in the position of secondary payer to the collateral source.

Locus of liability. Most malpractice cases impose liability directly on the individual doctor who was judged to be at fault. Tort law has never required that doctors carry insurance against such liability. Only a few states now require such coverage as a condition of practice, and a small percentage of doctors still "go bare"—that is, practice without malpractice insurance. In effect, in most states it is left up to the doctor to decide whether a patient seriously injured by him will ever be able to collect the large judgment for full compensation to which the patient is entitled under tort doctrine. However, the vast majority of physicians are risk-averse enough to carry substantial malpractice insurance. Because the insurance premiums do not depend on the negligence experience of the individual practitioner, the real source of compensation for injured patients is not the careless doctor who is the focus of the tort system, but the group of doctors in the specialty or region who are defined by the malpractice carrier as the appropriate pool for this insurance coverage.

Under workers' compensation, the legal locus of liability is the employer—the business enterprise—not the individual worker, supervisor, or executive who might have been personally responsible for the accident. The employer is explicitly required to carry workers' compensation insurance or to provide evidence of its own capacity for self-insurance, as well as security for such insurance. But because of the size of most business entities and the incidence of injuries in many industries, the accident experience of the individual firm provides an actuarial basis for varying the premiums charged for workers' compensation insurance. Consequently, this liability system preserves a considerable financial incentive for the individual firm to improve its workplace injury record.

Procedure for establishing liability. The malpractice system relies on the civil jury to make the crucial decisions about fault and damages on the basis of a case developed in a formal public trial by the lawyers acting for each side. Although workers' compensation programs do not take the precise form of the NLRB model upon which the AMA's administrative fault proposal is based, they are designed to be easily available to workers trying to collect benefits for their injuries without having to use lawyers, and to offer a comparatively informal administrative hearing that reduces the time and legal expense for resolving the vast majority of contested claims.

Viewed against that broader backdrop, it is clear that the AMA's specific proposal of administrative fault addresses only the last procedural component of the program, leaving the crucial substantive features of malpractice law largely untouched. The individual doctor would be responsible for an injury only if he had erred in his medical treatment, and the patient who suffered injuries as a result would be entitled to full compensation for all the losses inflicted, both financial and psychological. The AMA recommends a number of additional legal reforms, most prominently in the area of damages: a collateral source offset and a reasonably generous, inflation-adjusted cap on pain and suffering awards. The system would develop clearer, more systematic guidelines for determining exactly what is meant by full tort compensation of the injured victim, but the basic legal principle would not be diminished.

Given that setting for the administrative fault idea, the reaction it will evoke is easy to imagine. In the United States there is an historical affinity between our fault-based, make-whole tort law and the court-centered, jury-dominated system of civil justice—an affinity of such long standing that it now appears to be "natural." Legislators will be very reluctant to deliver into the hands of a single bureaucratic hearing officer the authority now wielded by the jury to make findings of fact on which will rest the fate of both the doctor who may be judged negligent and the patient who may be seeking millions of dollars in compensation for tangible losses. Serious concern will also arise about replacing the continuing cross-section of popular views expressed by ad hoc jury panels with a single agency that might become too responsive to the point of view of doctors, who are the agency's principal organized constituency. The experience with medical disciplinary boards does not immediately allay that concern. The insistent question that will have to be answered in the inevitable constitutional challenge (if not before) is, what do injured patients get in return for providing doctors a new adjudicative forum, one in which the medical community would feel more comfortable?

One possible quid pro quo is the offer of free public legal representation to injured patients to try to establish liability of the doctor. For too long the sentiment underlying legislative policy in this area is that we have far too many spurious claims—in medical parlance, "false positives"—being filed by patients. Hence the appeal of devices like medical review panels, which would screen out invalid claims before too much damage was done to the doctor. But as the Harvard study demonstrates, there is a far higher incidence of valid claims *not* filed by patients who have suffered actual damage at the hands of their doctors. The AMA's proposal, modeled on the organization of the General Counsel to the NLRB, responds to the problem of the "false negative" by providing more accessible legal relief to many patients. This innovation would be particularly helpful to those who suffer modest injuries with a potential level of damages that would make the case unrewarding for a private attorney to undertake. That representation gap is exacerbated in the many jurisdictions that now offset collateral source benefits against tort awards, reducing even further the net economic recovery from tort suits, and then require the private attorney to secure expensive "certificates of merit" and/or medical review before having a chance to establish the patient's claim in court.

Under the proposed AMA regime medical fault and scientific causation would be just as difficult to prove against a doctor and a liability insurer resisting claims they believe they could defeat. Against the highly paid and sophisticated defense bar, the board's general counsel would be able to offer only modest professional salaries to recruit a staff that would likely be composed primarily of recently admitted attorneys looking for valuable litigation experience before going on to lucrative private practice. Any patient with a worthwhile case—characterized by good evidence of fault, severe injuries, and large damages—would therefore be better advised to utilize the services of a high-priced personal injury specialist to obtain maximum value from the claim. Yet it is precisely these catastrophic injuries that are most in need of care and attention in the design and reform of a mandatory public tort regime. The value to injured patients of the services of private versus government attorneys would be even greater if the elimination of collateral source benefits and the constraints on pain and suffering damages, both sought by the AMA, were combined with the principle of considering the successful plaintiff's attorney fees as an independent element of tort damages.[6]

The AMA proposal offers a second quid pro quo to patients for administrative fault. This is the promise of more effective protection against future medical injuries. In my opinion the major institutional virtue of the proposal is the way that it would knit together decision making about negligent events that produce compensation for affected patients with judgments that trigger discipline for affected doctors. But in evaluating how effective these preventive efforts are likely to be, even by an agency armed with all the new statutory weapons that the proposal anticipates, recall how sharply the scope of physician regulation is limited. The focus is on identifying and eliminating a tiny number of especially poor doctors rather than on trying to enhance the quality of care provided by the vast majority of typical doctors. It is worth noting that the AMA does not contemplate that even the improved medical board it envisions will be authorized to define and enforce elevated standards of practice for the profession: presumably doctors do not have sufficient confidence in any government agency to entrust it with that role.[7] Patients and their attorneys may be pardoned, then, for feeling similar qualms about entrusting such a body with the final say about the quality of medical care that was provided to them.

Notwithstanding these cautionary observations, the administrative fault proposal is interesting and worthy of serious consideration. We must devise better procedures for adjudicating issues of science and technology within our legal system.[8] Indeed, the issue of causation is just as significant a problem in malpractice litigation as is physician carelessness, as evidenced by such questions as whether cerebral palsy that develops in an infant was, in fact, the result of an admitted failure to monitor and detect fetal distress during the period of delivery years before.[9] At the same time we must recognize that altering one aspect of the present malpractice system—even a feature as central as the forum in which legal doctrines are applied to concrete cases—falls far short of addressing all the dissatisfactions of either doctors or patients with the present tort/fault regime. The AMA proposal helpfully alters the terms of the debate by forcing us to confront a far-reaching alternative to the traditional litigation approach to personal injuries. In that respect it is a welcome diversion from the heated but ultimately fruitless controversy over which peripheral tort doctrines should be preserved or "reformed." In the same spirit of exploring for fundamental alternatives, then, I shall tackle some additional deeply embedded features of malpractice law.

Organizational Liability

If a state were to adopt the AMA's proposed system of administrative fault, these results would probably ensue:

- More accurate determinations would be made about liability and causation in individual disputes but without any major shift in aggregate outcomes.
- Malpractice claim rates would rise, because patients who suffer less serious and damaging injuries would be able to utilize state-provided legal representation to establish their doctor's negligence and consequently to recover compensation.
- The amount of tort recovery would be more predictable, and some protection would be provided against huge awards for pain and suffering. This would enhance the insurability of malpractice liability, but it would not materially reduce total patient recoveries or doctor premiums, especially if the state adopted my proposal to make patient legal fees compensable as part of a broader reform of damages law.

In sum, under an administrative fault system the average doctor would practice with a greater risk of a smaller tort award for negligent treatment. Doctors (unlike patients) would have more confidence in the judgments of the new tribunal administering the law, as compared with the frustration they experience over occasional ill-founded jury verdicts. However, it is doubtful that doctors would ultimately feel that much of the tangible burden of malpractice law had been removed from their shoulders.

That burden has two basic ingredients: the incidence of tort suits and the cost of malpractice insurance. Neither of these factors would be materially lessened by substituting administration for litigation of malpractice claims. Doctors would still have to subject themselves to depositions and cross-examinations; they would still be required to hear their professional performance being impugned by witnesses and lawyers, only this time in front of a medical board with authority over their license to practice. And whether or not a doctor experienced any such claims or verdicts arising out of his own work, he would still have to pay the (rising) premiums for liability insurance against the future occurrence of that contingency.

Let us turn first to the premium issue. The practical problem presented by malpractice premiums is their size relative to physician revenues. Annual premiums for all physicians practicing in this country average over $15,000, and range up to $200,000 for obstetricians and surgeons in cities like New York and Miami. For a doctor just starting a practice or wishing to wind down his professional career, having to pay insurance premiums of five- or six-figure amounts is extremely onerous. The physician's fee schedules do get adjusted over time to generate the revenues needed to cover this standard cost of practice; but sudden huge lurches may occur in the volatile market for malpractice insurance, forcing individual doctors in a variety of settings to ante up $50,000 or more in additional premiums. Because physician fees billed to future patients—as allowed by Medicare, Blue Cross, and other health insurance schemes—cannot be immediately adjusted to accommodate such an increase in practice costs, the result is a substantial drop in the net personal income of the doctor and his or her family. In reality, then, physicians cannot enjoy full insurance protection against the vicissitudes of the tort liability system. Moreover, many doctors experience this untoward effect on their incomes even if they have not been personally involved in a meritorious tort claim.

The source of the problem is the insurance classification system. Insurers typically try to devise smaller, more refined risk categories, which will permit them to market coverage at lower rates to the preferred groups. In the case of medical malpractice, a pediatrician or an internist in a rural area is a much better risk than an obstetrician or surgeon in a big city. This disparity exists *not* because obstetricians and surgeons are inherently more accident-prone, or because rural areas are more likely to attract higher quality doctors than those found in the big cities. Rather, the difference in premium rate stems from two factors: the inevitable human errors of a doctor in a high-risk specialty are more likely to produce serious patient injuries, and the legal system in urbanized areas is likely to translate patient injuries into more tort claims and higher damage awards. But whatever the explanation, the problem remains that the pool of obstetricians in New York City or neurosurgeons in Miami is simply too small to be able to cover even a tiny number of severe and costly injuries without extracting from each member of the pool very high insurance premiums. The higher these malpractice premiums are relative to gross and net revenues from practice, the worse will be the dislocation from any sudden sharp increase in premiums for the group.

Perhaps the key intellectual influence on the evolution of tort liability over the last several decades, even within the framework of the fault principle, has been the sentiment of scholars and judges that more expansive liability can safely be imposed on the enterprise, which can obtain insurance against the risk and distribute the burden of the liability across the broad pool of the enterprise's constituencies.[10] Even in the fields of product and environmental liability, substantial dislocation has been experienced by firms as these insurance markets tried to adjust to the recent growth in the tort burden.[11] But the product and environmental areas at least enjoyed the luxury of a substantial number of participating business enterprises to bear the increased legal liability and insurance costs. By contrast, roughly three-quarters of all malpractice claims are brought against individual physicians[12] in a health care system that is still one of the last outposts of the independent entrepreneur.

Given that diagnosis of the problem, the nature of the solution follows quite naturally. We must find a way to make the overall health care system pay for and distribute the cost of malpractice insurance without having to funnel the premiums through the coffers of individual doctors. The technique I favor is to make the hospital or other health care organization primarily liable for all *accidental* (negligent, not intentional) injuries inflicted on patients due to malpractice committed by anyone affiliated with the institution, whether or not the actor is technically an employee of the hospital. In other words, for purposes of personal injury policy, the relationship of hospital and affiliated physicians should be deemed to be the functional equivalent of the relationship of an HMO to its staff physicians. In the HMO context, individual obstetricians or surgeons are not expected personally to pay the large malpractice premium required for their medical specialties, which are much riskier than those of the pediatrician or internist. Likewise, we do not expect that the pilots or mechanics working for an airline company should personally pay the substantial premiums that would be required for insurance against instances of careless behavior in these jobs, slipups that are far riskier than those which might be committed by a flight attendant or passenger agent working for the same airline. Instead, under this proposal each doctor in every specialty is treated as a member of a single firm engaged in the enterprise of health care, with the organization responsible for collecting revenues from the patients who receive the benefits of its services and for purchasing the insurance required to protect against the risk of serious injuries that occur. The analogy, again, is to pilots or mechanics, who are assumed as a matter of course to be parts of the larger enterprise of air travel, with the firm assuming immediate responsibility for injuries caused by the mistakes of its workers, and paying for those costs through revenues collected from all passengers on its flights.

Although this proposal constitutes a fundamental reorientation of the malpractice system, it goes with the grain of several trends and developments in the last two decades. The evolution of hospital liability over the last century can be summarized quickly.[13] Historically, hospitals were not inviting targets for tort litigation because of legal immunities enjoyed by charitable and governmental institutions, and because of the judicial assumption that hospitals were not responsible for the medical (as opposed to the administrative) side of patient care. By the early sixties, courts had largely cleared away these initial legal obstacles to a hospital's liability for the negligence of its own employees. However, the vast majority of treatment decisions and procedures were still the responsibility of doctors who were legally independent practitioners with only patient admitting privileges in the hospital. To avoid this "independent contractor" limitation on vicarious liability, many states adopted one or both of two doctrinal devices. The concept of "ostensible authority" is used to hold hospitals liable for negligence committed in emergency, radiology, anesthesia, or other services for which a hospital has directly contracted with outside practitioners to provide for its patients. The concept of direct "corporate liability" has been adopted to make hospitals liable for their own negligent failure to check the credentials and monitor the performance of surgeons, obstetricians, and others who are granted the privilege of admitting their own patients into a hospital for necessary procedures.

At the beginning of the nineties, then, a variety of legal openings exist for a tort claim against a hospital, usually accompanying the claim against a negligent doctor. My impression is that most suits against hospitals are lodged to allow the patient to tap the much larger insurance policy of the hospital, rather than risk a failure to collect on a possible multimillion-dollar jury award because of coverage limits in the doctor's liability policy.[14] Yet of the $7 billion paid annually for malpractice premiums, roughly two-thirds come from physicians, while hospitals and other health care institutions pay only one-third.

A related trend that affects malpractice insurance itself is "channeling"—a system in which the hospital provides insurance coverage out of its own policy for all or part of the malpractice liability of its attending physicians. Channeling programs have been adopted by a number of hospitals on a voluntary basis because the aggregate amount of premiums can be reduced on account of self-insurance or economies of scale. Some have adopted the system in order to recruit and retain doctors in higher-risk specialties and regions. A few states, such as New York, have recently gone further, requiring hospitals to purchase excess coverage (coverage for over $1 million per claim) for their medical staff.[15]

The more typical state response to this concern, though, has been to create a Patient Compensation Fund (PCF). PCF's are financed by charges to doctors, hospitals, or carriers and provide liability insurance coverage above a fairly low ceiling—such as $100,000—on the doctor's personal responsibility. In many states the PCF is part of a broader malpractice law that also imposes a limit on total patient recovery, even for economic losses from the fund—$500,000, say, or $1 million—thus triggering the serious constitutional and policy concerns I discussed earlier.[16] Aside from the rather offensive ceiling feature, however, the PCF has the legitimate aim of permitting doctors to limit their premium practice costs to a defined amount, while offering injured patients access to an insurance pool that will distribute the burden of the most serious injuries across a much larger constituency.[17]

My proposal for full-scale organizational liability goes considerably beyond any of these tort and insurance developments. The individual hospital would be exclusively liable for all the damages resulting from negligent treatment of any patients in the hospital by its affiliated doctors, employees or not.[18]

Such a bold move toward enterprise liability in the malpractice litigation-insurance system would have two immediate advantages. On the insurance side, it would greatly ease the problem of raising the funds needed to pay for malpractice insurance. Even though $5 billion in annual physician premiums is a hefty sum, it is less than 1 percent of the nation's annual expenditures on its health care system, now topping $600 billion. Large urban hospital enterprises (or groups of smaller suburban or rural hospitals) are much better able to absorb future jumps in liability premiums, which are a relatively small proportion of overall hospital operating revenues. They are certainly well equipped to handle the increase in comparison with the individual physician who practices in a high-risk setting and who may have to come up with $100,000 to pay a malpractice premium bill as a condition to beginning practice for the year.

On the litigation side, assigning tort liability to a single entity would also reduce the administrative burden by channeling all tort claims for an incident against a single party. Nearly 25 percent of malpractice claims now have two or more defendants.[19] Many of them involve the hospital, whose legal responsibility for the actual carelessness of admitting physicians on the premises has been gradually expanding under a number of doctrinal theories. Such hospital liability, and, to an even greater extent, the PCF idea, insulate the high-risk specialties such as obstetrics from much of the cost burden of compensating the truly catastrophic cases, while still leaving the doctor in the suit as the immediate legal target for the initial losses on the claim. Any case with multiple defendants is much more complicated, time-consuming, and expensive because of the presence of several actors, insurers, and lawyers with their differing tactical interests, which must be reconciled with each other as well as with the plaintiff. One virtue, then, of clearly fixing the legal responsibility for the injury on a single entity is to simplify the litigation process and thereby reduce the attendant costs.

Still, the idea generates some troublesome questions. First, should the reallocation of responsibility be *mandated* across the board by the legislature rather than allowed to emerge step by step through voluntary agreements between hospitals and their medical staffs? Second, should the liability of the health care organization be *exclusive*, thereby relieving the individual physician of a legal incentive to be careful in his own professional performance?

The first objection may recall the discussion in Chapter 5 of the contractual alternative to mandatory tort law. I expressed concern about the imbalance in the relationship between doctor (or hospital) and patient, assuming that the power tilt in favor of the health care provider would lead inevitably to a no-liability situation if freedom of contract over liability were permitted. However, that concern is of little relevance in the doctor-hospital context. Once nonwaivable rights for the patient are guaranteed, doctors and hospitals should be capable of negotiating freely and on an equal footing about how to allocate legal and insurance responsibilities for accidents among themselves. If enterprise-based tort litigation can in fact deliver on its promise of savings for all in insurability and administrability, why not rely on the market to generate such savings to the greatest extent possible?

Such insurance-channeling programs have in fact been voluntarily adopted in a variety of settings. But these programs have encountered several practical obstacles, one of which is the problem of paying for the new allocation of responsibility in the existing network of medical reimbursement programs. The cost of malpractice liability for delivering babies, for example, is currently built into the fees charged by obstetricians for their work. If liability were shifted to the hospital, obstetric fees would have to be sharply reduced, while hospital charges for the mother and baby would be increased to cover the added institutional expense. The problem arises because the hospital and the doctors associated with it have little direct control over the size of their fees, which are fixed in the reimbursement schedules of a host of health care insurers, public and private, state and federal. This difficulty does not exist when the doctors are salaried employees of a university hospital or an HMO, for example, for in that situation all the revenues from obstetric or surgical services flow into a single institutional account, from which the costs of liability can be borne. (Note also that in the HMO setting the salaried doctors are never obliged by contractual agreement to pay indemnity to the organization; consequently, the doctors do not have to purchase individual insurance and obtain higher salaries to absorb this employment expense.)

Unlike HMO's, the vast majority of doctors and hospitals operate financially independent of each other. For this group the major transaction costs of reconstructing the many reimbursement schedules constitutes a potent inertial force in favor of the legal status quo.[20] Consequently, supporters of the move toward organizational liability must recognize that such a transition as a matter of tort policy is far less likely to be accomplished by private, incremental action than by an across-the-board public policy that deals with both sides of the equation.

The second major question to address is whether it is sound policy to relieve the individual doctor of personal liability for his own carelessness, even if the alternative regime is more efficient in the short run. After all, the behavior of an organization consists only of the acts of the human beings that make it up. Shouldn't we try to increase rather than decrease the level of personal care and attention of doctors in the hazardous world of modern medicine? If so, how can we afford to relax the tort incentives now trained on doctors?

The case for organizational liability rests on a contrary premise: tort sanctions in health care are most usefully focused on institutions rather than individuals.[21] Portions of that argument have appeared at various points in this book, and I shall now attempt to draw them together.

Let us first consider the prospect of malpractice litigation from the doctor's perspective. Most malpractice suits arise in connection with momentary inadvertent slips or mistakes that are hardly influenced by the threat that an adverse tort verdict might materialize years later. Even with respect to conscious medical choices about what level of precaution to employ, the doctor rarely has a financial incentive to scrimp on safety for the patient. Additional tests or more complicated procedures usually entail more work and greater fees for the doctor.

Even if a physician were inclined to shirk his or her responsibility to the patient, most of the personal incentives provided by tort law would continue to exist under a regime of organizational liability. The patient-victim would still inflict uninsurable costs on the doctor—in income, stress, and professional stigma—by litigation undertaken to establish the fault of the doctor so that the patient could collect from the hospital. Moreover, it is already the case in the current individualistic tort regime that the patient collects the monetary award not directly from the careless doctor, but from the doctor's liability insurer, and ultimately from funds generated by the health care insurance system to pay for the malpractice premiums.

Yet the inadvertent mishaps of the individual doctor, even if they are not deliberate and only minimally deterrable, are dangerous and need to be contained to the extent possible. The best vehicle for identifying and dealing with such incidents is the organization in which the doctor practices. The memory of the institution can serve to record and piece together patterns in a host of apparently idiosyncratic incidents. The collective wisdom of the hospital team can be pooled to devise feasible procedures and technologies for minimizing the ever-present risk of occasional human failure by even the best doctors; for example, by developing systems to monitor a patient under anesthesia or a fetus during delivery in order to detect and avoid sudden oxygen deprivation and consequent irreversible brain damage. Not only does the organization have a greater capacity to establish such quality assurance programs, but it is also more likely to do so in response to the incentives created by tort liability. Many health care institutions are so large that they do not have to carry outside insurance; those that have outside coverage experience enough claims to constitute a credible actuarial base for sizable variations in the price of insurance sold to institutions depending on their relative safety records.[22] In the more competitive, market-oriented health care environment of the nineties, the prospect of such a payoff might well induce hospitals to make more substantial investments of time, effort, and money in quality assurance programs.

Many observers might concede that hospital liability has initial comparative advantages over physician liability but still feel reluctant to eliminate the doctor's legal responsibility for his own negligence. My response to that concern is that our goal should be to focus tort liability and incentives on the institution, the point at which they are most likely to be effective. In so doing, we will in turn induce the institution to train its organizational pressures on the physician to adhere to the highest practice standards. That is in effect what happens now in the relationship of hospitals to their house staff, nurses, and other employees, and in the relationship of HMOs to their entire complement of physicians. (Recall as well the analogy of the relationship between the airline company and the pilots or mechanics whose errors might cause a plane crash.) If a staff member's negligence causes injury to a patient, the patient would sue and collect from the institution, which in turn would use appropriate personnel management techniques—in selection, training, supervision, discipline, and termination—to achieve a higher level of care from its employees. Indeed, that phenomenon already exists among independent doctors, notably in the efforts by certain physician-owned carriers to conduct in-depth peer review of the practices of doctors involved in troublesome malpractice incidents. One possible result of a highly unfavorable review is that the negligent doctor will lose insurance coverage and consequently the ability to practice. The assumption of organizational liability is that the ideal setting for peer review is the immediate hospital environment in which the doctor practices. The institution must be empowered and encouraged to employ the necessary managerial tools to reduce substandard care by physicians permitted to use its facilities. And unlike a tort award, the suspension of the doctor's valuable hospital admitting privilege is a loss that cannot be insured against.

Stating the case for organizational liability so baldly immediately raises the hackles of physicians and their associations. They contend that most doctors are not employees and do not want to be treated as employees. They are independent professionals who must be free to exercise their own medical judgment, not forced to comply with the edicts of hospital administrators. If the price of the hospital's bearing the responsibility for physician negligence is to grant authority to the hospital over the standards of treatment by the independent practitioner, doctors may well reject that price as too steep. It is evident, then, that the physicians' impulse to preserve their autonomy is another steep obstacle to voluntary steps toward organizational liability and authority, no matter how much more effective an instrument this may be for patient safety.

My response to this final objection is that it nostalgically evokes a health care world that has long since passed. The present troubling reality is that the professional judgment of independent doctors is regularly challenged in the courtroom and second-guessed by *ad hoc* lay juries, as well as by hospital and governmental administrators.[23] The essence of the AMA's administrative fault proposal is to move malpractice cases into a forum that would permit a more informed professional appraisal of the quality of the medical treatment under attack. The major thrust of current legislative and regulatory efforts to spur more aggressive risk management programs is to require each hospital to establish peer review committees whose job would be to set standards of physician practice, to monitor regularly the level of performance by all doctors working in the hospital, and to deal stringently with problem cases as they appear, taking measures that could include "firing" doctors from the hospital. In the present network of arrangements the one feature that has lagged far behind the other changes in the relationship of doctors and hospitals is the current assignment of tort liability and the related responsibility for obtaining malpractice insurance. This gap has produced the variety of deleterious effects described above. My proposal for a system of explicit organizational liability is designed to bring the world of the courtroom into closer correspondence with the world of the hospital operating room.

No-Fault Patient Compensation: Promise and Pitfalls

Suppose we were to take the second step away from the traditional regime of tort/fault liability by adding the concept of *organizational* liability to the *administrative* forum proposed by the AMA. That raises the further question of whether to retain the core substantive condition to liability—proof of fault on the part of the individual doctor. After all, organizational liability is simply an attenuated version of fault. The entity that is held liable to pay for the damages is only vicariously accountable for the actual carelessness of the doctor or other actor who would not be legally or financially responsible for the injuries. So why not complete the circle by dispensing entirely with the fault requirement, establishing a full-blown program for compensating all patients injured as a result of medical treatment, irrespective of the presence or absence of negligence in the treatment?

A no-fault program would respond to the other major problem felt by doctors under the present malpractice regime. Doctors want to be relieved not only of the financial burden of malpractice premiums, but also of the emotional burden of adversarial litigation with their patients and the risk of having their professional competence stigmatized by a jury verdict. At the same time, patient-victims would be relieved of the burden of demonstrating the fault of their own doctor, against the doctor's vigorous personal and legal resistance, in order to gain access to the pool of insurance funds that the health care system now accumulates to compensate at least some victims of iatrogenic injuries.

No-fault patient compensation for medical accidents, modeled on workers' compensation for workplace accidents, evoked considerable interest in the early seventies when the malpractice crisis first loomed on the horizon.[24] New Zealand adopted a version of categorical no-fault compensation for the victims of medical accidents as a feature of its broader social insurance approach to all accidental injuries.[25] Sweden followed suit with a separate, self-contained patient compensation scheme.[26] But in the United States the no-fault idea was a nonstarter in the medical area, even in states that adopted some degree of no-fault compensation for motor vehicle accidents.[27] This absence of interest was not merely a testimonial to the effective political resistance the personal injury bar has regularly been able to mount against any erosion of its tort preserve. Even some of the most prominent scholarly devotees of no-fault, commenting from a variety of intellectual perspectives, expressed grave doubts about the viability of the concept in the context of medical accidents.[28] The consensus was that in spite of its initial appeal, no-fault patient compensation was simply not feasible.

That verdict was rendered at a time when the annual malpractice claim rate was roughly 1 per 35 doctors, and when liability premiums totaled roughly $1 billion annually. Now claims are running at more than 1 suit per 10 doctors every year, and annual malpractice premiums have reached $7 billion. So it is not surprising that medical no-fault is back in vogue. Other countries have furnished examples: Finland has adopted a program largely modeled on Sweden's,[29] and a government commission in Canada has proposed a somewhat different version there.[30] In this country the states of Virginia and Florida have legislated no-fault compensation for babies who suffer severe brain or neurological damage during delivery, one of the major trouble spots in present-day malpractice.[31]

A no-fault program is made up of a network of components, including limited scheduled benefits, informal administrative processing and adjudication of claims, and an enterprise for channeling the payment and financing of the compensation for injured victims. Administration of claims and the financing mechanism were canvased in the sections dealing with administrative fault and organizational liability. Taking that earlier discussion as a given, let us now address the core proposal that a victim should be entitled to at least some compensation from the actor, irrespective of the presence or absence of fault on the actor's part.

That principle itself may be adopted in a number of forms. The standard version is the one now in operation in workers' compensation schemes for workplace injuries: the program is mandatory rather then voluntary, comprehensive rather than limited to specific types of injuries, and exclusive rather than supplementary to a still-available tort remedy (at least with respect to the employer who provides the no-fault insurance). Yet none of these features of contemporary workers' compensation is intrinsic to the no-fault concept. Indeed, there are no-fault programs that take the *opposite* tack in each of these respects. No-fault motor vehicle accident compensation, for example, is almost always superimposed on the existing tort system; it rarely replaces the latter entirely. The Virginia and Florida schemes of no-fault compensation for neurologically impaired babies are confined to this one type of accident, and participation in even this sharply limited program is at the election of the obstetrician or hospital. I shall not address this range of issues here, even though they would be important in any blueprint of a no-fault proposal. Instead I will focus on the more fundamental choice between the concepts of fault and no-fault and evaluate their respective merits in providing sensible compensation for medical injuries and effective prevention of those injuries.

Compensation

The traditional case for no-fault emphasizes its comparative advantage in providing more generous compensation, facilitated to some extent by expected administrative economies in delivering the benefits. Under a standard no-fault scheme victims of all medical accidents would be eligible for compensation solely because of the nature of the losses they have suffered, not because their injuries were fortuitously produced by the carelessness of a doctor or nurse—an eligibility criterion that consumes more money in legal disputes than is spent in financial benefits for those patients who eventually pass this test.

This program has immediate appeal as a matter of compensation principle. But the evident increase in the number of victims who would be compensated raises the first major objection to no-fault: it would be far too expensive for medical accidents. The New York and California studies found that for every negligently injured patient, at least three more are injured for reasons other than provider negligence. Even for injuries that are due to substandard treatment, only one in sixteen victims receives any compensation from the tort system. Since doctors and hospitals now lament that they cannot afford to pay the $7 billion in premiums required by a tort system that has the range of built-in restrictions on coverage discussed above, the last thing health care providers would elect is a no-fault program that promises coverage to nearly *fifty* times the current number of tort recipients.

Let us consider this argument from two perspectives, one of principle and one of fact. At the most fundamental level, the claim that we cannot afford to pay for the cost of patient injuries is simply wrong. If medical accidents occur and patients are injured, the cost will be "afforded" somehow, either by the immediate victim and family or by alternative sources of community support. Ironically, a significant portion of the cost is actually generated by and handled within the health care system itself. About one-quarter of total malpractice damages flow from the expenses of medical treatment and rehabilitation,[32] so the only policy issue is deciding from whose pockets these monies are to come.

Suppose it were decided that the nation was not prepared to pay any more than the current $7 billion malpractice premium bill in compensating patient losses under a no-fault scheme. Perhaps that amount might even be doubled to account for the presumed savings in unnecessary "defensive" medicine induced by the current tort system. This leaves open the question of what criteria to use for distributing these funds. The current social judgment embedded in the tort system is that a selected few victims—those injured by demonstrably careless treatment—will collect *full* compensation for *all* their injuries, whether these injuries are modest or grave, economic or noneconomic, covered by collateral sources or entirely uninsured. This tort principle seemed quite appropriate as long as the issue was defined as an attempt to achieve corrective justice between innocent patient and careless doctor by deciding which person should bear the burden of the patient's injuries. But once it is acknowledged that the compensation burden is actually borne collectively by patients through the premiums they pay their health insurers, which then pay the fees of doctors, who in turn pay liability premiums to malpractice insurers, which finally pay benefits to patients who are injured, a quite different set of criteria should seem equitable for distributing the limited funds our political economy is prepared to make available to the victims of iatrogenic injuries.

The target of the available funds should be meeting the tangible needs of injured victims. Money would be provided to pay the bills for medical treatment and physical or vocational rehabilitation that is needed to heal the injuries as quickly as possible. In addition, income would be made available to replace the lost earnings that victims had relied on to support themselves and their families. Finally, rather than simply cap or scale down pain and suffering damages from a comparatively high dollar figure, following the example of workers' compensation such noneconomic redress would be confined to the severely and permanently disabled, with strictly limited benefits specified in an age-adjusted schedule of physical impairments.

In sum, an explicit disability insurance program would give priority to compensating the catastrophic losses of the few people who were most seriously injured, rather than try to insure the modest losses of the much larger number of people who were only moderately harmed. The New York State study, for example, found that nearly half its injured patients were back at work within one month of their initial admission to the hospital, and more than three-quarters were back within six months.[33] The most sensible policy assumption of any system of mandatory insurance is that people are typically able to absorb small setbacks out of their own resources or out of broadly available benefits such as sick pay. Consequently, the object of social concern should be the individual and family who suffer a devastating loss that only the broader community can effectively bear.[34] From this perspective, the single worst idea in malpractice reform is the imposition of a ceiling—typically a fixed dollar amount that is not adjusted to years of subsequent inflation—on the total amount that can be paid to any one victim for all medical and rehabilitation costs, nursing care, and lost earnings. Such statutory provisions achieve cost containment objectives at the expense of the small, politically powerless group of younger, more severely injured victims of medical accidents. Far more rational and appealing conservation criteria are available for stretching the limited amount of resources made available for patient disability benefits.

First, such compensation should be available only to the minority of injured patients whose disability endures for some moderately extended time. In the case of no-fault patient insurance a time-based screening criterion is essential, if only to facilitate disentangling the medical costs and lost earnings that are specifically attributable to the iatrogenic injury from the losses that would normally be expected to flow from the underlying illness and its treatment and recuperation. A six-month dividing line would be a reasonable transition point from the short-term disability protection that people can be expected to secure for themselves and the long-term disability benefits such as Social Security Disability Insurance that the community mandates for everyone's protection.

Next, mandatory patient compensation should reimburse only longer-term losses that are not covered by other sources of public and private loss insurance, on the assumption that these other sources are more accessible and efficient conduits for redress than a liability scheme that still requires judgments about the *cause* of (if not the *fault* for) the injury for which benefits are being sought. The Harvard study found that with respect to long-term losses, even though over 85 percent of medical costs were covered by insurance, only 20 percent of the lost earnings of injured patients were replaced by other nontort sources.[35]

Finally, although providing unlimited coverage for long-term medical and rehabilitation costs incurred by injured patients might be appealing, the pattern set by other modes of public and private disability insurance suggests that only a designated proportion of net lost wages should be replaced. If we followed the example of no-fault workers' compensation, we would reimburse two-thirds of gross earnings (or 80 percent of net earnings) up to a ceiling set somewhere between 100 and 150 percent of the state's average wage.

The last criterion recalls the principle of cost sharing that is implicit in the design of all no-fault schemes, a principle that has two justifications in the intellectual framework of compulsory insurance policy. One objective is to bring about the most equitable distribution of benefits and burdens under such programs. In the current tort system, which replaces all lost earnings, however high they may be, damage awards paid to those with higher incomes are much greater in amount than those paid to people with smaller incomes. This disparity in the size of monetary awards might seem fair when we look at the cases *ex post* and observe that the higher-earning victim's losses are much larger than the other's. However, the spread is much less appealing when the situation is viewed *ex ante*, at the time when the tort costs are being paid for. The financial burden of malpractice insurance (or of product liability insurance for pharmaceutical manufacturers) ultimately falls on individuals who pay the premiums for health insurance (or the bill for prescription drugs). Yet the prices charged for these services or products do *not* vary according to the incomes of the consumers who must pay for this form of disability insurance as one component of the purchase price. So designing a patient compensation scheme with the scope of income replacement restricted more or less to the average earnings in the community results in much greater equity. Those with higher incomes, of course, retain the option of purchasing voluntarily the additional disability protection they think they need to protect their incomes.

A second justification for shifting from full compensation to some form of cost sharing is that doing so reduces the risk of moral hazard on the part of victims whose behavior might otherwise be altered if they realized that all the financial losses from an injury would be made up from the external source. Many observers doubt that this is a significant factor in inducing careless behavior in the production of the original injury, at least in the medical context, where most serious iatrogenic injuries are inflicted on patients who are comparatively passive recipients of treatment. The more substantial problem arises in the aftermath of the medical accident. At that point the patient's decision about how much rehabilitation to undergo or whether and when to return to work are important determinants of the total economic loss that will be occasioned by the original injury. These decisions illustrate the virtue of *coinsurance*, which requires the individual to bear a share of his lost earnings in order to create some incentive to reduce the total amount of his earnings losses.

One major undertaking of the Harvard study was to determine whether a no-fault program designed within parameters like those described above would be even conceivable in financial terms. For that purpose we interviewed in 1989 a cohort of patients who had been injured in 1984. We spoke not simply to patients who had been injured due to provider negligence and who consequently had potentially litigable claims, but also to patients (three times the number of the negligently injured group) whose injuries had occurred without identifiably careless treatment, but whose losses would be potentially compensable under a no-fault scheme. Our objective was to document all the economic losses suffered by those patients from 1984 through 1988, as well as all the compensation they received for those losses from various forms of health and disability insurance, in order to calculate past and future losses for the rest of the injured patients' life expectancy.

We found that the most seriously disabling (including fatal) injuries were more likely than not to have been caused by a provider's negligence and were therefore potentially litigable under the present tort system. We also learned that those claims which actually entered the tort process were disproportionately likely to include extremely great economic losses. So the true gap between losses compensable under fault and under no-fault was much smaller than first appeared from looking only at pure rates of adverse events and negligent adverse events without controlling for the differences in the resulting physical impairments and financial losses. Next, when we focused on the critical economic losses—the medical costs and lost earnings that occurred in longer duration cases (cases lasting longer than six months from the time of hospital admission) that were not reimbursed by other insurance sources—the estimated compensable financial losses, in discounted present values, were surprisingly modest: just over $400 million in 1989.[36] This estimated figure is comparatively small in light of the total amount spent on malpractice insurance (in both direct premiums and self-insurance), which was over $1 billion in New York (admittedly one of the highest-cost malpractice states, along with Florida and Michigan).

Of course, there are some major differences in the two figures. Roughly 60 percent of malpractice expenditures are spent on administration and litigation. Of the remainder about 50 percent is spent on pain and suffering and other noneconomic losses. The other substantial item of economic loss is household work, which we estimated would cost $450 million in New York on the somewhat unrealistic footing that household time should be valued at the market wage payable to the group of injured women patients in our study. But even granted these caveats—that some compensation would be required for lost household production, that some scheduled benefits might be paid for loss of enjoyment of life due to physical impairment, and certainly that a great deal of money would be necessary to administer a no-fault program—the Harvard study clearly demonstrates that a policy shift from tort/fault to no-fault patient compensation is a financially viable option in the catalogue of alternatives to present-day malpractice litigation.

Administration

Advocates of no-fault programs assume that a major reason such programs could compensate many more victims for about the same amount of money is the considerable savings in administrative expenses that they would offer. Administration is unquestionably a major item in the overall malpractice bill. In addition to the business costs of accumulating the insurance funds by selling liability coverage and collecting and investing the premiums, the legal and other claims adjustment expenses required to distribute the insurance money to injury victims amounts to between 55 and 60 percent of the total expended in the claims process.[37] That proportion is roughly three times the administrative share of claims expenditures in workers' compensation.[38] The second argument for no-fault, then, is that dispensing with the inquiry about the negligence of doctors and other health care providers will free up additional funds from administrative economies; as a result, it will be possible to increase the scope and generosity of disability insurance provided to all injured patients.

It is this issue that generates the second major objection to the no-fault patient compensation idea. Critics claim that the anticipated administrative savings cannot be extrapolated from the occupational setting. Instead, they argue, in the medical context determining the *cause* of the patient's injury would typically be as difficult as the determination of the doctor's *fault* under the current system. If that be the case, the result of adopting a no-fault scheme would be even higher administrative costs, because under such a regime a larger number of patients would be lodging equally contentious claims.

There is unquestionably a significant difference between a no-fault program that compensates workers (or motor vehicle users) for injuries "arising out of and in the course of employment" (or while using a motor vehicle) and a no-fault program for injured patients. Unlike the employee who goes to work or the driver who gets into a car, the patient who enters a hospital is already suffering from an underlying illness, which may itself be capable of producing the disabling losses in question. If someone breaks a leg from a fall at work or in a motor vehicle collision, he enters the hospital for treatment but may emerge with a permanent limp. The consequences of this disability are properly chargeable to the health care system only if the disability was caused by the treatment received in the hospital rather than by the original accident. Indeed, it is evident that at least some of the medical expenses and the earnings lost from work must have been the product of the initial unhealthy condition, the treatment for it, and the patient's recuperation. Deciding whether medical treatment produced a worsening of the original condition and, if so, disentangling the financial consequences of the iatrogenic injury from the underlying illness, require delicate judgments about what transpired inside the hospital, and how the treatment altered the path that the patient's condition otherwise would have been expected to follow.

The problem is more complex than simply identifying which if any losses—episodes of lost work and earnings, for example—were caused by medical management. Equally difficult conceptual issues arise concerning which losses are properly attributable to a specialized program of liability for health care injuries. Doctors often undertake medical treatment that is known to be traumatic because such intervention is necessary to arrest and cure a disease even more life threatening than the treatment; consider radical chemotherapy for cancer, for example. Consequently, for a determination of liability it cannot suffice to decide that a particular episode of disability was the consequence of—arose out of and in the course of—medical treatment. The disability must fall outside the range of intended or expected consequences of the treatment. To illustrate, suppose in the example of the broken leg that the limb had become seriously infected, and that by the time the injured party arrived at the hospital gangrene had set in. Imagine further that a medical judgment was made that amputating the leg was necessary to save the patient's life, and that the patient consented to the operation. Although in a sense it is true that the amputation directly caused the loss of the leg, from the point of view of liability policy one would certainly not conclude that medical treatment was the relevant cause of the loss. The patient's initial unhealthy condition required the intervention, so the underlying condition must be deemed the true cause of the loss of the leg. Only if the infection that led to the amputation had been the effect of treatment provided inside the hospital would the loss properly be the responsibility of a no-fault patient compensation scheme.

In fact, not even in this hypothetical case of an identifiably iatrogenic injury should all the costs of the disability be compensable. The initial condition of a broken leg would itself normally have produced some hospital and medical expenses and lost earnings during the period of treatment and recuperation. Only the additional injuries from infection and amputation would be attributable to the health care system. In practice it would likely be too costly and burdensome to have a patient compensation program always try to isolate precisely which of the immediate economic consequences were attributable to the original unhealthy condition and which to the iatrogenic injury, even after determining that such an injury had occurred. Instead, the program would feature an across-the-board rule that no-fault insurance is available only after a certain period of disability had run, perhaps six months. Such a trigger would not only finesse a particularly troublesome aspect of the causal inquiry, but it would also concentrate the program's resources on longer-term disability, which should be the focus of mandatory insurance under either a fault or no-fault liability criterion.

The target of a patient compensation program, then, is the unintended or unexpected adverse consequence of medical care, not the inevitable or regular consequence of appropriate treatment designed to ameliorate a patient's original condition, treatment that would still have been undertaken even if one had known, *ex ante*, of the harmful consequences that would flow from the medical intervention. However, drawing the line between unintended and inevitable consequences is not tantamount to conducting an inquiry about the doctor's fault. Let us consider two cases to illustrate the difference. In the first, a patient has a breast lump that a biopsy indicates is malignant.

On the recommendation of her doctor the patient agrees to a mastectomy. Once a more complete examination of the tissue is possible after the surgery, the earlier diagnosis is revised: the lump is benign. In the second case, a patient is diagnosed with a condition that is best treated with a particular drug. However, when the patient uses the prescribed drug, it becomes evident for the first time that he is susceptible to a reaction to the drug that is even worse than the original illness, which might have been addressed with a different although less effective treatment. Under the tort/fault system, which would scrutinize the doctors' behavior from the perspective of the situations as they appeared at the time the treatment decisions were made, in neither of these cases would negligence be found, because the medical judgments were perfectly reasonable in light of the information available about the risks and benefits of the courses of treatment. But under no-fault patient compensation, which allows consideration of the situation with the aid of hindsight, it is evident that the harmful events—the severe drug reaction and the removal of a normal breast—were not inevitable results of treatment required to cure the patients' condition, unlike the removal of a gangrenous leg. If either of the resulting disabilities fit within the benefit structure of the program, it would be compensable.

Ultimately it is not possible to design a program for pure no-fault patient compensation. My examples to this point have all consisted of positive (though harmful) consequences of medical intervention—acts of commission. The particularly difficult cases in the medical setting are instances of omission, in which the harmful consequence is attributable to a failure properly to diagnose and treat the patient's condition in the first place.

Consider the example of a patient undergoing treatment for cancer who dies in the hospital as a result of the malignancy. The death is caused by the original condition, not the treatment. Contrast this with a case in which the patient dies as the result of an inadvertent overdose of chemotherapy, a positive medical intervention. The matter becomes more complicated, though, if the cancer in the first example was a curable one, such as an early Hodgkin's lymphoma, that was not properly diagnosed or treated in the hospital. In that instance, even though it may be descriptively accurate to conclude that cancer was the factual cause of death, legal policy would judge the significant cause to be the doctor's failure to interrupt the natural development of the tumor.

Our notion of causation must be broadened, then, to include what might be called *moral* or *policy* causation, what should have happened, as opposed to purely *factual* causation—what did or might have happened. If causation is so broad, however, we must ensure that a self-contained patient compensation program does not slide into becoming general social insurance for every disability or fatality that medical care did not prevent or cure. One measure for preventing this is to establish criteria that specify what *should* have happened, thereby distinguishing the properly compensable cases from the noncompensable ones. The easy cases are those in which treatment was impossible. If a disease cannot be cured, it should be the responsibility of broad-based social insurance, public or private, to pay for the victim's losses from such diseases. This role should not be assigned to a patient compensation program, which is supposed to shoulder the health care system with only the costs of disabling injuries that are attributable to its own operations. Suppose, though, that the disease could have been cured if it had been treated by the top practitioner in one of the major teaching hospitals of the world. Under that *optimal care* standard, compensation should be available for any disability that could probably have been avoided by some doctor, somewhere. That would likely be a very expensive compensation program. To avoid going that far by choosing to compensate only disabilities that would have been cured by the *reasonable care* expected from the average doctor in an actual practice setting, it is necessary to reinstate the fault principle as the basis for compensating at least this category of iatrogenic injuries.

The foregoing cases illustrate the conceptual and practical difficulties that confront efforts to transplant the no-fault model into the medical setting. But the fact that there are real difficulties in designing such a liability alternative is not a sufficient reason for sticking rigidly to the tort *status quo*. Indeed, tort law itself must grapple with the same knotty causal questions. Once a court decides that a doctor was at fault in the standard of care provided, it must then make the second determination of whether it was actually the medical negligence that caused the harm to the patient for which damages are sought. Such harm would of course include a failure to cure a disease that should have been manageable. In a series of cases over the last decade dealing with this issue, known as "loss of a chance,"[39] courts have grappled more and more frankly with the problem of what to do about a patient who came to his doctor with an existing cancer or heart disease, but who now argues that the doctor's failure properly to diagnose or treat the condition deprived him of a real (though perhaps a less than fifty-fifty) chance of survival. In any event, even though questions of causation can be conundrums in either the tort or the no-fault setting, the evidence is that the causal inquiry is generally far less difficult than is the additional fault judgment that tort law must undertake. The medical reviewers in the Harvard study found that only a small fraction (5 percent) of their causal judgments were "close calls," a mere quarter of the proportion of the difficult negligence judgments the doctors had to make.[40] Moreover, the results of the academic investigation in New York are corroborated by experience in Sweden and New Zealand, the two countries that have provided no-fault compensation for medical injuries over a decade. In both countries it has been possible to draw a causal dividing line without any pronounced administrative burden for the no-fault programs as a whole.

Prevention

Just as I concluded earlier that no-fault patient compensation was financially affordable, I am satisfied that it would be administratively feasible. This is not to deny that thorny questions of causation would be present in many cases. As part of our ongoing research efforts, the Harvard Medical Practice Study Group will analyze how the Swedish and New Zealand programs have handled the troublesome cases that turned up in our New York sample. We realize that since much more would be riding on such rulings in the United States because of the gaps and limitations in our health care and disability safety nets, legal contests here over close causal cases would undoubtedly be more heated than they are in the two no-fault countries. So even if eliminating the fault inquiry might conceivably slash the present administrative share of the claims dollar from nearly 60 percent to under 30 percent, that share could be reduced by another two-thirds (to 10 percent or less) if we also eliminated the inquiry about what caused the patient's injury and simply provided compensation on the basis of the type and magnitude of the losses suffered.[41]

Let us look at the example of the no-fault schemes adopted recently in Virginia and in Florida for babies who suffer neurological injuries during delivery.[42] These programs provide generous compensation for the resulting onerous medical and rehabilitation expenses, as well as modest replacement of earnings that will be lost in the future. It is estimated, however, that only a small fraction of infants born with cerebral palsy or other birth defects sustained these injuries as a result of medical treatment. Moreover, it is extremely difficult to identify the iatrogenic cases, because the symptoms of the condition often do not manifest themselves until years later.[43] Finally, from the vantage point of the disabled babies it appears arbitrary to redress the present losses of some babies but not others simply because of the way their respective injuries happened to come about years earlier.

More generally, we might ask whether it is reasonable to advocate a program guaranteeing patients redress for health care costs that stem from disabling injuries suffered inside the hospital, when there is no guarantee of health insurance coverage for the injuries or illnesses that brought the patient into the hospital in the first place? From a compensation perspective, there is no doubt that if we leave the tort/fault regime in search of a more equitable and administratively efficient system, our ultimate destination should not be a categorical program of no-fault benefits based on the cause of the injury, but rather a broad program of social insurance for all victims against especially pressing losses.[44]

The response in favor of a no-fault stopping point is that focusing financial responsibility for certain kinds of disabilities on the enterprises or activities that caused the injuries can make a substantial contribution to prevention of future injuries. The major shortcoming of social insurance is that by dispensing with individualized liability for the financial consequences of injuries caused by particular actors, leaving the costs to be distributed across the community as a whole, we lose the safety incentive that would otherwise be placed on individuals faced with the prospect of having to pay for injuries they could have avoided. So those who are uncomfortable with the idea of relying solely on ethical, market, and regulatory incentives to secure necessary levels of safety and quality in modern-day medicine should be wary of pure social insurance for medical injuries, as wary as they would be of blanket contract waivers of liability.

Ironically, a standard popular and political objection to a no-fault regime is that it would eliminate any legal incentive to maintain a high level of safety. That is fair comment about the operation of the New Zealand system, for example, and apparently about what is contemplated for Virginia. Under both programs the responsibility for patient injuries is diffused among all those who contribute to the insurance fund.[45] However, well-designed no-fault programs, such as workers' compensation, are as much a mode of individualized liability as is tort law. Under existing workers' compensation plans, as well as under what would be the most sensible arrangement for patient compensation, a particular employer or hospital is liable for injuries arising out of its own operations. While insurance against this liability would be available for organizations not large enough to shoulder the risk on their own, such insurance can be experience-rated in an actuarially credible way in order to maintain a potent incentive for the enterprise to prevent injuries and in that way avoid legal and financial liability.

The fact that both fault and no-fault liability can generate safety incentives is well recognized by tort scholars, if not in the popular debate. Although there is no shortage of armchair speculation about the likely similarities and differences in the fault and no-fault regimes, until recently only scant empirical material was available to confirm or refute the analytical preferences.

No empirical study of the few existing no-fault patient compensation schemes has ever been done. The only empirical investigation of the preventive impact of the current malpractice system is the Harvard study in New York.[46] Though there may be room for debate about the various statistical steps we took, our best judgment is that there was at least a modest level of injury reduction attributable to more intense use of the tort system against the hospitals in certain areas of the state. In addition, the no-fault program for workplace injuries has a relatively long track record, and recently the province of Quebec applied the no-fault model to motor vehicle injuries.[47] New studies of the impact of these alternative liability regimes provide evidence that is useful in weighing fault versus no-fault for the medical injury context.

The research from Quebec indicates that the province's shift in liability policy did increase the hazards on its highways. Motor vehicle *fatality* rates are considered the best measure of relative risk, because fatal incidents are least subject to the reporting effect induced by expanding entitlement to compensation. Quebec experienced increased fatality rates, estimated in two different studies at 7 percent and 14 percent, respectively.[48] There is sharp debate in the literature about whether these higher fatality risks are attributable to a reduction in driving precautions induced by no-fault itself—which the second study found responsible for a 10 percent increase in driving fatalities in the province—or to the new flat-rate price system for motor vehicle insurance, which was part of the Quebec program and which attracted larger numbers of higher-risk drivers onto Quebec highways. The earlier study found the flat-rate system to be the sole source of the higher fatality rate.

The result of this debate is significant because of the contrasting results from research in the workplace setting. In the most recent and comprehensive empirical analysis in this area, Professors Viscusi and Moore have demonstrated that existing no-fault workers' compensation programs can be credited with reducing by somewhere between 25 and 45 percent the number of fatalities that would otherwise have occurred in American workplaces.[49] This sharp difference in empirical result should not be particularly surprising. In contrast with the flat-rate first-party benefit paid to driver-victims under no-fault auto insurance, workers' compensation is designed on the third-party liability model. The employer is individually responsible for injuries that occur in its operations, and sizable employers are heavily experience-rated for the purpose of calculating their insurance premiums. As a result, an organization has considerable financial incentive to take the measures necessary to reduce hazards in its operations, including the human errors of its managers and employees.[50]

If, as I assume, any move from fault to no-fault in the medical arena would carry with it a shift in the focus of liability from the individual doctor to the hospital organization, not only is the workplace example much more pertinent than the motor vehicle case, but it is very likely that the law would achieve considerably greater leverage for prevention than it does under the current malpractice regime. The defendant hospital would still be responsible for all negligent injuries suffered by patients—that is, for all cases in which the incident would have been avoided had the individual doctor, nurse, or technician taken the necessary precautions. With respect to this subset of patient injuries, no-fault patient compensation would retain the present legal incentive for reasonable care. But no-fault goes further, imposing legal liability even in cases of entirely blameless accidents. To underscore the significance of this expansion of legal responsibility, recall the finding of the Harvard study that patients suffer three times as many disabling injuries when no identifiable party is at fault.

A natural reaction to the last observation is that such an extension of liability could not serve a prevention function for injuries without a discernible faulty actor, even though it would provide compensation to the victim. Non-negligent accidents are those in which the injury could not have been avoided by reasonable precautions. So what value is served by imposing a liability incentive on the health care provider to avoid unavoidable injuries?

The fallacy in that challenge is its static perspective on the medical accident problem. Malpractice law confines itself to enforcement of what the medical profession has adopted as appropriate procedures and precautions, given the current state of the art. But the practice of medicine is constantly evolving under the impetus of newly developed diagnostic and treatment techniques. Many iatrogenic injuries that were accepted as inevitable over a decade ago—heart block during cardiac surgery, for example—are now considered avoidable as a matter of course. The vital prevention role of a no-fault system, then, is to add a legal spur to existing incentives to undertake research and innovation in safer, more advanced medical techniques.

Of course, under a typical no-fault regime, including the one I would favor for the medical setting, there is a corresponding reduction in the level of sanctions imposed on a party responsible for a negligent injury that is now readily avoidable. The patient would be unable to recover large awards for pain and suffering, and the defendant's legal fees would be considerably smaller in the administration of any one claim under the proposed regime. However, it is unlikely that steep awards in individual cases are necessary to assure appropriate safety consciousness on the part of health care providers, who are insured in any event against the costs of huge awards, and whose overall liability-overhead costs under no-fault would likely be at or above the current level under the tort system. Indeed, the wider ambit of no-fault patient compensation would boost the odds that specifically negligent injuries would receive at least some compensation, because benefits would be payable for all injuries, even those in which the negligence that occurred is too difficult for patients to detect or to prove in court under the current system.

The more compelling concern relates to the nonpecuniary aspects of tort sanctions. Under the fault system a jury scrutinizes the behavior of the doctor, decides whether his care was substandard, then renders a quasi-moral judgment about his poor performance in the case at issue. The public stigma from this process adds a significant—and noninsurable—reputational concern to any worries the doctor might have about purely financial exposure under the law. A no-fault program, by contrast, leaves it to the health care system to decide whether it is worthwhile to invest in a particular safety precaution, or whether instead to bear the financial responsibility for risks that are now judged not reasonably avoidable. But because the health care provider must still pay for unavoidable injuries that do occur, there is a continuous financial incentive to seek and adopt safer modes of treatment.

I am convinced that this subtle legal reconstruction of the medical market would be a more effective and efficient instrument for increasing patient safety than the more dramatic morality play of tort litigation. The tort/fault model fuels the popular but false impression that the problem consists in finding and holding to account a few bad apples in the medical profession. It is understandable why this malpractice regime has elicited such a powerful defensive reaction from doctors. The individual physician is risk-averse when it comes to the personal and professional stigma of a negative legal verdict. The same doctor makes the majority of treatment decisions concerning his patient. Finally, the widespread availability of health insurance sharply reduces financial resistance from patient-consumers to the added cost of treatment precautions whose necessity is dubious. But the reason why malpractice litigation has been able to produce no more than a modest reduction in patient injuries is that tort law misconceives the medical accident phenomenon.

A large majority of iatrogenic injuries are not due to anyone's negligence. Most of the negligence that surfaces in the tort system consists of momentary inattention and inadvertent slipups rather than deliberate scrimping on the quality of patient care in order to enhance the doctor's personal and financial rewards. The prevention role of a no-fault program assumes that if the health care organization is obligated to pay for patient injuries, however they may occur, the claims and payments will provide a continuing opportunity for the institution to learn about how such injuries transpire and how best to avoid them in the future. Is there a record of erratic behavior by an individual provider, whose performance should be either improved or terminated as a result? Or was an injury primarily attributable to the normal routines or facilities of the institution, such as a pattern of diagnostic or prescriptive mistakes by residents near the end of their continuous thirty-six-hour shifts in the emergency room? From this perspective the most appropriate role of the law is to promote constant improvement in the standard operating procedures of all personnel in these complex organizations, not simply to single out for blame individuals whose mistakes unfortunately inflict serious patient injuries of a kind that are likely to be reviewed in the courtroom.[51]

One apparent difference between a fault and a no-fault regime is that a no-fault scheme may appear to exonerate the victim—who, as a party to the health care relationship, is in a sense a participant in the "production" of the accident—from any pressure to avoid accidents. Under a fault regime the victim bears the risk of any injuries that cannot be attributed to the carelessness of another actor. Moreover, to the extent that the victim's own carelessness was a contributing factor, some portion of the liability is attributed to him. As a result, under the tort system the victim has considerable personal incentive to avoid accidents and their uncompensated or only partially compensated harms. But under a pure no-fault regime the victim is entitled to redress for the injury in any event and has no liability-based incentive to avoid injuries even in cases in which he might have been able to do so.

The practical significance of this analytical difference between fault and no-fault liability is greatly attenuated in the medical setting. The role of the patient in the hospital is far more passive in relation to doctors, nurses, and others than is the role of the consumer in relation to the manufacturer of the products he uses, or the role of the worker in relation to his employer. Of course in some medical situations, particularly those involving the ingestion of drugs or the failure to follow medical directives in recuperation, injury could be avoided by greater patient care and attention. Yet how much incentive to exercise care is actually eliminated by telling a patient (or worker or consumer) that although he might suffer a painful, perhaps even fatal injury, he or his surviving dependents will be able to recover compensation for the losses? The standard law and economics contention—that guaranteed compensation for losses dilutes the potential victim's incentive to take appropriate precautions—appears to be most applicable when the asset at risk is merely money or property rather than life or limb.

However, policymakers who are convinced not only that victims' carelessness contributes to their injuries, but also that the prospect of legal recovery is a moral hazard that induces more accidents, can readily incorporate the appropriate corrections into the design of a no-fault program. My observation that it is important to include thresholds or limitations on benefits as an incentive for victim rehabilitation after an injury applies in this case as well: presumably such limits would perform the same role in motivating people to avoid injuries in the first place. A no-fault program could go even further, denying payment of all benefits in cases in which the fault of the victim reached a specified level. That level might be defined as willful or reckless behavior, as in most workers' compensation programs, or perhaps gross negligence on the part of the patient, if the moral hazard of no-fault appeared to be a truly serious problem in the health care setting.

Elective No-Fault

The foregoing appraisal of the characteristic strengths and limitations of the fault and no-fault models satisfies me that no-fault liability is likely to produce more, not less, prevention of medical injuries. This is certainly the case when the comparison is between an organization- ally based no-fault regime and the present tort system with its focus on the fault of individual doctors. Adding the clear-cut advantages of administrative no-fault over fault-based litigation as an instrument for more equitable and more economical compensation, it is unques- tionable that no-fault must now be taken seriously in the debate about the future of medical liability.

That is not to imply that we should immediately sweep away the existing malpractice system and institute full-blown no-fault in its place. It is understandable that policymakers would be reluctant to take such a fateful leap in the dark. As an intermediate step, Jeffrey O'Connell's idea of "elective no-fault"[52] is an appealing possibility and may be a promising opening move for easing into the new liabil- ity approach.

Elective no-fault would operate this way: the legislature would ex- plicitly empower hospitals and other health care organizations to of- fer their patients an administrative compensation scheme for iatro- genic injuries in return for a waiver of common law tort liability. The legislation would require that the benefits meet certain standards of generosity. This might mean full out-of-pocket medical expenses along with 80 percent of net lost earnings up to 150 percent of the state average, plus specified payments for the loss of enjoyment of life due to different physical impairments. Each participating health care facility would have to operate an effective quality assurance pro- gram that would include reporting all accidents and holding people accountable for all adverse events identified through the claims pro- cess. The claims administration procedure would have to meet ac- ceptable standards of neutrality and due process. The program would cover all injuries inflicted on the hospital's patients, even injuries caused by nonemployee doctors with admitting privileges to the hos- pital. Appropriate adjustments would have to be made in the health care reimbursement schedules for all the participants, for both hospi- tals shouldering the new liability and doctors being relieved of the old tort liability (so this kind of program is most likely to surface in uni- versity teaching hospitals or HMO's, where the doctors are already employed or insured by the health care organization). The data assembled by the Harvard Medical Practice Study Group could be used by insurance actuaries to make reasonable projections of the cost of the new no-fault insurance, which in turn would permit hospital administrators and medical personnel to judge whether it would be worthwhile to offer this new package to their patients in return for relief from the burdens of tort litigation. The patients, in turn, would have to be fully informed, in readable and intelligible terms approved by the state insurance department, about the nature of the tort rights they would be giving up as well as about the no-fault benefits they would be receiving before deciding whether to accept medical care offered under no-fault auspices or to patronize an institution and doctors still governed by the existing tort regime.

There are distinct advantages to this scenario for reform. The most obvious is the relative ease of persuading the public and politicians simply to permit patient and doctor a choice about no-fault, a choice made under carefully tailored and protective conditions,[53] as opposed to convincing them to mandate no-fault liability. The experience of the new system in the initial self-selecting institutions would be extremely useful in determining the best response to issues such as whether to specify that certain designated events will be compensable, or whether various kinds of losses should be compensated.[54] Finally, government policymakers monitoring the results of this contractual experiment and appraising the patterns in both the no-fault and the tort/fault environments would gain a more realistic understanding of the comparative advantages of the two liability systems before deciding that one regime is so far superior that it should be established as public policy for everyone.

The Limits of No-Fault

It should be apparent from this chapter that I consider the no-fault model a promising response to the current discontents with malpractice litigation. Yet I do not wish to oversell the virtues of no-fault, certainly not as a global solution to every aspect of the medical injury problem.

The fundamental positive argument for any liability system, including no-fault, has to be its value as an instrument for preventing injuries. If the choice is solely between fault and no-fault as alternative modes of liability, then no-fault has evident advantages as a source of compensation. Yet the various forms of public and private social insurance do even better at compensation than does any no-fault program. That is why I envisage that no-fault patient compensation would be a secondary source of benefits, kicking in only after injured patients had exhausted their primary loss insurance. Anyone who argues not simply that we should move away from tort/fault but also that we should stop at no-fault must assume that internalizing the cost of medical injuries will reduce the levels of injury enough to warrant the inevitable compromises on the compensation side that would occur when benefit payments are limited to those who can prove the often elusive factor of medical causation. I am convinced that liability rules have a preventive effect, based on the systematic evidence of their preventive impact on workplace and motor vehicle accidents. Furthermore, I am confident that it is possible to design a framework of liability in the medical field that would be sounder than the current malpractice regime. Indeed, as part of our ongoing research program, the Harvard Medical Practice Study Group is using our New York data base to simulate the operation of a no-fault experience rating formula that would generate prevention incentives considerably greater than those now provided by tort law.

Of course, even a no-fault scheme that is generally more effective than the existing malpractice system may not be the best vehicle for dealing with every type of medical injury. The limited value of medical no-fault is nowhere better illustrated than in the only two instances currently in place in this country—the Virginia and Florida programs for brain-damaged babies. Infant brain damage cases are among the most difficult for accurately deciphering medical causation, in particular because the symptoms of cerebral palsy often manifest themselves only years after the delivery. What is more, the fact that these state legislatures delegated the task of determining causation to their workers' compensation boards does not inspire great confidence, since those tribunals have a long history of difficulty in dealing with their own causation issues, such as determining whether certain long-latency diseases like lung cancer were produced by workers' exposure to conditions on the job. Even worse, no attention was paid in the design of the Virginia and Florida programs to the prevention objective, the sole valid justification for placing such serious obstacles in the way of obtaining compensation. Instead, the legislatures adopted the same kind of flat-rate pricing schemes that exacerbated the motor vehicle accident problem in Quebec.

It is no secret that the inspiration for the Virginia and Florida no-fault schemes was entirely political. Obstetricians feeling oppressed by malpractice litigation and insurance premiums had demanded relief. It seems clear in retrospect, however, that a better method for dealing with this small slice of the problem of medical accidents and tort litigation would be an explicit loss insurance program for all infant victims of cerebral palsy that would not require any effort to isolate the specific causes. The cost of such broader disability insurance would be greater than the cost of either fault or no-fault liability.[55] But because the bulk of infant brain damage costs are expenditures on medical care and rehabilitation, the health care system would simply be refinancing the cost of its own services.

The Virginia and Florida examples illustrate that no-fault liability is not the most attractive option in every situation, even after a decision is made to move away from the fault-based tort system. And even adoption of no-fault patient compensation would not entirely remove medical accidents from tort scrutiny. Any categorical no-fault scheme operates in a legal environment in which tort principles constitute the prevailing background norms. Given the multitude of actors typically involved in many accidental injuries and the fact that some but not all of these actors may be governed by no-fault, there are continual border skirmishes between the two systems. This phenomenon has been most evident in the case of workplace injuries. Injured employees regularly sue the manufacturers of defective products or toxic chemicals used in the workplace, even though the employee-employer relationship itself is governed exclusively by no-fault workers' compensation. The same boundary problems will surely arise in the context of medical no-fault, and they should be accounted for in the design of such a plan.

The major source of this tension will be prescription drugs and other products manufactured for the health care market (which the Harvard study found to be involved in a substantial minority of the patient injuries in its New York sample).[56] The recent case of *O'Gilvie v. International Playtex*[57] epitomizes the potential problem. A woman using tampons experienced symptoms of toxic shock syndrome. Alerted to the problem by the warnings on the product package, the woman immediately consulted her family doctor. The doctor misdiagnosed her condition as scarlet fever and prescribed treatment that did not prevent her death a day later. The family sued the tampon manufacturer, not the doctor, and won a jury award of $1.5 million in compensatory damages and $10 million in punitive damages, a verdict that was later upheld by the Tenth Circuit Court of Appeals.

The *O'Gilvie* case is only one stark illustration of the kinds of tort claims and verdicts that result from the involvement of manufacturers in medical responsibility for a patient's injuries. Along with the widely heralded "mass tort" disasters involving products such as the prescription drug DES and the Dalkon Shield, similar features and tensions appear in suits involving vaccines,[58] prescription drugs of a variety of types,[59] equipment used in hospitals,[60] and blood transfusions that may be infected with the AIDS virus.[61]

· Like surgical procedures, medication and equipment used to cure diseases often pose their own serious risks to the patient.

· Pharmaceutical manufacturers who launch new products on the market must rely on doctors, hospital nurses, or technicians to serve as "learned intermediaries" who must decide whether use of a drug is warranted for a particular condition, warn patients about the drug's potential risks, and deal quickly and effectively with any harmful reactions that do occur.

· Even when the immediate source of an injury is an apparent mistake made by the doctor, as in the *O'Gilvie* case, patients regularly try to sue the manufacturer along with the doctor—perhaps even instead of the doctor. They do so partly because it is easier to persuade a jury to award huge damages, including punitive damages, against a large corporation, and partly because it is easier to collect large sums of money from an enterprise whose assets far exceed the typically limited coverage in a doctor's insurance policy, and which is not protected by the damage caps or other constraints imposed by medical liability legislation.

· In reaction to spiraling litigation rates and costs, drug manufacturers have adopted some of the same defensive practices that doctors use. Products are withdrawn from the market irrespective of their net social value. Firms are hesitant to invest in research and development of new products that might prove generally beneficial since any new drug that turns out to be dangerous creates a risk of putting a company into bankruptcy on account of a flood of lawsuits.[62]

My purpose at this point is not to appraise the benefits and burdens of pharmaceutical litigation, nor to explore specific avenues for its reform. That endeavor would require a book of its own. I simply want to emphasize that the trends described here would be exacerbated by the institution of medical no-fault programs covering doctors and hospitals.

Any such program would impose considerably sharper limits on patient recovery, at least for pain and suffering, than exist now under either malpractice law or standard malpractice insurance coverage. Limits on potential recovery by any one patient can be defended on the ground that they make it possible to pay no-fault benefits to redress the basic financial needs of a much broader number of injured victims. However, the patient who has a severe injury unquestionably caused by fault is still likely to cast about for someone to sue. The example of the workplace demonstrates that the most likely candidate for such suits will be a product manufacturer.[63] Injured workers, who are already entitled to no-fault workers' compensation benefits paid for by their employer, now receive through third-party tort suits nearly half the total damages awarded in all product liability claims. Essentially the same efforts have been made to outflank the limits on no-fault benefits for military service-related injuries: witness the Agent Orange litigation against the manufacturers who supplied the federal government with the chemical.[64] The scenario would undoubtedly repeat itself if no-fault medical liability programs were enacted.

There are a number of ways to respond to this dilemma. The simplest solution, currently employed in Sweden, would be to establish a no-fault program for pharmaceuticals as well.[65] Interestingly, the National Childhood Vaccine Injury Act, enacted in 1986 by the U.S. federal government, establishes a limited version of such a scheme.[66] The program covers the principal vaccines that are required for children under public health immunization programs; for all permanently disabled infants it pays medical and rehabilitation expenses, projected lost wages, and even an amount for pain and suffering up to $250,000. But the distance yet to travel to no-fault drug liability is indicated by the fact that even in the vaccine situation, perhaps the best possible case for the exponents of no-fault, use of the program is left to the voluntary election of the injured victim. Victims retain the right to reject the no-fault benefits and to sue in court—albeit with significant constraints on potential tort recovery, a provision that the authors of the act hoped would minimize tort litigation in this area.

Assuming, then, that for the foreseeable future any no-fault medical liability program would have to operate side by side with a tort/fault system of liability for the manufacture of most drugs and equipment used in the health care system, boundary rules are required to delimit the respective spheres of responsibility. It is crucial that the designers of medical no-fault learn from the seventy-five years of experience and mistakes in dealing with the same issue in the workplace. In the occupational setting the injured worker first collects the no-fault benefits funded by the employer. With this guaranteed recovery as a base, the worker consults a lawyer, who institutes a suit against the manufacturer of, say, the machine tool or toxic chemical that was involved in the injury, seeking a large tort damage award (from which, by the way, the employer will be reimbursed for workers' compensation benefits paid). In response, manufacturers who observe that the employer is the immediate guilty party in the accident, like the doctor in the *O'Gilvie* case,[67] seek from the culpable employer a contribution to any tort award won by the employee. The employer, who financed no-fault benefits for all its employees in return for immunity from paying tort damages to any of them, naturally resists the third-party claim as an effort to finesse its own statutory immunity from tort suits. The result of this pattern has been decades of costly and largely fruitless litigation about which of the two liability insurance regimes will end up paying the injured employee and how much each share will be.

Having analyzed this problem in detail elsewhere, here I shall simply suggest what would be the easiest, most sensible solution. Take again the example of the *O'Gilvie* case, but this time in a world in which no-fault benefits were available for medical accidents. The survivors of the deceased patient would collect the defined benefits payable from the patient compensation fund. These benefits would automatically be offset against any tort award won against the manufacturer, thus casting product liability in the role of tertiary insurer, behind both secondary patient compensation insurance and the primary loss insurance available for health care costs and lost earnings. Just as the medical liability program would have no right to recoup its benefit payments even from the manufacturers of defective drugs or products, so also the manufacturers would have no right of contribution to their tort liability, even from careless doctors who were covered by the no-fault scheme. The consequence is that the patient would collect the same amount of compensation, wasteful litigation between the two insurance programs over which party is responsible for how much of the injury would be eliminated, and a reasonable level of incentives for prevention would still operate under each of the medical and pharmaceutical liability models. To the objection that this scheme still leaves drug manufacturers exposed to excessive liability in cases like *O'Gilvie*, my answer is that, if so, we should reexamine the tort rules relating to liability and damages in pharmaceutical cases, not permit incursions by drug manufacturers that would threaten a smooth-running no-fault system governing the relationship of patients to doctors and hospitals.

As this lengthy chapter has demonstrated, the road to no-fault patient compensation is long and rocky. Difficult judgments must be made about a number of crucial components of such a program. How should we define the causal connection that would entitle patient-victims to compensation? What categories and levels of compensation should be paid for the financial and nonfinancial losses from the injury? How can liability insurance arrangements be designed to offer health care providers appropriate incentives for safer and better quality medical care? What decision-making procedures will afford due process to the individual parties and sensible judgments about the issues in dispute, while keeping to a minimum the program resources spent on claims administration? And how should an island of no-fault be situated in the broader sea of tort liability?

It has taken fault-based malpractice law centuries to evolve its own answers to these and other issues, for better or for worse. It will require hard thought, not quick judgments, to fashion the ideal responses to these dilemmas in the no-fault context as well.

7

Afterword

The field of medical malpractice is a microcosm of the trends and tensions in legal liability generally. The product and environmental areas, for example, have also been subject to spiraling litigation rates and insurance premiums, sparking political pressures for broader tort reform and scholarly debates about the virtues and vices of the contractual, regulatory, social insurance, and no-fault alternatives to the tort regime. But medical malpractice has always been at the eye of the legal storm because of popular appreciation of the special personal stakes when a patient is moved to sue his or her doctor, charging negligence in the care that was provided.

Modern medicine is an inherently hazardous undertaking. The documented risk of medical injuries, even only those injuries caused by identifiable negligence, is high. We should not be surprised at that fact. We ask the health care system for more and more ambitious repairs of the ravages done to our bodies by time, by our living habits, and by our environment. In that quest we continually devise new techniques and equipment that are both promising and risky. We then put this sophisticated technology in the hands of doctors, nurses, and others whose occasional but inevitable human errors cause serious, often irreversible harm to their patients.

Many more negligent patient injuries are inflicted by the health care system than are ever compensated by the tort system. This is not to deny the regular occurrence of unfounded, even frivolous, malpractice claims. However, the sole in-depth study of the disposition of malpractice claims—involving suits against anesthetists—found that the tort process was reasonably accurate in both its payment and rejection decisions. The serious failing of our civil justice system is that it is unable to identify and redress such a high proportion of the potentially valid suits that patients are entitled to bring. From that perspective Professor Richard Abel has argued that the real tort crisis is not that there are too many legal claims but that there are too few.

Whether this gap is actually a problem, let alone a crisis, depends on our judgment about how much good the legal system does when it pays the tort claims that it now receives. I no longer believe there is much value in the search for corrective justice between individual patient and doctor, however much that value has influenced the shape of our tort principles. Whatever judicial doctrines might say, in reality the litigation system mandates a form of disability insurance that is paid for by the broader community of potential patients in order to give protection to some of the patients who will be injured in the course of their medical care. My criteria for appraising the worth of that liability insurance regime are whether it provides appropriate compensation for patients who were already injured, fosters effective prevention of possible future injuries, and delivers both compensation and prevention at acceptable administrative costs.

Present-day malpractice litigation misses these targets by a considerable margin. Most of the claims dollar goes toward legal fees, pain and suffering, and items that have already been compensated by various sources of primary loss insurance, rather than being spent on the critical financial needs of the most severely injured patients. This acknowledged flaw of tort law as a mode of compensation might be acceptable if the system were living up to its promise as an effective incentive for injury prevention. Unfortunately, the little empirical evidence that we have, as well as systematic analyses of the characteristic features of the tort process, lead to the conclusion that even though the threat of tort suits induces expensive reactions from doctors, there has been only a modest payoff in reducing injuries to patients.

In this book I have developed a two-track program for remedying the deficiencies in present-day malpractice law. One track consists of major renovations, rather than just minor tinkering, within the tort system. We must sharply revise the principles of tort damages in order to concentrate the available resources on meeting the actual financial losses of seriously injured victims: by offsetting against the award all payments secured from collateral sources, by scaling downward any payment for pain and suffering, and by treating successful plaintiffs' attorney fees as an independent category of compensable damages. We must also shift the focus of tort liability from the individual doctor to the hospital or other health care organization, so as to use the leverage of the tort sanction to elicit more effective quality assurance programs from the institutions that are in the best position to reduce the current unacceptable rate of iatrogenic injuries. These proposals satisfy what should be but has too often not been the acid test of fair and sensible tort reform: it should be designed to address the needs of the *patients* who both pay for and rely on tort protection, rather than respond only to the concerns of doctors, lawyers, and insurers who have the ear of the state legislators.

There are states—most conspicuously New York and Florida—in which the current situation seems to have gone beyond the help of even serious tort reform. In states like these the no-fault idea must be placed squarely on the agenda. I recognize that no-fault patient compensation is technically and politically more difficult to bring about than was workers' compensation; and as a long-time student of the occupational injury field, I am only too aware of the flaws in the workplace version of the no-fault model. But the proper question about no-fault for medical injuries is not whether it would be easy and ideal, but whether it would be better than what now transpires in real-life malpractice litigation. For the reasons developed at length in the previous chapter, I am persuaded that in the medical context an intelligently designed no-fault program can provide more equitable compensation, more effective prevention, and more economical administration.

One signal virtue of the Harvard study in New York is that the data gathered there make no-fault at least a "thinkable" idea. Concerned individuals must now address the competing arguments on their intrinsic merits, not simply dismiss this alternative as unfeasible. The current period of comparative stability in the malpractice arena offers us an opportunity for careful reflection on the question of whether there should be a fundamental reorientation in medical liability law. We must not be lulled into thinking that the current calm will endure indefinitely, however. Recall the figures that indicate there is a large pool of potential tort claims that is yet to be tapped by personal injury lawyers. We should hope that by the time the third malpractice crisis hits this country in the nineties our public policymakers will have fashioned a fairer and wiser legal structure than those in place in the seventies and eighties.

Notes

Case Index

General Index

Abbreviations

Florida Policy Guidebook
Barry L. Anderson, Patricia M. Danzon, Clark C. Havighurst, Charles E. Phelps, and Frank A. Sloan, *Medical Malpractice Policy Guidebook* (Henry G. Manne, ed., Jacksonville, Fla.: Florida Medical Association, 1985)

Harvard Study
Harvard Medical Practice Study Group, *Patients, Doctors, and Lawyers: Medical Injury, Malpractice Litigation, and Patient Compensation in New York* (Cambridge, Mass.: Harvard University, 1990)

HEW Report
U.S. Department of Health, Education, and Welfare, *Report of the Secretary's Commission on Medical Malpractice* (Washington, D.C.: U.S. Government Printing Office, 1973)

HHS Report
U.S. Department of Health and Human Services, *Report of the Task Force on Medical Liability and Malpractice* (Washington, D.C.: U.S. Government Printing Office, 1987)

1984 Claims Closed Survey
U.S. General Accounting Office, *Medical Malpractice: Characteristics of Claims Closed in 1984* (Washington, D.C.: U.S. Government Printing Office, 1987)

Notes

1. The Malpractice Crisis

1. "Videotaping Doctor Visits: Rx for Lawsuits?" *Wall Street Journal*, p. 17, col. 3 (November 25, 1987). The same sense of impending doom has been generated by our entire regime of tort litigation and liability insurance. Popular concern about the general liability insurance crisis was captured in the title of *Time*'s March 24, 1986, cover story, "Sorry, America, Your Insurance Has Been Canceled."

2. The Reagan administration's view of the vices in present-day tort law and the solutions it favored were set out in two reports published by the Justice Department's Tort Policy Working Group: *Report of the Tort Policy Working Group on the Causes, Extent, and Policy Implications of the Current Crisis in Insurance Availability and Affordability* (Washington, D.C.: U.S. Government Printing Office, 1986), and *An Update on the Liability Crisis* (Washington, D.C.: U.S. Government Printing Office, 1987). A popularized but astute expression of the same jaundiced appraisal of tort litigation is Peter W. Huber, *Liability: The Legal Revolution and Its Consequences* (New York: Basic Books, 1988). A somewhat more moderate position on possible changes in medical malpractice law was spelled out in the *HHS Report*.

3. A by-product of nearly two decades of concern about medical malpractice litigation and insurance has been extensive investigation of this particular area of personal injury law. I shall draw upon much of this material as the source for the empirical assertions I will make in this section and later in the book. It is useful at this point, then, to identify the major studies to which I will refer regularly.

   The first systematic government review was the *HEW Report*. A research report prepared for the HEW secretary's commission by Mark Kendall and John Haldi, "The Medical Malpractice Insurance Market," *HEW Report*, Appendix 494, contains a particularly useful description of the trends in malpractice insurance in the sixties. Another research report by Steven K. Dietz, C. Bruce Baird, and Lawrence Berul, "The Medical Malpractice Legal System," *HEW Report*, Appendix 87, gives a good sense of the trends in the legal system in the same decade.

   As the problems became more pronounced by the mid-seventies, the

American Insurance Association published its *Special Malpractice Review: 1974 Closed Claim Survey, Preliminary Analysis of Survey Results* (New York: AIA, 1975). This report was followed by the U.S. Department of Health, Education, and Welfare, *Medical Malpractice Claims: A Synopsis of the HEW/Industry Study of Medical Malpractice Insurance Claims* (Washington, D.C.: U.S. Government Printing Office, 1978); then by a more extensive claims review conducted by the National Association of Insurance Commissioners, *Malpractice Claims: Final Compilation, Medical Malpractice Closed Claims, 1975–1978* (Brookfield, Wis.: NAIC, 1980). The results of the NAIC empirical study of malpractice claims in the mid-seventies were summarized in M. Patricia Sowka, "The NAIC Medical Malpractice Closed Claims Study: Executive Summary," 45 *Connecticut Medicine* 91 (1981).

Marking the even more dramatic changes of the mid-eighties, the federal government commissioned and published a more up-to-date set of investigations. Several of these were conducted by the U.S. General Accounting Office (GAO), in particular, the empirical studies *Medical Malpractice: Insurance Costs Increased but Varied among Physicians and Hospitals* (Washington, D.C.: U.S. Government Printing Office, 1986); *Medical Malpractice: Six State Case Studies* (Washington, D.C.: U.S. Government Printing Office, 1986); and *1984 Claims Closed Survey*. The GAO also published a brief analytical report, *Medical Malpractice: A Framework for Action* (Washington, D.C.: U.S. Government Printing Office, 1987); and the Department of Health and Human Services issued a much more detailed examination of the issues in its *HHS Report*.

More recently the Institute of Medicine has produced a two-volume interdisciplinary report, Victoria P. Rostow and Roger J. Bulger, eds., *Medical Professional Liability and the Delivery of Obstetrical Care* (Washington, D.C.: National Academy Press, 1989). Finally, Frank A. Sloan and Randall R. Bovbjerg, *Medical Malpractice: Crisis, Response, and Effects* (Washington, D.C.: Health Insurance Association of America, 1989), updates many of the trends since the mid-eighties.

The issues of malpractice litigation and insurance costs vary greatly among the different states, with perhaps the starkest situations being those in New York and Florida. These two states have produced in-depth analyses of their own malpractice issues. Studies from New York include the New York State Department of Health, *Physician Malpractice Claims Closed, 1980–1983* (Albany, 1986); Report of the New York State Insurance Department on Medical Malpractice, *A Balanced Prescription For Change* (New York, 1988); Association of the Bar of the City of New York Ad Hoc Committee on Medical Malpractice, *Report on Recommendations for the State of New York* (New York: 1989); and the *Harvard Study*. Studies of the situation in Florida were done in the *Florida Policy Guidebook* and the Florida Academic Task Force for Review of the Insurance and Tort Systems, *Preliminary Fact-Finding Report on Medical Malpractice* (Gainesville, Fla.: 1987). The latter findings are presented in detail in David J. Nye, Donald G. Gifford, Bernard L. Webb, and Marvin A. Dewar, "The Causes of the Medical Malpractice Crisis: An Analysis of Claims Data and Insurance Company Finances," 76 *Georgetown Law Journal* 1495 (1988).

4. Kendall and Haldi, "Malpractice Insurance Market," p. 509, stated that malpractice insurance premiums for doctors totaled $32 million in 1960, at which time the cost for such insurance was $29 million for hospitals. The GAO study *Insurance Costs* estimated that the 1985 physician premiums were $3.4 billion, double the $1.7 billion of just two years earlier (p. 25), while hospital premiums were $1.34 billion, up from $850 million in 1983 (p. 39). The *HHS Report*, p. 147, relied on American Medical Association surveys which found that physician insurance costs actually totaled $3.8 billion in 1985 (to which would be added 40 to 50 percent more for hospital insurance costs). From 1985 through 1988, the average doctor's malpractice premiums rose by 50 percent; see Martin Gonzales and David Emmons, eds., *Socioeconomic Characteristics of Medical Practice, 1989* 7 (Chicago, Ill.: AMA Center for Health Policy Research, 1989). Assuming only modest growth in hospital liability expenses, total tort costs must have been over the $7 billion mark by 1988.

5. The banner front-page headline for the October 2, 1989, edition of *Barron's* read, "Medical Malpractice: End of the Nightmare." The story inside, Diana Henriques, "Just What the Doctor Ordered: The Crisis in Medical Malpractice Insurance Is Ending," p. 8, details recent premium declines and speculates on the reasons for them. A *New York Times* story by Milt Freudenheim, "Costs of Medical Malpractice Drop after an 11-year Climb," p. 1, col. 1 (June 11, 1989), and a *Wall Street Journal* article by James R. Schiffman, "Medical-Malpractice Insurance Rates Fall: Drop in Number of Claims Cuts Insurers' Costs," p. B1, col. 1 (April 28, 1989), had each presented the same picture several months earlier. Finally, a piece entitled "Improvement Continues for Medical Liability Insurance," in the St. Paul Fire and Marine Insurance Company's *Physicians' and Surgeons' Update* 1 (July 1989), documents trends in claims, payments, and premiums at this company—the largest national malpractice carrier—which operates in forty-two states and insures more than 20 percent of the nation's physicians (although none in such critical high-cost states as Florida, New York, or Michigan).

6. Patricia M. Danzon, *Medical Malpractice: Theory, Evidence, and Public Policy* (Cambridge, Mass.: Harvard University Press, 1985), refers (at 59–60) to surveys from 1956 and 1963 that determined that there were approximately 1.3 malpractice claims per 100 doctors each year. Mark C. Kendall, "Expectations, Imperfect Markets, and Medical Malpractice Insurance," in Simon Rottenberg, ed., *The Economics of Medical Malpractice* 167–192 (Washington, D.C.: American Enterprise Institute for Public Policy Research, 1978), reports (at 188) an annual claims rate of 1.7 per 100 doctors in 1966, 2.1 per 100 by 1970, and 4.1 per 100 by 1973. The American Medical Association's surveys of its members reported that the claims frequency rate rose to 8.0 per 100 by the early eighties, and over 10.0 per 100 by 1985 (*HHS Report*, p. 166). The GAO report *Six State Studies*,

p. 17, indicated that the annual claims rate against the St. Paul Fire and Marine Insurance Company was 16.5 per 100 insured doctors in 1984. In 1985 the St. Paul's claims rate jumped to 17.3 per 100 before dropping as low as 13.0 per 100 in 1988 (see St. Paul's *Physicians' and Surgeons' Update,* p. 1).

7. GAO, *1984 Claims Closed Survey,* p. 19, reported that 43.3 percent of all 1984 medical malpractice claims resulted in indemnity payments to the victim. Because many patients file claims against more than one provider but collect from only one, the aggregate success rate for patients is probably closer to 50 percent.

8. See Mark Peterson, *Civil Juries in the 1980s* (Santa Monica, Calif.: RAND Institute for Civil Justice, 1987), in particular pp. 20–25. It is noteworthy that the plaintiff victory rate in malpractice jury trials in San Francisco and Chicago was also doubling in that period, from about one-quarter to about one-half of the cases tried (p. 17). So the expected jury award, which is a function of both the estimated chance of victory and the size of award, was up twentyfold in San Francisco and fortyfold in Chicago in that quarter-century. And the current situation is not specific to these jurisdictions. Florida Academic Task Force, *Preliminary Fact-Finding Report,* pp. 147–150, revealed that plaintiffs won 54 percent of malpractice trials in the Miami area, with verdicts averaging nearly $900,000 from 1985 through 1987 as compared with an average $265,000 award in all tort cases in that region. The *New York Closed Claims Survey,* pp. 1–5, found that the average jury verdict in the state as a whole (not just the New York City area) rose from $58,000 in 1976–77 to $359,000 in 1983 (see Table F-2). Stephen Daniels and Lori Andrews, who reviewed a national sample of jury verdicts from 1981 to 1985 in obstetric and gynecological malpractice cases, found that the median (not the average) award was $390,000 per case (in 1985 dollars); see their "Shadow of the Law: Jury Decisions in Obstetrics and Gynecology," in Institute of Medicine, *Medical Professional Liability,* II, 161, 180.

9. See Michael G. Shanley and Mark A. Peterson, *Posttrial Adjustments to Jury Awards* (Santa Monica, Calif.: RAND Institute for Civil Justice, 1987), which found that 71 percent of total damages awarded by juries was eventually paid out following the post-verdict process.

10. The 1970 figure is from Danzon, *Medical Malpractice,* p. 151; the 1975 and 1978 numbers are from Sowka, "NAIC Executive Summary," p. 92; the 1984 figure is from the GAO's *1984 Claims Closed Survey,* p. 35; and the 1986 number is from Sloan and Bovbjerg, *Medical Malpractice,* p. 8.

11. The GAO reported that in 1984 the average settlement paid in New York was $105,000, and in Florida it was fully $140,000, versus $80,000 nationally for that year; *Six State Studies,* p. 18.

12. See Marshall Sella, "More Big Bucks in Jury Verdicts: Additions to the 1988 List," *American Bar Association Journal* 69 (July 1989), describing the $52 million verdict won by the noted litigator Joe Jamail in the 1988 case of Palacios v. Medical Arts Hospital of Houston (including a remarkable $26 million award for pain and suffering in the two years it took the

victim to die following a botched operation). See also Amy Dockser Marcus, "Juries Rule against 'Tort Reform' with Huge Awards," *Wall Street Journal*, p. B1, col. 3 (February 9, 1990), describing the case of a Vietnamese baby who entered a Los Angeles hospital for a routine hip X-ray, left the hospital with extensive brain damage, and was awarded $54 million in 1989 by a Los Angeles jury.

13. The most graphic illustration of this phenomenon is the situation in Florida, where the share of total malpractice expenditures contributed by million-dollar awards shot up from 4.5 percent in 1981 to 29.0 percent in 1986. See Nye et al., "Causes of the Medical Malpractice Crisis," p. 1552. Patricia M. Danzon, in her review essay, "Medical Malpractice Liability," in Robert E. Litan and Clifford Winston, eds., *Liability: Perspectives and Policy* 101–127 (Washington, D.C.: The Brookings Institution, 1988), summarizes (at 106–107) her earlier work documenting this trend on a national basis, particularly with respect to the pain and suffering component of the damage award.

14. See Office of National Cost Estimates, Health Care Financing Administration, "The National Health Expenditures, 1988," 11 *Health Care Financing Review*, no. 4, p. 1 (1990), which estimates expenditures on self-employed physicians' services to be $105 billion in 1988, and on hospitals (including their salaried physicians), $212 billion, out of a grand total of $540 billion in national health care expenditures of all types that year.

15. See Gonzales and Emmons, eds., *Socioeconomic Characteristics of Medical Practice, 1989*, pp. 6–7.

16. By mid-1987, the malpractice premium for a neurosurgeon in Dade or Broward County, Florida, was $192,000; for an obstetrician it was $165,000 (Nye et al., "Causes of the Medical Malpractice Crisis," p. 1502). The premiums paid in the New York City and Long Island areas of New York State have been close to those in the Miami area (see *Harvard Study*, pp. 1–2). Note that the excess coverage (from $1 million to $2 million on a claim) for New York doctors is actually paid for by the hospitals with which they are affiliated. Florida obstetricians across the entire state (not just in Dade/Broward) spent 23 percent of their gross practice revenues on malpractice insurance (Nye et al., p. 1506), roughly the same amount spent by all New York State obstetricians. Obstetricians in New York City pay 28 percent of their revenue for insurance: see Zachary Y. Dyckman, Jackson Knowlton, and Judy Anderson, *Report to the Medical Society of the State of New York: An Analysis of Medical Malpractice Insurance Expenses and Physician Income in New York and Selected States* 14 (Albany, N.Y.: 1985). Of course, the figures for neurosurgeons and obstetricians in the New York City and Miami areas depict the malpractice insurance situation in its most extreme form. Doctors in the rest of Florida pay premiums roughly half the size of those in the Miami area, and doctors in the low-risk specialties (such as family practice with no surgery) pay a premium that is about one-tenth that of neurosurgeons and one-eighth that of obstetricians (Nye et al., p. 1502). So there can be a spread of nearly 20 to 1 in the insurance premiums charged to doctors

practicing in the same state. And for a doctor working in a state with a much lower liability risk, such as Indiana, the entire premium range will be another order of magnitude lower than that of Florida or New York. In Indiana, for example, the range was roughly $1,000 to $11,000 in 1985; see GAO, *Insurance Costs* pp. 31–34.

17. An initial study by Bruce C. N. Greenwald and Marnie W. Mueller, "Medical Malpractice and Medical Costs," in Rottenberg, ed., *The Economics of Medical Malpractice*, pp. 65–86, found that physician fees actually increased more than the extra premiums. However, later research by Frank A. Sloan, "Physician Demand for Malpractice Insurance," in *Analysis of Survey Data on Physicians' Practice Costs and Incomes* 144 (Nashville, Tenn.: Vanderbilt Institute of Policy Studies, 1981), using a different methodology, found that by that time doctors' revenues had recovered only three-quarters the premium hikes of the mid-seventies, leaving the physician to absorb the remainder out of net earnings. Although similar econometric analysis of the physician fee reaction to the malpractice increases of the mid-eighties remains to be done, the trends in average premium increases and physician revenues depicted in Institute of Medicine, *Medical Professional Liability*, I, 106–112, suggest that doctors generally have been able to pass through the bulk of their added malpractice costs in this decade.

18. To return to the Florida data, the latest and most detailed available, a Miami obstetrician had to pay $30,000 in medical malpractice premiums in 1983, and $165,000 in 1987 (Nye et al., "Causes of the Medical Malpractice Crisis," p. 1502). In other words, the cost of malpractice insurance rose from 5.5 percent to 23.1 percent of gross revenues for all Florida obstetricians in just five years (Nye et al., p. 1506). Consequently, in spite of any long-term equilibrium adjustments that may have been made by the national health care system to the rising malpractice insurance bill, huge and abrupt changes in practice costs to doctors in these areas of high liability risk produced an immediate sharp drop in the net disposable income of the individual doctor and family. In effect, these physicians were deprived of much of the benefit of the insurance protection that they thought they were buying and that most judges and tort scholars assume has been absorbing and distributing the financial consequences of rising malpractice liability.

19. See F. Patrick Hubbard, "The Physicians' Point of View Concerning Medical Malpractice: A Sociological Perspective on the Symbolic Importance of 'Tort Reform,'" 23 *Georgia Law Review* 295, 331–332 (1989).

20. See Institute of Medicine, *Medical Professional Liability*, I, 104–109.

21. See Daniel N. Price, "Workers' Compensation: 1976–80 Benchmark Revisions," 47 *Social Security Bulletin* 3, 16 (July 1984); and William J. Nelson, Jr., "Workers' Compensation: Coverage, Benefits, and Costs, 1986," 52 *Social Security Bulletin* 34, 41 (March 1989).

22. The GAO's *1984 Claims Closed Survey*, pp. 52–53, found that 70.6 percent of claims were against individual physicians, 1.8 percent against nurses, 1.6 percent against dentists, and 0.8 percent against other occupational

categories, such as technicians, compared to 21.2 percent against hospitals and 4.0 percent against other institutional facilities, such as HMO's or nursing homes.

23. The videotaping story I related at the beginning of this chapter indicates the depth of feeling among doctors about their current malpractice plight and the possibility of a "brave new world" in the doctor-patient relationship. The most extensive research on the psychological effects of malpractice litigation on defendants has been published by Dr. Sara Charles and her associates: see Sara C. Charles, Jeffrey R. Wilbert, and Eugene C. Kennedy, "Physicians' Self-Reports of Reactions to Malpractice Litigation," 141 *American Journal of Psychiatry* 563 (1984); Sara C. Charles, Jeffrey R. Wilbert, and Kevin J. Franke, "Sued and Nonsued Physicians' Self-Reported Reactions to Malpractice Litigation," 142 *American Journal of Psychiatry* 437 (1985); and Sara C. Charles, Charlene E. Pyskoty, and Amy Nelson, "Physicians on Trial—Self-Reported Reactions to Malpractice Trials," 148 *Western Journal of Medicine* 358 (1988). Dr. Charles herself was the defendant in a tort suit, which she won. The proceedings are dramatically narrated in Sara C. Charles and Eugene Kennedy, *Defendant: A Psychiatrist on Trial for Medical Malpractice* (New York: Random House, 1986). An interesting comparative study is J. Douglas Peters, Steven K. Nord, and R. Donald Woodson, "An Empirical Analysis of the Medical and Legal Professions' Experiences and Perceptions of Medical and Legal Malpractice," 19 *University of Michigan Journal of Law Reform* 601 (1986).

24. This theme is developed in detail in Hubbard, "The Physicians' Point of View."

25. As quoted in ibid., pp. 344–345.

26. The assumption of the last several paragraphs is that medical malpractice law is an offshoot of a relationship between *individual* doctor and patient. This assumption is largely valid now as well as historically (see the GAO figures reported above in note 22). Even in most suits brought against hospitals and other facilities, the claims concern incidents in which an individual physician was alleged to be negligent. A lawsuit brought against an individual because of his personal behavior has an entirely different edge from a suit brought against a large organization that is handled by one of its officials. Motor vehicle accident cases also typically involve suits against individual drivers. Again, however, very different emotions are aroused by a proceeding in which only an individual's driving is impugned, in contrast to a case in which an individual's professional competence and self-identity are challenged. Liability insurance may remove the edge from the former, but it will not from the latter.

With some relatively recent exceptions, such as the doctrine of the "corporate" responsibility of the hospital to which I advert later, malpractice law is tailored to the peculiarly personal cast of the medical relationship. This will be a major theme of my analysis in this book. At the same time, important trends are transforming the health care system into a more organizational form. Increasing numbers of doctors work as employees for hospital corporations or health maintenance organizations, and patients act as consumers choosing one institutional provider over another. See Paul Starr, *The Social Transformation of American Medicine* (New York: Basic Books, 1982); and Clark C. Havighurst, "The Changing Locus of Decision Making in the Health Care Sector," 11 *Journal of Health Politics, Policy, and Law* 697 (1986). These changes in modern health care have important implications for the future of malpractice law and medical accident policy, an issue that I shall consider in Chapter 6. However, there is a considerable distance left to travel before the new model of doctor-patient relationship replaces the old one, either in fact or in the law.

27. See the estimates in Roger A. Reynolds, John A. Rizzo, and Martin L. Gonzalez, "The Cost of Medical Professional Liability," 257 *Journal of the American Medical Association* 2776 (1987).

28. The comment by Spence is quoted in Nye et al., "Causes of the Medical Malpractice Crisis," p. 1498. Among the more prominent expositions of this emphasis on the insurer's responsibility for the tort crisis are Sylvia Law and Steven Polan, *Pain and Profit: The Politics of Malpractice* (New York: Harper and Row, 1978), especially Chapter 9, "Malpractice Insurance: The Blood-Money Industry," 161 (a title that perhaps says it all); Ralph Nader, "The Assault on Injured Victims' Rights," 64 *Denver University Law Review* 625 (1988); Jay Angoff, "Insurance against Competition: How the McCarran-Ferguson Act Raises Prices and Profits in the Property-Casualty Insurance Industry," 5 *Yale Journal on Regulation* 397 (1988); and Ian Ayres and Peter Siegelman, "The Economics of the Insurance Antitrust Suits: Toward an Exclusionary Theory," 63 *Tulane Law Review* 971 (1989). The last three articles focus on the situation in personal injury liability insurance generally in the eighties, including medical malpractice insurance.

29. The reports of the New York Governor's Advisory Commission on Liability Insurance, *Insuring Our Future* (New York: 1986), and of the American Bar Association, *Commission to Improve the Liability Insurance System* (Chicago: ABA, 1989), contain a concise but sophisticated presentation of the nature of liability insurance and the reasons why changes in insurance premiums tend to be cyclical in character.

30. In fact, in 1988 a group of state attorneys general filed an antitrust suit against the major casualty insurers and the industry trade organization, the Insurance Services Office. This lawsuit sparked a scholarly debate between Ayres and Siegelman, "Economics of Insurance Suits," and George L. Priest, "The Antitrust Suits and the Public Understanding of Insurance," 63 *Tulane Law Review* 999 (1989), before the judge dismissed the action on the basis of the McCarran-Ferguson exemption. See *In re Insurance Antitrust Litigation*, 723 F. Supp. 464 (N.D. Cal. 1989).

31. See, for example, Scott E. Harrington, "Prices and Profits in the Liability Insurance Market," in Litan and Winston, eds., *Liability*, p. 42.

32. Detailed evidence to this effect is presented in Roger D. Blair and Scott D. Makar, "The Structure of Florida's Medical Malpractice Insurance

Market: If It Ain't Broke, Don't Fix It," 5 *Yale Journal on Regulation* 427 (1988).

33. The numbers in the text are taken from Sloan and Bovbjerg, *Medical Malpractice*, p. 3. A detailed picture of the malpractice insurance industry is presented in James R. Posner, "Trends In Medical Malpractice Insurance, 1970–1985," 49 *Law and Contemporary Problems* 37 (Spring 1986).

34. For the evidence about Florida, see Nye et al., "Causes of the Medical Malpractice Crisis"; for New York, see New York State Insurance Department, *Prescription for Change*, pp. 68–74. Further corroboration from New York is found in Governor's Advisory Commission, *Insuring Our Future*, p. 37; it details the spiraling claims experience of New York City, which is entirely self-insured, including for malpractice claims from the city's hospitals.

35. See the data presented in Harrington, "Prices and Profits," and in Richard N. Clarke, Frederick Warren-Boulton, David D. Smith, and Marilyn J. Simon, "Sources of the Crisis in Liability Insurance: An Economic Analysis," 5 *Yale Journal on Regulation* 367 (1988).

36. See California Medical Association, *Medical Insurance Feasibility Study* (San Francisco: Sutter Publications, 1977).

37. See Danzon, *Medical Malpractice*, pp. 22–25.

38. See *Harvard Study*. Chapter 5 of the study documents the elaborate steps we took to locate and analyze the hospital records and to corroborate the reliability and validity of our judgments based on those records.

39. See William Ira Bennett, "Pluses of Malpractice Suits," *New York Times Magazine* 31 (July 24, 1988) (emphasis added).

40. Danzon, *Medical Malpractice*, p. 74, found that urbanization was the most significant nonlegal variable associated with the frequency of malpractice claims.

41. On malpractice trends in Canada, see Don Dewees, Peter Coyte, and Michael Trebilcock, *Canadian Medical Malpractice Liability: An Empirical Analysis of Recent Trends* (Toronto: University of Toronto, 1989), especially Chapter 2, "The Problem: Malpractice Litigation Trends." For the United Kingdom, see Chris Ham, Robert Dingwall, Paul Fenn, and Don Harris, *Medical Negligence: Compensation and Accountability* 7–12 (Oxford: Centre for Socio-Legal Studies, 1988); and Frances H. Miller, "Medical Malpractice Litigation: Do the British Have a Better Remedy?" 11 *American Journal of Law and Medicine* 433 (1986).

42. Consider this simple comparison. Approximately 6,000 Americans die every year as a result of injuries suffered on the job. See Office of Technology Assessment, *Preventing Illness and Injury in the Workplace* 30–31 (Washington, D.C.: U.S. Government Printing Office, 1985). However, extrapolating the findings of the New York study (a statewide population estimate of nearly 13,500 fatalities) to the nation as a whole indicates that more than 150,000 Americans die every year as a result of accidents in hospitals. I should emphasize that a sizable proportion of that number are elderly patients who are already in poor health and whose demise is simply accelerated by whatever went wrong in their treatment. Perhaps a better index of the hazardous quality of modern health care is

the more than 30,000 severe disabilities inflicted annually on patients healthy enough to continue living with the permanent iatrogenic injuries they suffered. This injury toll is considerably greater than the analogous statistics for the nation's highways or workplaces.

43. See Frederick W. Cheney, Karen Posner, Robert A. Caplan, and Richard J. Ward, "Standard of Care and Anesthesia Liability," 261 *Journal of the American Medical Association* 1599 (1989). Essentially the same conclusion was drawn in an unpublished study by Henry S. Farber and Michelle J. White, "Medical Malpractice: An Empirical Examination of the Litigation Process" (1990). When these researchers compared the defendant hospital's own appraisal of the quality of care to the ultimate disposition of the claim, it turned out that when the hospital rated its care as good, two-thirds of the claims were dropped without payment; if the care rating was bad, 90 percent of claims were paid; and if the quality of care was ambiguous, paid settlements occurred in two-thirds of the cases. However, the average amount of settlement in the "bad" category was nearly 5 times higher than for the "good," and the "ambiguous" case settlements were 2.5 times as high as the "good."

44. This is the favored diagnosis of Kenneth S. Abraham, "Making Sense of the Liability Insurance Crisis," 48 *Ohio State Law Journal* 399 (1987).

Another important analysis of the mid-eighties tort crisis is George L. Priest, "The Current Insurance Crisis and Modern Tort Law," 96 *Yale Law Journal* 1521 (1987), as updated in "The Antitrust Suits and the Public Understanding of Insurance." Briefly stated, Priest's argument is that the recent escalation in the price of liability insurance is the result of a serious unraveling of the overall insurance pool: better risks have steadily turned to self-insurance arrangements of a variety of types, leaving the relatively poor risks to bear the higher costs of the now smaller pool, thereby propelling the adverse selection process even further. Priest goes on to argue that such opting out of the insurance pool is largely attributable to the inappropriate kinds of loss insurance that modern tort judges force enterprises to provide to their customers under the guise of tort liability. Priest traces the intellectual theory that has influenced modern judges in "The Invention of Enterprise Liability: A Critical History of the Intellectual Foundations of Modern Tort Law," 14 *Journal of Legal Studies* 461 (1985).

Priest provides persuasive documentation for his empirical account of the severe contraction of the insurance pool in the products field, although he has not yet supplied a firm analytic bridge between the supposed unsuitability of judge-made accident insurance for consumers and the evident unwillingness of enterprises to purchase liability insurance coverage against their own legal risks from tort litigation. But in any event, the Priest hypothesis does *not* square with the empirical facts of medical malpractice. It is true that in the seventies there was an unraveling of the commercial market for malpractice insurance, as large numbers of doctors shifted to newly created mutual carriers (see Posner, "Medical Malpractice Insurance"). That shift was completed by the early eighties, yet as we saw earlier in this chapter, in the brief span of two to three years the physicians' own carriers more than doubled the premiums they charged their principals. I believe that the explanation for what happened in medical malpractice is that insurers finally reacted (and to some extent overreacted) to the steadily increasing claims frequency, to the even faster-rising average payments in each successful claim, and to the very steep rise in the much less predictable large damage awards.

45. Consider, for example, the contrast in the following figures. The *Harvard Study* found that there was a 1 percent risk of a tort, that is, a negligently caused disabling injury to a patient, arising out of hospital treatment. Extrapolating from that base leads to the conclusion that of the approximately 40 million hospitalizations across the country each year, nearly 400,000 torts take place in American hospitals (see "1989 Statistical Abstract," Table 153). But only about 25,000 annual paid tort claims arise out of hospital stays (a figure calculated from the data in the GAO *1984 Closed Claims Survey,* pp. 20, 24–25). The gap between these two numbers gives a striking indication of a massive potential malpractice crisis that has not yet been witnessed.

2. The Tort/Fault Model

1. The potential use of private contractual initiatives in the medical area was the theme of a recent symposium in which many of the major scholars in this field canvassed the legal, economic, and health care dimensions of the medical malpractice problem. See Randall R. Bovbjerg and Clark C. Havighurst, eds., "Medical Malpractice: Can the Private Sector Find Relief?" 49 *Law and Contemporary Problems* 1 (1986).
2. If another actor, such as the victim or a third party, is also culpable, additional rules are fashioned to apportion the responsibility for the injury in some proportion to the multiple fault.
3. The major decision to this effect was Tunkl v. Regents of the University of California, 383 P.2d 441 (Cal. 1963). The same principle has been applied even in settings in which the waiver is asserted against a patient who is taking advantage of lower-cost services in a university clinic established for medical training purposes: see Emory University v. Porubiansky, 282 S.E.2d 903 (Ga. 1981).
4. I explore the no-fault model in detail in Paul C. Weiler, "Legal Policy for Workplace Injuries" (American Law Institute Working Paper, 1986). In Chapter 6 I will consider the value and limits of no-fault specifically for medical injuries.
5. For the classic explication of the concept of "negligence without fault," see Albert A. Ehrenzweig, "Negligence without Fault," 54 *California Law Review* 1422 (1966); and for a brief indication of how far FELA law has moved from its original commitment to a meaningful conception of "fault," see Guido Calabresi, *A Common Law for the Age of Statutes* 30–35, 203–210 (Cambridge, Mass.: Harvard University Press, 1982).
6. See generally Allan H. McCoid, "The Care Required of Medical Practitioners," 12 *Vanderbilt Law Review* 549 (1959); Joseph H. King, Jr., "In

Search of a Standard of Care for the Medical Profession: The 'Accepted Practice' Formula," 28 *Vanderbilt Law Review* 1213 (1975); Richard N. Pearson, "The Role of Custom in Medical Malpractice Cases," 51 *Indiana Law Journal* 528 (1976); and Page Keeton, "Medical Negligence—The Standard of Care," 10 *Texas Tech Law Review* 351 (1979). Robert C. Clark, "Why Does Health Care Regulation Fail?" 41 *Maryland Law Review* 1, 5–8 (1981), provides a perceptive account of how this particular rule of malpractice law accords with the general deference of lawyers and regulators to the presumed expertise and judgment of the medical profession.

7. If determining whether malpractice occurred is a matter not of medical judgment but of pure common sense—recognizing, for example, that sponges should not be left in a patient after an operation—specific evidence of deviation from a medical custom is not required: see, e.g., Toppino v. Herhahn, 673 P.2d 1297 (N.M. 1983).

8. The authority most frequently cited for this proposition is Judge Learned Hand's decision in The T.J. Hooper, 60 F.2d 737 (2d Cir. 1932).

9. 519 P.2d 981 (Wash. 1974).

10. See the review of the medical evidence in David M. Eddy, Lauri E. Sanders, and Judy F. Eddy, "The Value of Screening for Glaucoma with Tonometry," 28 *Survey of Ophthalmology* 194 (1983).

11. This was discovered through an extensive survey of ophthalmologists regarding their procedures both before and after *Helling*. See Jerry Wiley, "The Impact of Judicial Decisions on Professional Conduct: An Empirical Study," 55 *Southern California Law Review* 345 (1981).

12. Indeed, if the case were actually won by the plaintiff, the judgment would likely be paid by the common insurer of the two doctors, and the witness's own insurance premiums would increase at the same rate as those paid by the defendant doctor.

13. See, e.g., the formulation of the standard in such important decisions as Brune v. Belinkoff, 235 N.E.2d 793, 798 (Mass. 1968); and Blair v. Eblen, 461 S.W.2d 370, 373 (Ky. 1970). See also the more general discussion in Jon R. Waltz, "The Rise and Gradual Fall of the Locality Rule in Medical Malpractice Litigation," 18 *DePaul Law Review* 408 (1969).

14. This principle surfaces in present-day decisions in which the court refuses to allow mainstream doctors to define for the jury the standard of care to be required of such disciplines as chiropractic (see Kerkman v. Hintz, 418 N.W.2d 795 [Wis. 1988]), osteopathy (see Cardwell v. Bechtol, 724 S.W.2d 739 [Tenn. 1987]), and podiatry (see Dolan v. Galluzzo, 396 N.E.2d 13 [Ill. 1979]).

15. This situation inspired the controversial case of Ybarra v. Spangard, 154 P.2d 687 (Cal. 1944); see Warren A. Seavey, "Res Ipsa Loquitur: Tabula in Naufragio," 63 *Harvard Law Review* 643 (1950).

16. See Quintal v. Laurel Grove Hospital, 397 P.2d 161 (Cal. 1964); and Clark v. Gibbons, 426 P.2d 525 (Cal. 1967).

17. Or so it was asserted by Justice Utter of the Washington Supreme Court, concurring in Helling v. Carey, and by Justice Tobriner of the California Supreme Court, concurring in Clark v. Gibbons. These judges argued

that the better, simpler way for the law to pursue this desirable distributional role would be through a tort regime for medical accidents that was based frankly on strict liability of the defendant doctor.

18. The key early decision was Natanson v. Kline, 350 P.2d 1093 (Kan. 1960).

19. See Truman v. Thomas, 611 P.2d 902 (Cal. 1980).

20. See Alan Meisel, "The Expansion of Liability for Medical Accidents: From Negligence to Strict Liability by Way of Informed Consent," 56 *Nebraska Law Review* 51 (1977).

21. In particular in Canterbury v. Spence, 464 F.2d 772 (D.C. Cir. 1972); and Cobbs v. Grant, 502 P.2d 1 (Cal. 1972).

22. For valuable scholarly discussions of these policies, see Marjorie Maguire Shultz, "From Informed Consent to Patient Choice: A New Protected Interest," 95 *Yale Law Journal* 219 (1985); and Aaron D. Twerski and Neil B. Cohen, "Informed Decision Making and the Law of Torts: The Myth of Justiciable Causation," 1988 *University of Illinois Law Review* 607. Both articles make clear, however, that the effort to secure *ex ante* doctor disclosure (and as a consequence, true patient consent) through *ex post* liability for accidental physical injuries has not been a particularly fruitful tort law undertaking.

23. Expanded hospital liability has been pursued along two parallel doctrinal tracks. One employs a concept of "ostensible authority" to hold a hospital vicariously liable for the negligence of nonemployee physicians who staff the emergency room or other hospital facilities; see the review of the cases in Jackson v. Power, 743 P.2d 1376 (Alaska 1987). The other imposes direct "corporate" liability on the hospital for failing to screen and monitor the performance of accident-prone physicians treating their own patients in the hospital's facilities. See Insinga v. LaBella, 543 So.2d 209 (Fla. 1989), by which Florida became the eighteenth state to adopt this doctrine since the path-breaking decision in Darling v. Charleston Community Memorial Hospital, 211 N.E.2d 253 (Ill. 1965). Two useful reviews of these trends are Arthur F. Southwick, "Hospital Liability: Two Theories Have Been Merged," 4 *Journal of Legal Medicine* 1 (1983); and Diane M. Janulis and Alan D. Hornstein, "Damned If You Do, Damned If You Don't: Hospital Liability for Physicians' Malpractice," 64 *Nebraska Law Review* 689 (1985). The broader implications of this trend toward expanded hospital responsibility will be taken up in Chapter 6, in which I propose the adoption of a full-blown principle of *organizational* rather than *personal* liability for accidental patient injuries produced by doctor carelessness.

24. For a historical account of the development of this mind-set among tort theorists, see George L. Priest, "The Invention of Enterprise Liability: A Critical History of the Intellectual Foundations of Modern Tort Law," 14 *Journal of Legal Studies* 461 (1985).

25. See Chapter 1, note 7. Stephen Daniels and Lori Andrews, "The Shadow of the Law: Jury Decisions in Obstetrics and Gynecology Cases," in Institute of Medicine, *Medical Professional Liability and the Delivery of Obstetrical Care*, 2 vols., ed. Victoria P. Rostow and Roger J. Bulger, II, 161–193

(Washington, D.C.: National Academy Press, 1989), report (at p. 173) that in their national sample of jury verdicts from 1981 through 1985, plaintiffs won only 32 percent of medical malpractice cases, versus their 57 percent success rate in other civil litigation before juries.

26. In asserting that juries are basically *neutral* in appraising the contentions of patient and doctor about whether there was carelessness in the course of treatment, I do not mean to imply that jury verdicts always or even typically provide an *accurate* depiction of what happened. Indeed, there are grounds for skepticism about the ability of a present-day jury to assess the conflicting expert testimony in complex medical cases, although some of the most notorious examples pertain to the issue of causation rather than culpability. My point, rather, is that whatever may be the incidence of inaccurate jury verdicts, the mistakes are distributed randomly against both sides; they are not systematically tilted toward a finding that the doctor was at fault, resulting in tort recovery by the patient. In other words, assigning malpractice cases to an alternative tribunal with an expert scientific capacity of its own would probably not significantly reduce the odds (now around 30 percent in cases that go to trial) that the ordinary doctor would be judged to have been careless in the treatment that produced an injury to a patient.

27. See Mark C. Kendall, "Expectations, Imperfect Markets, and Medical Malpractice Insurance," in Simon Rottenberg, ed., *The Economics of Medical Malpractice* 167, 176 (Washington, D.C.: American Enterprise Institute for Public Policy Research, 1978).

28. See *HEW Report*.

29. For detailed accounts of the crisis of the seventies written from quite different points of view, see Sylvia Law and Steven Polan, *Pain and Profit: The Politics of Malpractice* (New York: Harper and Row, 1978); and Glen O. Robinson, "The Medical Malpractice Crisis of the 1970's: A Retrospective," 49 *Law and Contemporary Problems* 5, 6 (1986).

30. Several overviews of the trends in state malpractice legislation have been compiled. The best scholarly treatments are Robinson, "The Malpractice Crisis," and Randall R. Bovbjerg, "Legislation on Medical Malpractice: Further Developments and a Preliminary Report Card," 22 *U.C. Davis Law Review* 499 (1989).

Although I will not describe in detail the dozens of common law doctrines that state legislatures addressed in the seventies and eighties, or the various statutes designed to replace those doctrines, in this chapter I will sketch the important types of reform, the rationales offered for them, and the way that these changes fit into the strategy that states adopted for dealing with medical malpractice. Chapter 2 goes on to analyze the arguments in favor of and against legal reform in the context of the tort-fault model.

31. See *HHS Report*; see also David E. Sonenshein, "A Discovery Rule in Medical Malpractice: Massachusetts Joins the Fold," 3 *Western New England Law Review* 433 (1981).

32. These states include Delaware, Indiana, New Mexico, and South Dakota. See Robinson, "The Malpractice Crisis," p. 21, and Bovbjerg, "Legislation on Medical Malpractice," p. 524.

33. See *HHS Report,* p. 125; the latest such ruling is Hoffman v. Powell, 380 S.E.2d 821 (S.C. 1989). Frances E. McGovern, "The Variety, Policy, and Constitutionality of Product Liability Statutes of Repose," 30 *American University Law Review* 579 (1981), includes an extensive treatment of the experience with statutes of repose in the medical malpractice and architect-contractor contexts before such statutes entered the product liability debates. As indicated by the recent Utah decision in Sun Valley Water Beds v. Hughes & Son, 782 P.2d 188 (Utah 1989), statutes of repose will be struck down in the builder context if they are written so that the time may run out before the building has even collapsed.

34. See Sax v. Votteler, 648 S.W.2d 661 (Tex. 1983).

35. See Robinson, "The Malpractice Crisis," p. 22.

36. Typically the lawyer receives one-third of the award, although this percentage may vary depending on the lawyer's ability and the timing of the settlement. See Patricia M. Danzon, *Medical Malpractice: Theory, Evidence, and Public Policy* 190 (Cambridge, Mass.: Harvard University Press, 1985).

37. See, e.g., Ariz. Rev. Stat. Ann. §12-568 (West 1982); Haw. Rev. Stat. §671-2 (Supp. 1984).

38. See, e.g., Ind. Stat. Ann. §16-9.5-5-1 (Burns 1990) (15 percent of award); Or. Rev. Stat §752.150 (1983) (one-third of award); Tenn. Code Ann. §29-26-120 (1980) (one-third of award).

39. See, e.g., Del. Code Ann. Tit. 18, §6865 (1989); Cal. Bus. & Prof. Code §6146 (West 1990).

40. Fla. Stat. Ann. §768.56 (West 1986) (repealed). In Florida Patient's Compensation Fund v. Rowe, 472 So.2d 1145 (Fla. 1985), the Florida Supreme Court upheld the constitutionality of the law, which had just been repealed, and adopted the "lodestar" approach as the method of calculating attorney fees.

41. See F. Townsend Hawkes, "The Second Reformation: Florida's Medical Malpractice Law," 13 *Florida State University Law Review* 747, 771 (1985); Fla. Stat. Ann. §766.109(7) (West Supp. 1990).

42. See, e.g., Alaska Stat §09.55.536 (1985). But cf. Mattos v. Thompson, 421 A.2d 190 (Pa. 1980) (holding unconstitutional a statute providing for admissibility of the panel's verdict).

43. For results of empirical investigation, see Patricia Munch Danzon and Lee A. Lillard, "Settlement out of Court: The Disposition of Medical Malpractice Claims," 12 *Journal of Legal Studies* 345, 373–374 (1983); and Stephen Shmanske and Tina Stevens, "The Performance of Medical Malpractice Review Panels," 11 *Journal of Health Politics, Policy, and Law* 525 (1986). See the discussion of the constitutional issues later in this chapter. Jean A. Macchiaroli, "Medical Malpractice Screening Panels: Proposed Model Legislation to Cure Judicial Ills," 58 *George Washington Law*

Review 181 (1990), presents an extended defense of her model version of the screening panel idea; however, she does not explicitly address the results of empirical research done by scholars such as Schmanske and Stevens, who found that such panels substantially increase the cost and delay of disposing of malpractice claims without materially affecting claims frequency or severity.

44. See Robinson, "The Malpractice Crisis," p. 23; and Bovbjerg, "Legislation on Medical Malpractice," pp. 528–529.

45. See, e.g., Ark. Code Ann. §116-114–205 (1987); Fla. Stat. Ann. §766.102 (West. Supp. 1990); Wash. Rev. Code Ann. §7.70.030-.060 (West Supp. 1990).

46. See, e.g., Ala. Code §6-5-484 (1977).

47. See, e.g., Ariz. Rev. Stat. Ann. §12-563 (West 1982); Va. Code §8.01-581.20 (Supp. 1990).

48. See, e.g., Del. Code Ann. Tit. 18 §6854 (Supp. 1989).

49. See, e.g., May v. Moore, 424 So.2d 596, 602 (Ala. 1982) (holding that the term "same general neighborhood" refers to "national medical community"); Butler v. Alatur, 419 A.2d 938, 939–940 (Del. 1980) (permitting out-of-state practitioner to testify about local standards); Mitchell v. Angulo, 416 So.2d 910, 912–913 (Fla. Dist. App. 1982) (holding that "same or similar community" refers to national medical community).

50. See Jones v. State Board of Medicine, 555 P.2d 399 (Idaho 1976).

51. See, e.g., Ala. Code §6-5-548(a) (Supp. 1990); Mich. Comp Laws Ann. §600.2912(a) (West 1986).

52. See Sullivan v. Russell, 338 N.W.2d 181 (Mich. 1983) (finding that Michigan's assignment of the burden of proof to the malpractice plaintiff does not displace *res ipsa loquitur*).

53. Typical of the type of cases in which circumstantial evidence may be used to show negligence are those involving missed sponges, fire or explosion, or harm to healthy parts of the body. See, e.g., Del Code Ann. Tit. 18 §6853 (1989); Fla. Stat. Ann §766.102(4) (West Supp. 1990); Nev. Rev. Stat. §41A.100(1) (1989).

54. See Carson v. Maurer, 424 A.2d 825 (N.H. 1980); Jones v. State Board of Medicine, 555 P.2d 399.

55. Alan Meisel and Lisa D. Kabnick, "Informed Consent to Medical Treatment: An Analysis of Recent Legislation," 41 *University of Pittsburgh Law Review* 407 (1980), contains a careful tabulation and analysis of the informed consent legislation enacted by twenty-four states in the three years from 1974 to 1977.

56. See, e.g., Del. Code Ann. Tit. 18 §6852 (1989); Fla. Stat. Ann. §766.103 (West Supp. 1990); Idaho Code Ann. §39-4304–4305 (1985); Me. Rev. Stat. Ann. Tit. 24 §2905 (1990); Tenn. Code Ann. §29-26-118 (1980).

57. See, e.g., Pa. Cons. Stat. Ann. Tit. 40 §1301.103 (Purdon Supp. 1990); Wash. Rev. Code Ann. §7.70.050 (West Supp. 1990). See also LaCaze v. Collier, 434 So.2d 1039 (La. 1983) (incorporating patient need standard into Louisiana statute).

58. See, e.g., Iowa Code Ann. §147.137 (West 1989); La. Rev. Stat. Ann.

§40:1299.40 (West Supp. 1990); Ohio Rev. Code Ann §2317.54 (Page Supp. 1989). The effect of these statutes for liability purposes is unclear. See Robinson, "The Malpractice Crisis," p. 24.

59. 464 F.2d 772, 779–799 (D.C. Cir. 1972); see also Harnish v. Children's Hospital Medical Center, 439 N.E.2d 240 (Mass. 1982), an important restatement and endorsement of the patient perspective on the legal standard for disclosure.

60. See *HHS Report,* p. 109. State court cases reflecting this standard include the critical early decision in Natanson v. Kline, 350 P.2d 1093, and, post-*Canterbury,* Bly v. Rhoads, 222 S.E.2d 783 (Va. 1976); Henning v. Parsons, 623 P.2d 574 (N.M. App. 1980); and Woolley v. Henderson, 418 A.2d 1123 (Me. 1980).

61. See American Bank & Trust Co. v. Community Hospital, 683 P.2d 670 (Cal. 1984) (characterizing such payments as "windfalls").

62. Unfortunately, only a couple of states (including Arizona) give injured patients this reciprocal relief against errors in projected life expectancy. See Roger C. Henderson, "Designing a Responsible Periodic Payment System for Tort Awards: Arizona Enacts a Prototype," 32 *Arizona Law Review* 21, 46 (1990), for the best scholarly treatment of the subject of periodic payment.

63. See, e.g., Ala. Code §6-5-486 (1977); Del. Code Ann. Tit. 18 §6864 (1989). But cf. N.D. Cent. Code §26-40.1-16, repealed by S.L. 1983, ch. 332 §26 (repealing a periodic payments provision).

64. The classic work on this subject is John G. Fleming, "The Collateral Source Rule and Loss Allocation in Tort Law," 54 *California Law Review* 1478 (1966).

65. See, e.g., Cal. Civ. Code §3333.1 (West Supp. 1990); Wash. Rev. Code Ann. §7.70.080 (West 1990).

66. See, e.g., La. Rev. Stat. Ann. §40:1299.42 (West Supp. 1990); N.D. Cent. Code §26.1-14-11 (1989); R.I. Gen. Laws §9-19-34 (1984). This modification of the collateral source rule generally does not apply if the plaintiff had personally paid for the insurance or if the outside carrier had retained subrogation rights for tort claims. See, e.g., Ohio Rev. Code Ann. §2305.27 (Baldwin 1984).

67. Most of these states abolished or modified the collateral source rule for all tort claims.

68. The significance of the large award, particularly the pain and suffering component of the awards, is demonstrated by the calculations of Patricia M. Danzon in *Florida Policy Guidebook,* pp. 132–148.

69. See, e.g., La. Rev. Stat. Ann. §40:1299.42.B (West Supp. 1990); N.M. Stat. Ann. §41-5-6 (1989).

70. See, e.g., Cal. Civ. Code §3333.2 (West Supp. 1990); S.D. Codif. Laws Ann. §21-3-11 (1987).

71. See, e.g., Ind. Code Ann. §16-9.5-2-2.1 (1990); N.M. Stat. Ann. §41-5-6 (1989); Tex. Health & Safety Code. Ann. Art. 4590i §11.02 (Vernon 1985); Neb. Rev. Stat. §44-2825 (1988); Va. Code Ann. §8.01-581.15 (1984).

72. See, e.g., Ind. Code Ann. §16-9.5-2-2.1 (1990).

73. See Patricia M. Danzon, "The Frequency and Severity of Medical Malpractice Claims: New Evidence," 49 *Law and Contemporary Problems* 57, 58, 76 (1986).

74. These damage ceilings ranged in amount from $250,000 in Colorado (see Colo. Rev. Stat. §13-21-102.5 [West Supp. 1989]) to $1 million in Wisconsin (see Wis. Stat. Ann. §893.55 [West Supp. 1989]). Minnesota applied its new ceiling to all noneconomic losses *except* those classified as pain and suffering; see Minn. Stat. Ann. §549.23(2) (West 1988) ($400,000 limit on "intangible" losses such as emotional distress, embarrassment, and loss of consortium; this category does not include pain, disability, and disfigurement). Hawaii capped only damages awarded for pain and suffering, not for other noneconomic categories; see Haw. Rev. Stat. §663-8.7 (limiting pain and suffering damages to $375,000) (repealed by 1986 Haw. Sp. Sess. Laws, Act 2 §31). Some states allow their ceilings to be exceeded in cases of especially serious disablement and disfigurement; examples are the $500,000 ceilings in Alaska (see Alaska Stat. §09.17.010 [Supp. 1989]) and Massachusetts (see Mass. Gen. Laws Ann. Ch. 231 §60H [West Supp. 1990]). See generally Bovbjerg, "Legislation on Medical Malpractice," pp. 525–526, 543–544.

75. See, e.g., Kan. Stat. Ann. §60-3407 (West Supp. 1986); Tex. Rev. Stat. Ann. art. 4590i §11.04 (Vernon 1987); Wash. Rev. Code Ann. §51.32.075 (West 1990).

76. See the Justice Department's Tort Policy Working Group report, *An Update on the Liability Crisis* 90–93 (Washington, D.C.: U.S. Government Printing Office, 1987).

77. See Steven K. Dietz, C. Bruce Baird, and Lawrence Berul, "The Medical Malpractice Legal System," in *HEW Report.*

78. See M. W. Reder, "An Economic Analysis of Medical Malpractice," 5 *Journal of Legal Studies* 267 (1976).

79. Ibid., pp. 287–289. Although the law had some positive effect on premiums, its influence was not strong and became much fainter when the states of California and New York, where the pro-plaintiff tinge to the law was most pronounced, were removed from the analysis.

80. Roger Feldman, "The Determinants of Medical Malpractice Incidents: Theory of Contingency Fees and Empirical Evidence," 7 *Atlantic Economic Journal* 59 (1979). Feldman added three more doctrines to those studied by Reder, regarding the patient-physician privilege, remedies for unauthorized disclosure of information, and access of the patient's attorney to hospital records.

81. Ibid., pp. 62 and 64.

82. See Patricia M. Danzon, "The Frequency and Severity of Medical Malpractice Claims," 27 *Journal of Law and Economics* 115 (1984).

83. Ibid., p. 137. Danzon conceded that the degree to which these effects are supposedly attributable to the law is likely overstated because of the presence of other unmeasured factors in states that were associated with the adoption of pro-plaintiff legal positions.

84. See E. Kathleen Adams and Stephen Zuckerman, "Variation in the

Growth and Incidence of Medical Malpractice Claims," 9 *Journal of Health Politics, Policy, and Law* 475 (1984).

85. Ibid., pp. 484–485. Note that Adams and Zuckerman looked at only the seven basic common law doctrines and their statutory revision—*res ipsa loquitur*, the locality rule, *respondeat superior*, and the others—and did not consider the impact of the more prominent legislative reforms of damage rules, attorney fees, and so forth.

86. See Frank A. Sloan, "State Responses to the Malpractice Insurance 'Crisis' of the 1970s: An Empirical Assessment," 9 *Journal of Health Politics, Policy, and Law* 629 (1985).

87. The adoption of a screening panel as a prelude to a lawsuit had a negative and statistically significant effect on the level of premiums, while the requirement of arbitration and the revision of informed consent doctrines actually had a positive effect on premiums (ibid., p. 640). However, when Sloan looked at what he felt was the more appropriate measure—the rate of change in premiums rather than their absolute levels—the statistical significance of all these legal revisions disappeared (p. 642).

88. See Danzon, "The Frequency and Severity of Medical Malpractice Claims."

89. Ibid., p. 139.

90. See Danzon, "New Evidence."

91. Ibid., pp. 71–72 and 76–78.

92. See Frank A. Sloan, Paula M. Mergenhagen, and Randall R. Bovbjerg, "Effects of Tort Reforms on the Value of Closed Medical Malpractice Claims: A Microanalysis," 14 *Journal of Health Politics, Policy, and Law* 663 (1989).

93. Ibid., pp. 677–678.

94. The latter type of legislation includes, for example, rules that define the community of doctors whose norms of practice must be followed, and rules that specify when a doctor must disclose the risks of treatment.

95. See Robinson, "The Malpractice Crisis," p. 23.

96. This is evidenced by the fact that whereas earlier scholarly treatments of this topic focused on the medical context, more recent treatments have had to be much broader in compass. For examples of the former, see Martin H. Redish, "Legislative Response to the Medical Malpractice Insurance Crisis: Constitutional Implications," 55 *Texas Law Review* 759 (1977); Howard Alan Learner, "Restrictive Medical Malpractice Compensation Schemes: A Constitutional 'Quid Pro Quo' Analysis to Safeguard Individual Liberties," 18 *Harvard Journal on Legislation* 143 (1981); and David Randolph Smith, "Battling A Receding Tort Frontier: Constitutional Attacks on Medical Malpractice Laws," 38 *Oklahoma Law Review* 195 (1985). For examples of the latter, see Kenneth Vinson, "Constitutional Stumbling Blocks to Legislative Tort Reform," 15 *Florida State University Law Review* 31 (1987); and Richard C. Turkington, "Constitutional Limitations on Tort Reform: Have the State Courts Placed Insurmountable Obstacles in the Path of Legislative Responses to the Perceived Lia-

bility Insurance Crisis?" 32 *Villanova Law Review* 1299 (1987). The vast majority of the decided cases, however, still involve medical malpractice claims that are hindered or limited by the legislation under attack.

97. See Learner, "Restrictive Compensation Schemes," pp. 165–166.

98. States in which restrictions on malpractice damages have been struck down in recent years include Texas, Florida, Washington, Arizona, Kansas, and Oklahoma; these states joined Illinois, Ohio, North Dakota, Idaho, and New Hampshire, in which similar rulings were handed down in the seventies. Some states (such as Kentucky and Wyoming) have explicit prohibitions in their state constitutions against caps on damages in personal injury actions; others (Pennsylvania and Rhode Island, for example) have no such statutory damage caps now, but would, if they were so inclined, face unfavorable judicial precedents striking down other kinds of limitations on their malpractice laws. By contrast, the courts in Virginia and Maryland have recently upheld their damage caps, following the lead of earlier state court rulings in Indiana, Nebraska, and California. Not surprisingly, perhaps, in a recent decision the Louisiana Supreme Court, in the face of a strong dissent about the legislation, chose to duck this ticklish constitutional question. Citations to all the relevant decisions appear in subsequent notes to this section.

99. More detailed treatment can be found in the scholarly pieces cited in note 96 above.

100. See, e.g., Boyd v. Bulala, 877 F.2d 1191 (4th Cir. 1989) (upholding an absolute dollar limit on total damages of any kind in malpractice actions); Hoffman v. United States, 767 F.2d 1431, 1435–1437 (9th Cir. 1985) (upholding a California law setting a damage cap on noneconomic damages in malpractice actions); Fitz v. Dolyak, 712 F.2d 330, 332 (8th Cir. 1983) (upholding an Iowa statute of limitations applicable only to malpractice actions); Seoane v. Ortho Pharmaceuticals, Inc., 660 F.2d 146, 149–150 (5th Cir. 1981) (upholding a Louisiana statute requiring a medical panel review of malpractice claims); DiAntonio v. Northampton-Accomack Memorial Hospital, 628 F.2d 287, 291 (4th Cir. 1980) (upholding a Virginia malpractice law requiring notice and mediation); Woods v. Holy Cross Hospital, 591 F.2d 1164, 1173 (5th Cir. 1979) (upholding a Florida law requiring malpractice claimants to participate in a mediation process). One exceptional decision that has not been followed in any later case is McGuire v. C & L Restaurant, 346 N.W.2d 605, 613 (Minn. 1984), in which a damage cap in a so-called dram shop act was found to violate both the state and federal equal protection clauses.

101. The Supreme Court has not engaged in forthright substantive due process analysis since the end of the era epitomized by cases such as Lochner v. New York, 198 U.S. 45 (1905).

102. See, e.g., Fein v. Permanente Medical Group, 695 P.2d 665 (Cal. 1985), *appeal dismissed*, 106 S.Ct. 214 (1986). A recent case applying *Fein* is Franklin v. Mazda Motor Corp., 704 F.Supp. 1325 (D.Md. 1989) (upholding Maryland's $350,000 cap against due process challenges under both the federal and the state constitutions). The Supreme Court dis-

missed the appeal in *Fein* for want of a substantial federal question. Justice White asserted that the Supreme Court should take the case in order to resolve the *quid pro quo* debate; see 106 S. Ct. at 216. For a general discussion of that doctrine, see Redish, "Legislative Response," pp. 784–790.

103. See, e.g., *Fein* at 686.

104. See, e.g., *Fein* at 681, n. 18.

105. See, e.g., Duke Power Co. v. Carolina Environmental Study Group, 438 U.S. 59, 88 (1978), in which the Supreme Court confronted but did not decide the issue.

106. The federal district court ruled that the statute violated the Virginia constitution's jury trial guarantee, which was found to be equivalent to the federal guarantee. See Boyd v. Bulala, 647 F. Supp. 781, 786 (W.D. Va. 1986). The court then allowed the Commonwealth of Virginia to intervene to reargue the constitutional issue. In its second decision, the court held that the statute violated the federal constitution's jury right as well. See Boyd v. Bulala, 672 F. Supp. 915, 918–921 (W.D. Va. 1987). Although the Seventh Amendment to the federal Constitution does not impose jury requirements on state court trials (see New York Central Railroad Co. v. White, 243 U.S. 188 [1917]), the amendment applies to all federal court cases, whether or not jurisdiction is based on diversity. See Byrd v. Blue Ridge Rural Electric Cooperative, Inc., 356 U.S. 525 (1958). However, in Boyd v. Bulala, 877 F.2d at 1196, the Fourth Circuit reversed the district court's interpretation of the effect of the Seventh Amendment and followed the intervening ruling of the Supreme Court of Virginia in Etheridge v. Medical Center Hospitals, 376 S.E.2d. 525 (Va. 1989), upholding the Virginia law under the state constitution. See also, to the same effect for Maryland law, Franklin v. Mazda Motor Corp., 704 F.Supp. at 1330–1335; and Potomac Electric Power Co. v. Smith, 558 A.2d 768 (Md. Sp. App. 1989) (upholding a damage cap on noneconomic damages in a nonmedical wrongful death action); and for a malpractice damage cap in the Virgin Islands, see Davis v. Omitowoju, 883 F.2d 1155 (3d Cir. 1989).

107. For a description of the resurgence of state constitutionalism, see generally William J. Brennan, Jr., "The Bill of Rights and the States: The Revival of State Constitutions as Guardians of Individual Rights," 61 *New York University Law Review* 535 (1986); and Symposium, "The Emergence of State Constitutional Law," 63 *Texas Law Review* 959 (1985).

108. See Kenyon v. Hammer, 688 P.2d 961 (Ariz. 1984); Austin v. Litvak, 682 P.2d 41 (Colo. 1984); Smith v. Department of Insurance, 507 So.2d 1080 (Fla. 1987); Aldana v. Holub, 381 So.2d 231, 234 (Fla. 1980); Clark v. Singer, 298 S.E.2d 484 (Ga. 1983); Jones v. State Board of Medicine, 555 P.2d 399 (Idaho 1976), *cert. denied*, 431 U.S. 914 (1977), *on remand* Jones v. State Board of Medicine, Nos. 55527 and 55586 (4th Dist. Idaho, Nov. 3, 1980); Wright v. Central Du Page Hospital Association, 347 N.E.2d 736 (Ill. 1976); Kansas Malpractice Victims v. Bell, 757 P.2d 251 (Kan. 1988); Farley v. Engelken, 740 P.2d 1058 (Kan. 1987); Gale v. Providence Hos-

pital, 325 N.W.2d 439 (Mich. App. 1982); State ex rel Cardinal Glennon Memorial Hospital for Children v. Gaertner, 583 S.W.2d 107 (Mo. 1979); White v. State, 661 P.2d 1272 (Mont. 1983); Jiron v. Mahlab, 659 P.2d 311 (N.M. 1983); Carson v. Maurer, 424 A.2d 825 (N.H. 1980); Arneson v. Olson, 270 N.W.2d 125 (N.D. 1978); Simon v. Saint Elizabeth Medical Center, 355 N.E.2d 903 (Ohio 1976); Reynolds v. Porter, 760 P.2d 816 (Okla. 1988); Mattos v. Thompson, 421 A.2d 190 (Pa. 1980); Boucher v. Sayeed, 459 A.2d 87 (R.I. 1983); Lucas v. United States, 757 S.W.2d 687 (Tex. 1988); Sofie v. Fibreboard Corp., 771 P.2d 711 (Wash. 1989) (striking down a cap on tort damages generally); and Hoem v. State of Wyoming, 756 P.2d 780 (Wyo. 1988). In Williams v. Kushner, 549 So.2d 294 (La. 1989), a vigorous dissent declared that the Louisiana cap was invalid, but the majority avoided the issue by finding that the plaintiff's settlement had made the constitutional challenge moot. Most recently, the Kansas Supreme Court has apparently reversed direction by upholding a $250,000 cap on noneconomic damages that applies to all personal injury actions *except* medical malpractice: see Samsel v. Wheeler Transport Services, Inc., 789 P.2d 541 (Kan. 1990).

109. See *New York Central Railroad Co.*, 243 U.S. at 197.
110. See *Duke Power Co.*, 438 U.S. at 88.
111. Often judicial dissents in cases upholding malpractice legislation are the most strongly worded. See, e.g., *Fein* at 687–694 (Bird, C.J., dissenting). For a discussion of the quid pro quo theme, see Learner, "Restrictive Compensation Schemes," pp. 166–206. The states in which courts have explicitly recognized an alleged lack of a quid pro quo include California, Colorado, Florida, Idaho, Illinois, Kansas, New Hampshire, New Mexico, North Dakota, Ohio, and Wisconsin.

    As further evidence of that sentiment, it is interesting to note that in recent years judges have been much more willing to uphold revisions to the collateral source rule against constitutional challenges, in cases such as Barme v. Wood, 689 P.2d 446 (Cal. 1984); Lambert v. Sisters of Mercy Health Corp., 369 N.W.2d 417 (Iowa 1985); Baker v. Vanderbilt University, 616 F.Supp. 330 (M.D. Tenn. 1985); and Bernier v. Burris, 497 N.E.2d 763 (Ill. 1986) (but see *contra*, Farley v. Engelken, 740 P.2d 1058 [Kan. 1987]). A serious policy issue about the collateral source rule (which I will address in detail in the next chapter) must be faced; but whatever the verdict on that score, in all these cases the plaintiff-victims whose tort recovery is being reduced are receiving redress from other programs for their particular losses.

112. See Kenyon v. Hammer, 688 P.2d 961, and White v. State, 661 P.2d 1272.
113. See Carson v. Maurer, 424 A.2d 825.
114. See Boucher v. Sayeed, 459 A.2d 87, and Barme v. Wood, 689 P.2d 446 (Mosk, J., dissenting).
115. See Arneson v. Olson, 270 N.W.2d 132.
116. See Cal. Civ. Code §3333.1–.2 (West Supp. 1990).
117. See *American Bank & Trust*, 683 P.2d 670.
118. See Roa v. Lodi Medical Group, Inc., 695 P.2d 164 (Cal. 1985).

119. See *Fein*.
120. See *Barme*.
121. See notes 83–87 above.
122. See *Fein;* Johnson v. St. Vincent Hospital, Inc., 404 N.E.2d 585 (Ind. 1980); Prendergast v. Nelson, 256 N.W.2d 657 (Neb. 1977); Otero v. Zouhar, 697 P.2d 493 (N.M. App. 1984); State ex rel. Strykowski v. Wilkie, 261 N.W.2d 434 (Wis. 1978).
123. See Wright v. Central Du Page Hospital Association; Carson v. Maurer; Arneson v. Olson; Simon v. St. Elizabeth Medical Center.
124. See Smith v. Department of Insurance, 507 So.2d 1088; and Lucas v. United States, 757 S.W.2d 692.
125. Almost all the cases that struck down legislation under the quid pro quo argument, as well as some of the cases that did not, cited either *Duke Power* or state cases upholding workers' compensation schemes.
126. See Macchiaroli, "Medical Malpractice Screening Panels," pp. 197–222. As noted above, in Florida the jury trial right has also been used to strike down a damage cap limitation. See Smith v. Department of Insurance, 507 So.2d 1088.
127. See Cardinal Glennon Memorial Hospital, and Wright v. Central Du Page Hospital Association; see also DeLuna v. St. Elizabeth's Hospital, 540 N.E.2d 847 (Ill. App. 1989) (invalidating Illinois's certification requirement).
128. See Mattos v. Thompson and Aldana v. Holub. The Wyoming Supreme Court threw out the state's ten-year-old screening panel requirement in Hoem v. State of Wyoming, 756 P.2d 780.
129. Among the cases decided along these lines between 1987 and 1989 are *Boyd* and *Etheridge* in Virginia, *Franklin* and *Smith* in Maryland, *Lucas* in Texas, *Bell* in Kansas, *Smith* in Florida, *Sofie* in Washington, and *Williams* in Louisiana. (Full citations for these cases appear in notes 106 and 108 above.)

3. Serious Reform in the Tort/Fault Model

1. In the last several years, participants in the political debate about tort reform both in the medical area and generally have produced a large volume of reports and analysis concerning the pros and cons of different tort reforms. I cite here the volumes with which I am most familiar.

   The Reagan administration produced the two publications of the Justice Department's Tort Policy Working Group—*Report of the Tort Policy Working Group on the Causes, Extent, and Policy Implications of the Current Crisis in Financial Availability and Affordability* (Washington, D.C.: U.S. Government Printing Office, 1986); and *An Update on the Liability Crisis* (Washington, D.C.: U.S. Government Printing Office, 1987); as well as the *HHS Report.* From the states issued the 1986 Report of the New York Governor's Advisory Commission, *Insuring Our Future* (New York: 1986); the Report of the Massachusetts Governor's Task Force on Liability Issues, *Liability in Massachusetts: Toward a Fairer System* (Boston: 1986);

and the Florida Academic Task Force for the Review of the Insurance and Tort Systems, *Discussion Draft on Medical Malpractice Reform Alternatives* (Gainesville, Fla.: 1987).

The medical profession has provided several reports: three from the American Medical Association Special Task Force on Professional Liability and Insurance, *Professional Liability in the '80s* (Chicago: October 1984; November 1984; and March 1985); and more recently the AMA/Specialty Society Medical Liability Project, *A Proposed Alternative to the Civil Justice System for Resolving Medical Liability Disputes: A Fault-Based, Administrative System* (Chicago: AMA, 1987). The legal profession generated the American Bar Association Special Committee on Medical Professional Liability, *Report to the House of Delegates* (Chicago: ABA, 1985); the American College of Trial Lawyers, *Report of the Task Force on Litigation Issues* (New York: ACTL, 1986); the ABA *Report of the Action Commission to Improve the Tort Liability System* (Chicago: ABA, 1987); and the Association of the Bar of the City of New York, Ad Hoc Committee of Medical Malpractice, *Report on Recommendations for the State of New York* (New York: 1989). Finally, from the business community, A Statement by the Research and Policy Committee of the Committee for Economic Development, *Who Should Be Liable? A Guide to Policy for Dealing with Risk* (New York: CED, 1989).

These documents contain virtually all the possible arguments to be made for and against the various reforms that have been proposed within the present tort regime. (In the next section I present my own appraisal of these proposals and arguments.) However, although abolition and replacement of the tort/fault model is not seriously contemplated in the current political and governmental debates, it is certainly a live option in the scholarly community. Subsequent chapters, therefore, contain extensive discussion of two versions of this more fundamental alteration of the medical liability regime.

2. The most sophisticated exponent of this position is Ernest J. Weinrib; his most important work on the subject is to be found in "Toward a Moral Theory of Negligence Law," in Michael D. Bayles and Bruce Chapman, eds., *Justice, Rights, and Tort Law* 123 (Boston: D. Reidel Publishing Company, 1983); "Causation and Wrongdoing," 63 *Chicago-Kent Law Review* 407 (1987); and "Understanding Tort Law," 23 *Valparaiso University Law Review* 485 (1989).

3. 60 Mass. (6 Cush.) 292 (1850).

4. 199 P.2d 1 (Cal. 1948).

5. See the figures presented in Chapter 1, note 22.

6. Indeed, without such insurance coverage not only would the doctor suffer severe financial reverses from tort liability for even occasional accidents, but the most seriously injured patients would probably be unable to collect financial benefits from a formal legal verdict in their favor. Consequently, some states and many hospitals require that doctors purchase liability coverage before being permitted to practice in the state or hospital.

7. Although the text emphasizes that the malpractice insurer is the major player and payer in malpractice litigation, I do not wish to shunt the individual doctor entirely off the stage. Recall that a distinctive feature of malpractice litigation is that the defendant-doctor is a human actor, being sued as a result of something that happened while he or she was caring for a patient; consequently it is the doctor's professional performance and reputation that is challenged at trial. Even though tort policy must acknowledge and attempt to accommodate the special psychological features of the malpractice controversy, these characteristics provide little support for the corrective justice rationale for the regime. Since the major impact of the personal uninsured consequences of malpractice litigation are visited upon the doctor by the mere fact of being sued, the consequences are borne equally by doctors who are the subject of the majority of claims that ultimately are found to be without merit.

8. As I observed earlier, one of the sources of the contemporary malpractice crisis is the fact that these insurance systems moved out of synchronization with each other. The sharp increases in malpractice premiums in the mid-eighties seemed necessary to accommodate steady increases in claims and awards. However, the new malpractice insurance institutions that evolved in the wake of the mid-seventies crisis—"bedpan mutuals," patient compensation funds, and joint underwriting associations—were often underfunded in their early years because of the "long tail" feature of medical malpractice claims. Moreover, the insurers' earnings on their reserves for future claims declined with real interest rates in the mid-eighties, a development that put even more pressure on the premium component of the total revenues. Yet at the very time when these factors coalesced to produce major jumps in the malpractice premiums charged to doctors, medical cost containment programs were making it much more difficult for doctors to pass on this increased cost of practice to their patients and the patients' health insurers. Caught in the middle of these different insurance programs, doctors directed most of their ire at tort law and lawyers.

9. The principal expositions of this view of the tort system are Guido Calabresi, *The Costs of Accidents: A Legal and Economic Analysis* (New Haven: Yale University Press, 1970); Steven Shavell, *Economic Analysis of Accident Law* (Cambridge, Mass.: Harvard University Press, 1987); and William M. Landes and Richard A. Posner, *The Economic Structure of Tort Law* (Cambridge, Mass.: Harvard University Press, 1987). The major book-length treatment of malpractice law by Patricia M. Danzon, *Medical Malpractice: Theory, Evidence, and Public Policy* (Cambridge, Mass.: Harvard University Press, 1985), operates within the same efficient insurance frame of reference.

10. See Chapter 1, note 12.

11. In rather casually tracking reported personal injury decisions, for example, I turned up several cases from the last two or three years featuring awards of that magnitude. All these cases involved babies who were brain-damaged during delivery: Reilly v. United States, 665 F. Supp. 976

(D.R.I. 1987) ($11 million award by trial judge); Henry v. St. John's Hospital, 512 N.E.2d 1042 (Ill. App. 1987) ($10 million jury award upheld on appeal); Mather v. Griffin Hospital, 540 A.2d 666 (Conn. 1988) ($9 million jury award upheld on appeal); Merrill v. Albany Medical Center Hospital, 512 N.Y.S.2d 519 (App. Div. 1987) ($12.4 million jury verdict, eventually reduced to $6.1 million on appeal); Boyd v. Bulala, 678 F. Supp. 612 (W.D. Va. 1988); *reversed*, 877 F.2d 1191 (4th Cir. 1989) ($9 million jury verdict, eventually cut back to $750,000 under Virginia's damage cap, which was sustained as constitutional).

12. Evidence of the fact that juries systematically award significantly higher tort damages to the victims of medical accidents than to the victims of motor vehicle accidents suffering from the same injuries can be found in Audrey Chin and Mark A. Peterson, *Deep Pockets, Empty Pockets: Who Wins in Cook County Jury Trials* (Santa Monica, Calif.: RAND Institute For Civil Justice, 1985); and in Thomas B. Metzloff, "Researching Litigation: The Medical Malpractice Example," 51 *Law and Contemporary Problems* 199, 235–236 (1988).

13. See Ivy E. Broder, "Characteristics of Million Dollar Awards: Jury Verdicts and Final Disbursements," 11 *Justice System Journal* 349 (1986); and Michael G. Shanley and Mark A. Peterson, *Posttrial Adjustments to Jury Awards* (Santa Monica, Calif.: RAND Institute for Civil Justice, 1987).

14. As illustration from the medical context, in Baez v. Dombroff, 530 N.Y.S.2d 847 (App. Div. 1987), the plaintiff, who was left with disfigured breasts after a botched breast-reduction operation, originally won a $2.625 million jury award, saw the award cut to $1.5 million by the trial judge, and was still left with $750,000 by the court of appeals for her entirely nonfinancial loss. This amount is even more impressive in view of the fact that New York State is exceptional in the degree to which it empowers its judges to review the appropriateness of original jury verdicts. An even starker example from the nonmedical context is Delosovic v. City of New York, 541 N.Y.S.2d 685 (Sup. 1989). A mother who witnessed the instant killing of her two young children by a truck at a crosswalk was originally awarded $25 million by the jury. Although the appellate court eventually reduced this verdict against the city to $2.5 million, or only a tenth of the original award, that amount, together with settlement payments from other defendants, left the mother with nearly $4 million in total damages for her emotional distress.

15. See the calculations by Patricia M. Danzon in *Florida Policy Guidebook*, pp. 128–142.

16. Compare for example the *Delosovic* case with Fortman v. Hemco, Inc., 259 Cal.Reptr. 311 (Cal. App. 1989), in which a jury awarded $25 million to a three-year-old child who was left brain-damaged and paraplegic with a conscious life-expectancy of seventy-one years and estimated medical and rehabilitative expenses of more than $16 million. More systematically, the *1984 Closed Claims Survey* found that of all the malpractice victim categories in tort litigation the victims of "major" or "grave" permanent total disabilities recouped the smallest proportion of their economic losses.

17. Malpractice insurance is sold within segmented pools of specialties practicing in a single state or metropolitan region within a state. In most states there are fewer than five hundred obstetricians in active practice. Those in which there are more—California, New York, Texas, and Florida, for example—are subdivided into several different insurance regions. See Institute of Medicine, *Medical Professional Liability and the Delivery of Obstetrical Care*, 2 vols., ed. Victoria P. Rostow and Roger J. Bulger, I, 16–17, 99 (Washington, D.C.: National Academy Press, 1989).

18. That was the case in Louisiana, for example: see Williams v. Kushner, 549 So.2d 294, 307–308 (La. 1989).

19. See Council of Economic Advisers, *Economic Report of the President*, Table C-58 (Washington, D.C.: U.S. Government Printing Office, 1990).

20. See Danzon, *Medical Malpractice*, pp. 169–170. Up-to-date summaries of the scope and coverage of medical care and lost earnings protection of accident victims are presented in working papers prepared for the American Law Institute's Tort Reform Project by Kenneth S. Abraham, Troyen Brennan, and Lance Liebman.

21. See Patricia M. Danzon, "The Frequency and Severity of Medical Malpractice Claims: New Evidence," 49 *Law and Contemporary Problems* 57, 72, 77 (1986); and Frank A. Sloan, Paula M. Mergenhagen, and Randall R. Bovbjerg, "Effects of Tort Reforms on the Value of Closed Medical Malpractice Claims: A Microanalysis," 14 *Journal of Health Politics, Policy, and Law* 663, 678 (1989).

22. Unhappily, the recent trend has been in precisely the opposite direction: see Jeffrey O'Connell and James Guinivan, "An Irrational Combination: The Relative Expansion of Liability Insurance and Contraction of Loss Insurance," 49 *Ohio State Law Journal* 757 (1988).

23. Many economic analyses of the tort system assume that the moral hazard of overgenerous tort compensation arises from providing a significant inducement to the kind of careless victim behavior that produced the original accident. For a presentation and critique of this view, see Gary T. Schwartz, "Contributory and Comparative Negligence: A Reappraisal," 87 *Yale Law Journal* 697, 710–721 (1978). Even those who are skeptical of this prognosis in the medical context, in which most serious iatrogenic injuries are inflicted on patients who are largely passive recipients of their doctors' treatment, will concede that this problem can be significant in the aftermath of a medical accident in which the patient's own decisions about what rehabilitation to undertake, or whether and when to go back to work, will be important determinants of the total financial loss that flows out of the original medical accident and iatrogenic injury.

24. I explore the complicated arrangements for accommodating workers' compensation and product liability when they are related to the same injury in Paul C. Weiler, "Workers' Compensation and Product Liability: The Interaction of a Tort and Non-Tort Regime," 50 *Ohio State Law Journal* 825 (1989).

25. See *1984 Claims Closed Survey*, pp. 32–35. If the injury was more serious, another five months would elapse between claim and disposition. I

should note, however, that these median time frames have actually dropped somewhat since the mid-seventies: see M. Patricia Sowka, "The NAIC Medical Malpractice Closed Claims Study: Executive Summary," 45 *Connecticut Medicine* 91, 97 (1981), indicating that the period from incident to payment was thirty-seven months in 1975 and forty-six months in 1978.

26. See Ronald Conley and John Noble, "Workers' Compensation Reform: Challenge for the 80's," *Research Report of the Interdepartmental Workers' Compensation Task Force*, I, 57 (Washington, D.C.: U.S. Government Printing Office, 1982). Of course, a large number of workers' compensation benefits are paid for relatively minor lost-time injuries, and the shorter processing periods for these cases would pull down the overall average. But even the uncontested claims for permanent disabilities were paid within a month and a half, and the contested claims within five months. Only the controverted fatality claims took a long time for disposition—an average of eighteen months. Even so, this is only *half* the median time for *all* medical malpractice claims, fatal or nonfatal, serious or minor.

27. By contrast, Robert L. Bombaugh, "The Department of Transportation's Auto Insurance Study and Auto Accident Compensation Reform," 71 *Columbia Law Review* 207, 230 (1971), Table 10, depicts the department's findings regarding the total cost of operating the automobile liability system in 1968. The expenses included not simply the claims expenditures by victims and insurers (which were roughly equal in amount), but also the insurers' brokerage commissions and other acquisition costs, and the underwriting and investment expenses of the firms (the last two items were about equal to the claims-processing and litigation expenses of the two sides). Similarly, Jeffrey O'Connell, "An Alternative to Abandoning Tort Liability: Elective No-Fault Insurance for Many Kinds of Injuries," 60 *Minnesota Law Review* 501, 504–512 (1976), draws on a variety of sources to depict a breakdown much the same as Bombaugh's of the liability insurance dollar for motor vehicle, medical malpractice, and defective product cases. O'Connell found that the litigation costs of plaintiff and defendant in the malpractice and product areas amounted to a larger share of the premium dollar than did general overhead, although the latter was still a substantial component of the two liability programs.

28. This estimate in the 40–45 percent range is derived from a variety of sources. A recent and meticulous examination of the question is James S. Kakalik and Nicholas M. Pace, *Costs and Compensation Paid in Tort Litigation* (Santa Monica, Calif.: RAND Institute for Civil Justice, 1986). The authors conclude that for non-auto torts as a whole, the net compensation remaining in the hands of the victim amounted to 43 percent of the overall private and social expenditures for processing and reimbursing the claims (a share significantly smaller than the 52 percent left in the hands of motor vehicle victims; see Figure S.2, p. xiii). Medical malpractice is an important representative instance of the more complex and contentious non-auto tort cases.

The only figures I have seen specifically for the medical malpractice situation, drawn from the mid-seventies, are those reported by O'Connell, "Elective No-Fault Insurance," pp. 506–509, and the *Report of the Special Advisory Panel on Medical Malpractice, State of New York* 250–252 (New York: 1976). These sources put the net compensation to the victim at approximately 40 percent, after adjusting the figures to exclude the general overhead catergory. In an article in the October/November 1977 edition of its in-house newsletter, "Questions and Answers about Medical Malpractice Insurance," *Malpractice Digest* 1, 2–3, St. Paul Fire and Marine Insurance Company broke down the expenditure of its premium dollar into 22.5 percent on commissions, profits, taxes, and general overhead, and 28.6 percent on claims handling expenses, leaving 48.9 percent available to be paid to the plaintiff-victim. Assuming that the plaintiff in turn must pay out approximately one-third of the award for lawyer's fees and legal costs, roughly 42 percent of St. Paul's claims-processing and reimbursing expenditures are left as net compensation in the hands of the victim. None of these medical malpractice figures make any allowance for the social costs of the court system or the personal costs in time spent by victims and doctors contesting the claims, categories that Kakalik and Pace found to be significant in size; consequently it is apparent that the estimate in the text of an administrative cost share of between 55 and 60 percent of the claims dollar is a conservative one.

29. See George L. Priest, "The Current Insurance Crisis and Modern Tort Law," 96 *Yale Law Journal* 1521, 1560 (1987). Priest estimates that "Blue Cross-Blue Shield first-party health insurance administrative costs are 10% of benefits; SSI disability insurance administrative costs are 8% of benefits; Workers' Compensation disability insurance administrative costs are (a much-criticized) 21% of benefits."

30. *1984 Claims Closed Survey* at pp. 36–37. In 1984, 37.5 percent of all claims were resolved before any suit was initiated (and of these about 36 percent produced a payment); 50.6 percent were settled after suit but before trial (53 percent of these involving a payment); and another 1.5 percent were settled at trial but before the jury verdict.

31. Ibid., 46–47.

32. For example, see the recent case of Mercy Hospital of Laredo v. Rios, 776 S.W.2d 626 (Tex. App. 1989), upholding a jury award of $700,000 specifically for the pain and suffering of a baby who suffocated to death in an hour in the defendant hospital.

33. In Blum v. Airport Terminal Services, Inc., 762 S.W.2d 67 (Mo. App. 1988), an award of $1.5 million was upheld on behalf of a young single man whose plane had crashed. The award covered both the terror experienced before the crash and the three days' pain and suffering from the time of the crash until he died.

34. In DiRosario v. Havens, 242 Cal. Rptr. 423 (Cal. App. 1987), the parents of a seven-year-old girl were awarded $2.1 million in damages when their daughter was killed by a car negligently driven by a doctor. Com-

pare Yates v. Pollock, 239 Cal. Rptr. 383 (Cal. App. 1987), holding that if a doctor-defendant is sued for medical negligence, total damages for all family members (in this case, a widow and five children) would be confined by the $250,000 statutory cap applicable to all nonpecuniary damages from a single malpractice incident.

35. For example, in Georgacopoulos v. University of Chicago Hospitals and Clinics, 504 N.E.2d 830 (Ill. App. 1987), a woman who suffered brain damage during an operation received $3.5 million for her own pain and suffering during the balance of her life, which was expected to last from two to twenty years; in addition, her husband received another $750,000 for loss of consortium. There is a debate in the cases over whether "loss of enjoyment of life" is a category of damages conceptually distinct from pain and suffering, or only a component of that category. Riding on the resolution of the issue is the question of whether such damages may be paid to a person who is totally comatose and unable to appreciate any of these losses. For a recent review of the contrasting decisions across the country, see McDougald v. Garber, 524 N.Y.S.2d 192 (App. Div. 1988); *reversed*, 538 N.Y.S.2d 937 (1989).

36. Pain and suffering damages represent nearly 50 percent of damages paid in product liability cases as well. See the calculations by Danzon in *Florida Policy Guidebook*, pp. 128–142; and W. Kip Viscusi, "Pain and Suffering in Product Liability Cases: Systematic Compensation or Capricious Awards?" 8 *International Review of Law and Economics* 203 (1988).

37. See the discussion in Stanley Ingber, "Rethinking Intangible Injuries: A Focus on Remedy," 73 *California Law Review* 772, 778–786 (1985); and David W. Leebron, "Final Moments: Damages for Pain and Suffering Prior to Death," 64 *New York University Law Review* 256 (1989). Randall R. Bovbjerg, Frank A. Sloan, and James F. Blumstein, "Valuing Life and Limb in Tort: Scheduling 'Pain and Suffering,'" 83 *Northwestern Law Review* 908, 937 (1989), present a table that graphically displays the huge disparity in jury verdicts for pain and suffering awards, controlling for the category of injury in their sample from Florida and Kansas City. The article by Bovbjerg, Sloan, and Blumstein, which appeared some time after this chapter was first written, reflects a point of view on this problem that is largely in accord with my own.

38. For a representative statement, see Bingaman v. Grays Harbor Community Hospital, 699 P.2d 1230, 1233 (Wash. 1985). New York State is an exception to the pattern described in the text, since it adopted in 1986 a new statutory standard that requires the judge to ask whether a jury award "deviates materially from what would be reasonable compensation."

39. Recall the case of Baez v. Dombroff, in which breasts disfigured by a breast reduction operation were initially valued by the jury at $2.625 million, by the trial judge at $1.5 million, and by the appeals court at $750,000. Similarly, but in a nonmedical context, in *Delosovic* a jury award of $25 million for the distress of a mother who saw two of her young children killed by a truck was reduced to $2.5 million (to which

was added more than a million dollars from a settlement with other defendants in the case). Finally, in Duren v. Suburban Community Hospital, 495 N.E.2d 51 (Ohio Com. Pl. 1985), an award of $1 million for the pain and suffering experienced by the deceased for less than twenty-four hours was reduced on appeal to $500,000. At the same time the Ohio damage cap was struck down by the court as unconstitutional in order to sustain the overall award.

40. A table in Randall R. Bovbjerg, "Legislation on Medical Malpractice: Further Developments and a Preliminary Report Card," 22 *U.C. Davis Law Review* 499, 543 (1989), summarizes what happened. Between 1975 and 1977 there were sixteen legislated damage caps. Fifteen of these were just for malpractice cases, and of this group only four were confined to pain and suffering (most prominently California's $250,000 limit). However, in 1986 and 1987 twenty-two states enacted such legislation, twelve specifically for malpractice claims; of this group, nineteen caps were confined to pain and suffering damages.

41. Among the most frequently quoted statements on this subject are Louis L. Jaffe, "Damages for Personal Injury: The Impact of Insurance," 18 *Law and Contemporary Problems* 219 (1953); and the dissenting opinion of Justice Traynor in Seffert v. Los Angeles Transit Lines, 364 P.2d 337, 344 (Cal. 1961).

42. A recent and useful review article on market valuation of risk is Ted R. Miller, "Willingness to Pay Comes of Age: Will the System Survive?" 83 *Northwestern Law Review* 876 (1989). Michael J. Moore and W. Kip Viscusi, *Compensation Mechanisms for Job Risks: Wages, Workers' Compensation, and Product Liability* 47–49, 77–81 (Princeton, N.J: Princeton University Press, 1990), contains the latest econometric study of the net difference in employee wage rates produced by variations in the risk of nonfatal injuries. The wage premiums associated with the riskier jobs permit a calculation of the implicit monetary value placed on avoiding such injuries by workers who must choose how much it is worth to them to take the risks. Abstracting from the economic losses covered by workers' compensation insurance, Moore and Viscusi found that workers "valued" the nonpecuniary consequences of the typical lost time injury (thirteen days off the job) at about $20,000.

43. For reasons explained in Philip J. Cook and Daniel A. Graham, "The Demand for Insurance and Protection: The Case of Irreplaceable Commodities," 91 *Quarterly Journal of Economics* 143 (1977); and Samuel A. Rea, Jr., "Nonpecuniary Loss and Breach of Contract," 11 *Journal of Legal Studies* 35 (1982).

44. See Patricia M. Danzon, "Tort Reform and the Role of Government in Private Insurance Markets," 13 *Journal of Legal Studies* 517 (1984).

45. See Andrews v. Grand & Toy Alberta Ltd., 83 D.L.R.3d 452, 475–478 (1978), in which the Supreme Court of Canada endorsed this particular rationale for an award of pain and suffering damages (adopting the argument of A. I. Ogus, "Damages for Lost Amenities: For a Foot, a Feeling, or a Function?" 35 *Modern Law Review* 1 [1972]). The Court also held

that such awards should be capped at $100,000, a figure that has now been raised to approximately $200,000 to keep it in line with subsequent price inflation in Canada.

46. Selection of the actual monetary figure could draw upon the work of labor economists who determine the negative value that people place on different risks by noting the magnitude of the compensating wage differentials needed to attract and hold them in risky jobs. See, e.g., Miller, "Willingness to Pay," and Moore and Viscusi, *Compensation Mechanisms.*

47. This should not be viewed as a farfetched example, as evidenced by these recently reported cases: Burge v. Parker, 510 So.2d 538 (Ala. 1987) (a boy is awarded $445,000 from a doctor for the loss of his big toe, in addition to a $200,0000 settlement with the railroad involved in the same accident); Rattenborg v. Montgomery Elevator Company, 438 N.W.2d 602 (Iowa App. 1989) (a sixteen-year-old girl wins $500,000 for a permanently damaged finger); and Treadway v. Uniroyal Tire Company, 766 P.2d 938 (Okla. 1988) (a middle-aged man wins $750,000 for an impaired wrist that leaves him with a permanently weakened grip).

48. See, e.g., Danzon, "Tort Reform and the Role of Government," pp. 527–530, and Bovbjerg, Sloan, and Blumstein, "Valuing Life and Limb," pp. 938–952.

49. For example, compare the cases cited in note 47, awarding $500,000 to $750,000 for injured toes, fingers, or wrists, with the jury award in Hazelwood v. Beauchamp, 766 S.W.2d 439 (Ky. App. 1989), in which a farmworker whose hand was caught and crushed in a hay baler was awarded only $250 by the jury for the resulting pain and suffering.

50. For brief descriptions and appraisals of the AMA schedule, see Deborah A. Stone, *The Disabled State* (Philadelphia: Temple University Press, 1984); and Ellen Smith Pryor, "Flawed Promises: A Critical Evaluation of the American Medical Association's *Guides to the Evaluation of Permanent Impairment,*" 103 *Harvard Law Review* 964 (1990). This schedule has attracted considerable criticism in the workers' compensation context, primarily because these medical decisions are used as a proxy for the loss of earnings capacity by permanently and partially disabled workers. See Monroe Berkowitz and John F. Burton, Jr., *Permanent Disability Benefits in Workers' Compensation* (Kalamazoo, Mich.: W. E. Upjohn Institute for Employment Research, 1987); and Ellen Smith Pryor, "Compensation and a Consequential Model of Loss," 64 *Tulane Law Review* 783 (1990).

51. See Bovbjerg, Sloan, and Blumstein, "Valuing Life and Limb," pp. 953–956. A vehicle for producing these profile values could be a body composed of experienced judges, lawyers, insurers, doctors, and others, whose product would then be adopted by the state legislature or the state supreme court. An obvious analogy to what I have in mind is the work of the U.S. Sentencing Commission, which produced presumptive sentencing guidelines for different offenses and offenders. See Stephen Breyer, "The Federal Sentencing Guidelines and the Key Compromises upon Which They Rest," 17 *Hofstra Law Review* 1 (1988). I am satisfied that these more explicit criteria for jury decisions about pain and suffer-

ing would successfully meet the technical constitutional challenges considered in Chapter 2; see Bovbjerg, Sloan, and Blumstein, "Valuing Life and Limb," pp. 969–974. The underlying policy concern felt by many judges about containing this type of tort damages should be allayed by the proposal I make later in this chapter concerning defendants' paying for successful plaintiff's attorney fees.

52. See James S. Kakalik, Elizabeth M. King, Michael Traynor, Patricia A. Ebener, and Larry Picus, *Costs and Compensation Paid in Aviation Accident Litigation* 39–64 (Santa Monica, Calif.: RAND Institute for Civil Justice, 1988).

53. Recall the case of Fortman v. Hemco, which produced a highly publicized $24 million judgment for a badly injured child with a seventy-one-year life expectancy, of which $6 million was for pain and suffering. Assuming the standard one-third contingency fee, the net $16 million recovery for the child covered just the estimated medical bills and left nothing to the child for future earnings losses, let alone actual loss of enjoyment of life.

54. In 1987 California amended this part of its legislation to increase the allowable fee to 25 percent of any amount between $100,000 and $600,000 (with the 10 percent ceiling applicable only above $600,000). See the comments on this change in Jackson v. United States, 881 F.2d 707, 708–709 (9th Cir. 1989).

55. See Danzon, *Medical Malpractice*, p. 197.

56. The situation is actually somewhat more complicated than the text may suggest. The fact is that filing a spurious claim or motion "wastes" the resources not only of the plaintiff's attorney but also of the defendant, who is obliged to respond. The contingent fee is no guarantee against tactical use of the legal system to extract an offer of settlement from a defendant or insurer, which may find it cheaper to pay than to fight. However, that malfunction of the adversarial system of civil justice is not attributable to the contingent fee arrangement. It occurs as or more often under the hourly fee arrangement that is standard on the defense side, in which tactical maneuvering by the defense not only imposes substantial costs on the plaintiff, but also increases the defense attorney's own fee from his client. So a remedy for this problem is not to regulate the contingent fee payable to the plaintiffs' attorney, but to penalize this type of unethical conduct whenever and under whatever circumstances it occurs. I suggest some measures of this sort later in the chapter.

57. For a sustained argument to this effect, see Lester Brickman, "Contingent Fees without Contingencies: *Hamlet* without the Prince of Denmark?" 37 *UCLA Law Review* 29 (1989).

58. See F. Townsend Hawkes, "The Second Reformation: Florida's Medical Malpractice Law," 13 *Florida State University Law Review* 747, 769–772 (1985).

59. See Kakalik et al., *Aviation Accident Litigation*.

60. See William J. Curran, "The Lawyer's Role in Medical Malpractice Claims," 296 *New England Journal of Medicine* 24, 25 (1977).

61. See Steven K. Dietz, C. Bruce Baird, and Lawrence Berul, "The Medical Malpractice Legal System," in *HEW Report*, Appendixes 113–120; and Herbert M. Kritzer, Austin Sarat, David M. Trubek, and William L. F. Felstiner, "Winners and Losers in Litigation: Does Anyone Come out Ahead?" in *Civil Litigation Research Project Final Report, Part C* 29, 59 (Madison, Wis.: University of Wisconsin Institute for Legal Studies, 1987).

62. Insurer expenditures on attorney fees and litigation costs rose from $4,000 per case in 1978 (see National Association of Insurance Commissioners, *Malpractice Claims—Final Compilation: Medical Malpractice Closed Claims, 1975–1978* 47 (Brookfield, Wis.: NAIC, 1980) to $11,000 per case in 1984 (see *1984 Claims Closed Survey*, p. 20). This increase occurred at a significantly faster pace than the increase in average payments for successful claims, which rose from $45,000 in 1978 to $81,000 in 1984. Recall that payment for a successful claim is the base on which the patient attorney's contingent fee is calculated.

63. Note that enactment of a collateral source offset or of a pain and suffering scale to contain tort damages serves also to reduce the total fees earned by plaintiff attorneys, because these measures reduce the award base to which the one-third share formula is applied. But that outcome does not help the injured plaintiff, whose share of any cutback in damages is twice the size of his lawyer's.

64. The argument was first made by Jeffrey O'Connell: see "A Proposal to Abolish Defendants' Payment for Pain and Suffering in Return for Payment of Claimants' Attorneys' Fees," 1981 *University of Illinois Law Review* 333. Later expositions of the idea appear in John Leubsdorf, "Recovering Attorney Fees as Damages," 38 *Rutgers Law Review* 439 (1986); and Thomas D. Rowe, Jr., "Attorney Fees" (American Law Institute Working Paper, 1990).

65. The Florida provision, which was enacted in 1980, was repealed in 1985 because the doctors who had originally pressed for the reform found that in practice they could not collect their attorney fees when they won, although they occasionally had to pay million-dollar attorney fees if the patient won: see Thomas R. Tedcastle and Marvin A. Dewar, "Medical Malpractice: A New Treatment for an Old Illness," 16 *Florida State University Law Review* 537, 541, n. 36 (1988). Ironically, in Florida Patient's Compensation Fund v. Rowe, 472 So.2d 1145 (Fla. 1985), the Florida Supreme Court upheld the constitutionality of this provision just as it was being repealed by the state legislature. In that decision the court also established criteria for calculating the reasonable attorney fees owed to the prevailing party. However, because the Florida act governed all malpractice claims that had "accrued" in the five-year period between enactment and repeal, subsequent jurisprudence in Florida still provides helpful experience in the operation of a fee-shifting rule in personal injury litigation governed by the contingent fee.

66. Doctors are understandably troubled by the fact that a sizable proportion of malpractice claims appear upon close examination of the medical

records to be unfounded. But identification of a medical injury, let alone doctor negligence, is difficult, particularly without access to the records and the actors. A recent empirical study, Henry S. Farber and Michelle J. White, "Medical Malpractice: An Empirical Examination of the Litigation Process" (unpublished, 1990), found that the malpractice litigation process did a reasonably good job of screening out the majority of unfounded claims once the parties and their counsel were given access to the medical records. The question of what the law should do if the plaintiff's decision to initiate or prolong litigation was unwarranted and culpable, rather than reasonable but mistaken, is one I shall take up shortly.

67. As observed in note 65, the experience in Florida indicates that in practice many patients end up not paying most of the defendant insurer's legal expenses because the legal bills are much greater than the victim's assets. By contrast, the doctors (actually, their insurers) do have to pay the often hefty legal fees of successful patients (see, e.g., Good Samaritan Hospital Association, Inc. v. Saylor, 495 So.2d 782 [Fla. App. 1986], upholding a $1.1 million fee for 2,000 hours of work at $275 an hour, with a contingency multiplier of two). A sense that this disparity in the collectibility of legal fees was costly and unfair led physicians' organizations in 1985 to push for repeal of the reform that they had secured in 1980 in the hope of deterring some malpractice claims. However, there are enough malpractice victims with some assets that would be available to pay at least some of the defense bill, and they would feel enough concern over the prospect of having to seek protection of family assets under Chapter 9 of the bankruptcy laws, to make the disincentive problem from a two-way fee-shifting rule a real one.

4. Prevention of Medical Injuries

1. See authorities cited in Chapter 1, notes 37–39. See also Robert W. Dubois and Robert H. Brook, "Preventable Deaths: Who, How Often, and Why?" 109 *Annals of Internal Medicine* 582 (1988), which found that a significant fraction of the deaths in the twelve hospitals they studied would have been prevented if the patients had not received poor care. According to the majority verdict of their three-member expert panels, 27 percent of the deaths would not have occurred; by unanimous verdict, 14 percent could have been prevented.

2. Most prominent in the malpractice field is Patricia M. Danzon, *Medical Malpractice: Theory, Evidence, and Public Policy* 226 (Cambridge, Mass.: Harvard University Press, 1985); see also William B. Schwartz and Neil K. Komesar, "Doctors, Damages, and Deterrence: An Economic View of Medical Malpractice," 298 *New England Journal of Medicine* 1282 (1978). Peter A. Bell, "Legislative Intrusions into the Common Law of Medical Malpractice: Thoughts about the Deterrent Effect of Tort Liability," 35 *Syracuse Law Review* 939 (1984), is skeptical about a purely economic model of tort incentives (see pp. 949–965); but he contends that tort litigation influences physician behavior through a rather different psycho-

logical process, involving fear of personal and professional stigma rather than of financial penalty (pp. 973–990). For another helpful review of the issues covered in this chapter, see Randall R. Bovbjerg, "Medical Malpractice on Trial: Quality of Care Is the Important Standard," 49 *Law and Contemporary Problems* 321 (1986).

3. This is not to suggest that tort law is necessarily the best policy instrument for curing such a malfunction in the health care market. An alternative might be to improve the operation of the market directly by making detailed information about the comparative risk of different health care providers available to consumers. For an initial effort of this kind, see U.S. Congress, Office of Technology Assessment, *The Quality of Medical Care: Information for Consumers* (Washington, D.C.: U.S. Government Printing Office, 1988). The pros and cons of retrenching on mandatory tort liability in favor of more voluntary contractual arrangements will be explored in the next chapter.

4. For the most comprehensive recent catalogue of arguments against the assumed safety effects of tort law, see Stephen D. Sugarman, *Doing Away with Personal Injury Law: New Compensation Mechanisms for Victims, Consumers, and Business* 3–34 (New York: Quorum Books, 1989).

5. See the latter part of Chapter 3.

6. This point is emphasized by Peter Huber in his book *Liability: The Legal Revolution and Its Consequences* (New York: Basic Books, 1988) and in his earlier writing.

7. For a recent description and careful appraisal of the methodology and results of this body of research, see Donald Dewees and Michael Trebilcock, "The Efficacy of the Tort System: A Review of the Empirical Evidence" 20–34 (American Law Institute Working Paper, 1989).

8. For a representative statement of this conventional view, see Versteeg v. Mowery, 435 P.2d 540 (Wash. 1967). Cases that explicitly exculpate a doctor who adheres to the views of a "respectable minority" of practitioners, even within specific branches of allopathic medicine, include Chumbler v. McClure, 505 F.2d 489 (6th Cir. 1974); Borja v. Phoenix General Hospital, Inc., 727 P.2d 355 (Ariz. App. 1986); and Estate of Smith v. Lerner, 387 N.W.2d 576 (Iowa 1986).

9. See, for example, Hood v. Phillips, 554 S.W.2d 160 (Tex. 1977).

10. See *Harvard Study,* Chapter 7.

11. Such tort incentives will be even more forceful to the extent that the tort system assesses punitive damages against the defendant, i.e., makes an award against the doctor or hospital that is substantially higher than the losses suffered by the patient. Indeed, recent economic analysis of punitive damages seeks to justify these awards as a mechanism for overcoming the inevitable shortfall in litigation and thus raising the expected tort sanction to the optimal level; see Jason S. Johnston, "Punitive Liability: A New Paradigm of Efficiency in Tort Law," 87 *Columbia Law Review* 1385 (1987); and Robert D. Cooter, "Punitive Damages for Deterrence: When and How Much?" 40 *Alabama Law Review* 1143 (1989). Sizable punitive awards have been rendered in recent malpractice cases: Mercy

Hospital of Laredo v. Rios, 776 S.W.2d 626 (Tex. App. 1987) (jury award of $1 million in punitive damages upheld, for gross negligence of hospital nurses resulting in suffocation death of infant); Birchfield v. Texarkana Memorial Hospital, 747 S.W.2d 361 (Tex. 1987) (jury award of $1.2 million in punitive damages for baby born blind due to defective oxygen equipment, upheld by Texas Supreme Court and then trebled under state's consumer protection legislation); and Adams v. Murakami, 268 Cal. Rptr. 467 (Ct. App. 1990) (upholding jury award of $750,000 in punitive damages against a psychiatrist whose neglect of an institutionalized mental patient led eventually to the patient's giving birth to a severely retarded child). But such awards are sufficiently rare in the medical context that I have not undertaken a detailed treatment of them in this book. For my own views about how standards of punitive damage should be revised in tort law generally (a matter of pressing concern for the manufacturers of prescription drugs and other products used in the health care sector), see Chapter 22 of the American Law Institute, *Compensation and Liability for Product and Process Injuries: Proposed Final Report*, vol. 2 (Philadelphia: ALI, 1991).

12. See *Harvard Study*. On the one hand, the perceived risk of suit per 100 doctors was twice the actual risk in New York State, and the perceived risk of a suit arising out of a negligent injury was 60 percent, at least ten times the true risk. On the other hand, the doctors surveyed had an accurate sense of the distribution of tort risk by region and by specialty, and those who had been sued at least once had a 60 percent greater estimate of the litigation risk than did those who had never been sued. See *Harvard Study*, Chapter 9, pp. 15–20.

13. See Danzon, *Medical Malpractice*, pp. 141–143. Ironically, the greater concern expressed recently about the tort system is that the standard of medical custom is an obstacle to recent government and private efforts to contain the nation's soaring health care costs: see, e.g., E. Haavi Morreim, "Cost Containment and the Standard of Medical Care," 75 *California Law Review* 1719 (1987).

14. My views on this issue have been greatly influenced by Mark F. Grady, "Why Are People Negligent? Technology, Nondurable Precautions, and the Medical Malpractice Explosion," 82 *Northwestern University Law Review* 293 (1988).

15. In discussions about the relationship between tort law and personal carelessness, I often refer to a phenomenon reported in a U.S. Department of Transportation Automobile Insurance and Compensation study, *Driver Behavior and Accident Involvement: Implications for Tort Liability* 176–181 (Washington, D.C.: U.S. Government Printing Office, 1970). This report describes empirical research done in 1962 on the driving performance of adult white male drivers in Washington, D.C. The drivers and their vehicles were followed and filmed for a couple of miles, and the drivers' performances were evaluated by police officers and traffic safety experts. In just five minutes of urban driving, the drivers in the sample (which was biased toward presumably more cautious middle-aged,

white-collar professionals) committed an average of *nine* driving errors of at least four different types; the vast majority of the drivers fell in the range of six to fifteen errors of two to five types. But when the drivers' accident records from police and insurance files were checked against this test experience, there was little difference between the error rates of drivers who had had no accidents over the previous several years and those who had had two or more accidents. Furthermore, there was no significant difference in error rate between drivers who had previously been involved in a culpable accident versus a nonculpable accident.

The general point is that all drivers are prone to human errors such as speeding, changing lanes without signaling, following the car in front too closely, and turning improperly. Fortunately all but a small proportion of these errors take place in situations in which no accident results. Contrast the slips and mistakes of a neurosurgeon or an obstetrician, which transpire in a much less forgiving environment in which irreversible harm can and does occur, producing major tort claims as a consequence. This difference in risk potential also explains the huge disparity in claims and insurance costs of neurosurgeons and obstetricians versus those of internists and pediatricians.

16. The Report of the Board of Trustees of the American Medical Association, *Study of Professional Liability Costs* (Chicago: AMA, 1983), indicates that even after the substantial increases in malpractice premiums of the early seventies, fewer than 3 percent of doctors "go bare" in the sense of being entirely uninsured, and that the bulk of these are in low-risk categories such as general practice. A number of jurisdictions—Florida, Pennsylvania, and New York, for example—have included in their recent malpractice reform legislation a requirement that doctors carry substantial insurance coverage as a condition of practice (see F. Townsend Hawkes, "The Second Reformation: Florida's Medical Malpractice Law," 13 *Florida State University Law Review* 747, 781–783 [1985]), as many states had done earlier for the operation of motor vehicles. Whatever practical difference such laws may make, they are clear legal corroboration of the assertion that malpractice litigation now functions as the port of entry into a program of mandatory disability insurance.

17. The most extensive analytical treatment of the function of liability insurance in the tort regime and the effect it may or may not have on safety incentives provided by tort law, is Steven Shavell, *Economic Analysis of Accident Law* 186–261 (Cambridge, Mass.: Harvard University Press, 1987). Danzon, *Medical Malpractice*, pp. 118–136, also provides an illuminating account of the relationship between insurance and prevention, with reference specifically to medical accidents and liability.

18. See Danzon, *Medical Malpractice*, pp. 129–130; Bell, "Legislative Intrusions," pp. 954–956; and Linda Darling, "The Applicability of Experience Rating to Medical Malpractice Insurance," 38 *Case Western Reserve Law Review* 255 (1987).

19. See Darling, "The Applicability of Experience Rating," for a detailed description of the New York plan and a brief sketch of the Massachusetts

legislation. The Massachusetts law, as well as various proposals for implementing experience rating in that state, are analyzed in the decision of the hearing officer on behalf of the Commissioner of Insurance, *Opinions, Findings, and Decision on Medical Malpractice Rates for Physicians and Surgeons* 136–151 (1987).

20. I discuss the potential uses of experience rating in Canadian workers' compensation in Paul C. Weiler, *Protecting the Worker from Disability: Challenges for the Eighties* 110–128 (Toronto: Government of Ontario, 1983). The specific features and operation of the current experience rating program in American workers' compensation, designed by the National Council of Compensation Insurers (NCCI), are described in Richard B. Victor, *Workers' Compensation and Workplace Safety: The Nature of Employer Financial Incentives* (Santa Monica, Calif.: RAND Institute for Civil Justice, 1982). The NCCI program begins to take account of an individual firm's experience when the firm pays a workers' compensation premium of at least $2,500, a point that even relatively small employers in the more dangerous industries can reach. However, at that lower level the experience rating formula makes only a minor adjustment in the employer's premium: see NCCI, *ABCs of Revised Experience Rating* (New York: NCCI, 1989).

21. Recall the findings in the study done for the U.S. Department of Transportation on the high incidence of driving errors committed by ordinary, reasonably safe drivers (see note 15).

22. See John E. Rolph, "Some Statistical Evidence on Merit Rating in Medical Malpractice Insurance," 48 *Journal of Risk and Insurance* 247 (1981); Blaine F. Nye and Alfred E. Hofflander, "Experience Rating in Medical Professional Liability Insurance," 55 *Journal of Risk and Insurance* 150 (1988); and Frank A. Sloan, Paula M. Mergenhagen, W. Bradley Burfield, Randall R. Bovbjerg, and Mahmud Hassan, "Medical Malpractice Experience of Physicians: Predictable or Haphazard?" 262 *Journal of American Medical Assocation* 3291 (1989). The last study had available the most comprehensive data base—all malpractice claims lodged in Florida between 1975 and 1988—and used physician claims experience for incidents occuring between 1975 and 1980 to predict the distribution of claims from incidents in the years 1981–1983.

23. See Frank A. Sloan et al., "Malpractice Experience," Table 5.

24. A revealing demonstration of this appears in a recent study by Frederick W. Cheney, Karen Posner, Robert A. Caplan, and Richard J. Ward, "Standard of Care and Anesthesia Liability," 261 *Journal of American Medical Association* 1599 (1989). A team of topflight anesthesiologists carefully reviewed a large national sample of insurance files for claims against practitioners of their specialty in order to determine independently whether substandard care had been provided to the claimant patients. In cases in which substandard care had occurred and caused an injury, 82 percent of the patients received some liability payment; the percentage was even greater for cases in which there was a permanent disabling injury. But payment was also made in 42 percent of the cases

in which the care appeared to have been appropriate. That finding did *not* imply that the tort system was making inaccurate judgments about these cases: the average size of payment for disabling injuries in the appropriate-care cases was only one-fifth of what it was for similar injuries caused by substandard care. The carriers evidently found it sensible to settle even the dubious claims for a modest amount of money rather than pay the legal expenses and court the risks of a jury trial. But from the point of view of the anesthesiologists who were involved in these cases, to use the tactical settlements as a basis for surcharges on their insurance premiums for the future simply added further insult to the injury of having had to face and defend these lawsuits in the past. See also the recent study by Henry S. Farber and Michelle J. White, "Medical Malpractice: An Empirical Examination of the Litigation Process" (unpublished, 1990), which documents essentially the same pattern of litigation results from 300 malpractice claims of all types filed against a single medical center over a decade.

25. The Florida Academic Task Force for Review of the Insurance and Tort Systems reviewed the distribution of all past malpractice claims in that state from 1975 through 1986 (see Table 35 of its *Preliminary Fact-Finding Report on Medical Malpractice* 141 [Gainesville, Fla.: 1987]). To the question, how many doctors were successfully sued six or more times during that period—that is, at a rate of at least one paid claim every two years—the answer is only 24 doctors (about 0.1 percent of the over 20,000 total of Florida practitioners), and these doctors produced only 0.3 percent of total paid claims and 2.3 percent of total payments.

26. In effect, the insurer says to doctors, "If you are careless now and your carelessness produces both an injury and a lawsuit, and if the lawsuit is one of a defined number of such claims within a five-year period, then once all these claims are resolved eight to ten years later, you will be subject to a surcharge on your malpractice premium." That kind of premium threat is far less immediate than what most of us face under motor vehicle insurance, for example. For a revealing demonstration in a different context of how the time discount factor erodes the financial threat of even fully experience-rated liability insurance, see Donald N. Dewees, "Economic Incentives for Controlling Industrial Disease: The Asbestos Case," 15 *Journal of Legal Studies* 289 (1986).

27. For an illuminating description and analysis of these carriers, see William B. Schwartz and Daniel N. Mendelson, "The Role of Physician-Owned Insurance Companies in the Detection and Deterrence of Negligence," 262 *Journal of American Medical Association* 1342 (1989). The Massachusetts Medical Society did, in fact, secure an experience-rating system modified along these more qualitative lines, pursuant to legislative amendments that came into effect in 1990; see Massachusetts General Laws, Chapter 175A, Section 5C.

28. Termination of coverage can be a substantial penalty for doctors, for reasons described in William B. Schwartz and Daniel N. Mendelson, "Physicians Who Have Lost Their Malpractice Insurance," 262 *Journal of Amer-*

ican Medical Association 1335 (1989). Consequently this penalty is applied to only the most accident-prone doctors. However, as the statistics in note 24 demonstrate, these "bad apples" produce only a tiny fraction of tort claims and payments.

29. Although the payoff might seem to be significantly greater from varying the premiums paid by doctors in the higher-risk categories of medical malpractice (urban obstetricians and neurosurgeons, for example), a large portion of their high premium rates are due to the magnitude of damage awards and the small size of the insurance pool, factors that do not reflect the level of care of the doctors concerned. Stronger constraints would therefore have to be placed on the experience rating formula in these risk categories to keep them actuarially sound and fair to the physicians practicing in those specialties.

30. See AMA, *Study of Professional Liability Costs*, which reports that physicians with a claim against them averaged three days in depositions, court appearances, and meetings with attorneys, and also that of this group one in eight hired his own lawyer in addition to the one provided by the insurer. The Harvard study found a somewhat greater time loss, the modal period being three to five days and the average time lost slightly over five days; see *Harvard Study*, Table 9.9.

31. Further elaboration of this point appears in Mark Grady, "Why Are People Negligent?"; and in Howard A. Latin, "Problem-Solving Behavior and Theories of Tort Liability," 73 *California Law Review* 677 (1985).

32. See John H. Eichhorn, Jeffrey B. Cooper, David J. Cullen, Ward R. Maier, James H. Philip, and Robert G. Seeman, "Standards for Patient Monitoring during Anesthesia at Harvard Medical School," 256 *Journal of American Medical Association* 1017 (1986), authored by anesthesiologists at the nine Harvard teaching hospitals. They had been consulted by the Risk Management Foundation of Harvard's "captive" insurance carrier, which was concerned about the incidence and high costs of anesthesia-related accidents (composing 4 percent of total malpractice claims and 8 percent of total payments). As a result, the group developed a set of standards and procedures for closer monitoring of patients under anesthesia, designed to prevent loss of oxygen and other typical mishaps in that setting. Although the new procedures required additional personnel and equipment, the estimated extra cost was only $5 per anesthesia case, a small fraction of Harvard's "premium" of $53 per case. However, it is highly unlikely that this set of precautions (which has been endorsed by the American Society of Anesthesiologists) would have emerged from individual physicians' reflections on their own clinical experience, even if the doctors were strongly motivated to avoid personal tort liability. The process required, instead, a collective effort by an organization that was only indirectly governed by malpractice law.

33. For a detailed review of these studies, see Dewees and Trebilcock, *Efficacy of the Tort System*.

34. Tort law purports not simply to secure the appropriate level of precautions in medical treatment, but also to influence other aspects of the

physicican-patient relationship—in particular by requiring doctors to make their patients fully aware of information that is reasonably necessary for meaningful consent to a proposed course of treatment. This would appear to be an ideal area in which the law could significantly influence doctor behavior. The legal doctrine of informed consent is relatively new, it applies across the entire spectrum of medical practice, it is both controversial and well known, and doctors do consciously decide to adopt a standard routine for handling the issue with their patients. Nevertheless, a recent survey of empirical research on the general topic of informed consent, Alan Meisel and Loren H. Roth, "Toward an Informed Discussion of Informed Consent: A Review and Critique of the Empirical Studies," 25 *Arizona Law Review* 265 (1983), finds little corroboration of the expectation that tort law would make a real difference in this area of physician behavior (pp. 273–274).

35. See Jerry Wiley, "The Impact of Judical Decisions on Professional Conduct: An Empirical Study," 55 *Southern California Law Review* 345 (1981).

36. See Daniel J. Givelber, William J. Bowers, and Carolyn L. Blitch, "*Tarasoff*, Myth and Reality: An Empirical Study of Private Law in Action," 1984 *Wisconsin Law Review* 443. The actual decision is Tarasoff v. Regents of the University of California, 551 P.2d 334 (1976), which replaced an earlier California Supreme Court ruling in the same case, reported under the same name at 529 P.2d 553 (1974).

37. To a considerable extent, the difference in their conclusions was due to the respective researchers' contrasting views about the significance of the fact that doctors in *other* states also altered their behavior in the judicially prescribed direction (compare Wiley, "Impact of Judicial Decisions," 377–380, with Givelber et al., "*Tarasoff*," 489–490). Did that prove that the legal pronouncements of these state supreme courts were even more powerful because of their external impact? Or that court rulings were unnecessary to induce changes in behavior occurring in jurisdictions not bound by the court's edicts? It is interesting to note that any impact of *Tarasoff* came from only the first ruling, requiring a warning to the victim: this was the only pattern observable in the questionnaire responses, not the broader range of "reasonable" measures ordained by the supposedly authoritative second *Tarasoff* ruling.

38. Apparently OSHA has influenced employers to make a substantial investment in safety and health: see Ann P. Bartel and Lacy Glenn Thomas, "Direct and Indirect Effects of Regulation: A New Look at OSHA's Impact," 28 *Journal of Law and Economics* 1 (1985); and Ann P. Bartel and Lacy Glenn Thomas, "The Costs and Benefits of OSHA-Induced Investments in Employee Safety and Health," in John D. Worrall and David Appel, eds., *Workers' Compensation Benefits: Adequacy, Equity, and Efficiency* 41 (Ithaca, N.Y.: ILR Press, Cornell University, 1985).

39. W. Kip Viscusi, "The Impact of Occupational Safety and Health Regulation, 1973–1983," 17 *Rand Journal of Economics* 567 (1986), the only study of the longer-term effects of OSHA over the first decade of its existence, found that enforcement of the law produced a net reduction of 5 to 6

percent in total workdays lost due to injuries, with a somewhat stronger effect on more severe injuries. Bartel and Thomas, "Costs and Benefits of OSHA-Induced Investments," calculated that a doubling of the OSHA inspection rate would produce 25 percent more compliance with the law and 90 percent greater employer investment in safety and health, but only 2 percent fewer workdays lost due to injury. Leon S. Robertson and J. Philip Keeve, "Worker Injuries: The Effects of Workers' Compensation and OSHA Inspections," 8 *Journal of Health Politics, Policy, and Law* 581 (1983), are slightly more optimistic about the efficacy of workplace safety regulation. When they controlled for the coincident increases in workers' compensation benefits in the late seventies that induced the reporting of more "subjective" injuries such as back cases, the net effect of OSHA on the more objectively demonstrable lacerations and fractures was stronger. But the point remains that according to the evidence available so far, the actual safety gain from additional legally mandated precautions in the workplace is marginal. Some of the reasons why this is so are discussed in detail in Weiler, *Workplace Injuries*, pp. 82–95.

40. The most recent example of this genre is the two-volume report of the Institute of Medicine, Victoria P. Rostow and Roger J. Bulger, eds., *Medical Professional Liability and the Delivery of Obstetrical Care* (Washington, D.C.: National Academy Press, 1989).

41. See American Medical Association Special Task Force on Professional Liability and Insurance, *Professional Liability in the '80s* 16 (Chicago: October 1984; November 1984; and March 1985).

42. See Roger A. Reynolds, John A. Rizzo, and Martin L. Gonzalez, "The Cost of Medical Professional Liability," 257 *Journal of American Medical Association* 2776 (1987). This study was conducted using two distinct methodologies. The first was based on an AMA survey of a broad and representative sample of its members. The doctors were asked whether and to what extent they had responded to concerns about tort liability by changing their patterns of practice from 1983 to 1984 in four different respects—increased record keeping, more tests and procedures, more follow-up visits, and more time spent with the patient during the visit. The additional financial costs of the practice changes in that year were then totaled (an estimated $4,600 for the average physician) and compared to the increased malpractice premium for that year (on average, $1,300 per physician). The ratio of the 1983–84 changes in practice costs to premium increases was then applied to the absolute level of physician malpractice premiums in 1984 ($3 billion) to produce an estimate of $10.6 billion as the total cost of defensive medical practices.

The study's second methodological approach was to calculate the observed relationship between differences in malpractice premiums paid by the same doctor sample (premiums serving as a proxy for the differential risk of litigation), and the variation in use of and charges for a wide variety of standardized medical procedures in the specialties represente.¹ by the doctors. Again, the estimates were made for the 1983–84 changes in price and utilization, as well as for the absolute levels of the two factors. Once the malpractice premium effect had been established for both price and utilization, the two factors could be recalculated on the assumption that liability was fixed at zero. The difference between the actual cost and the notional cost of price times utilization was assumed to be the defensive component of expenditures on this group of procedures. The same ratio was then applied to all expenditures on physician services in that year to produce an estimated $9.1 billion cost of defensive medicine.

Regardless of the merits of either of these methodologies, it is intriguing that the figures they generate are surprisingly close. And the fact that the second number ($9.1 billion) is somewhat lower than the first ($10.6 billion) offers further corroboration of the findings, because the second methodology incorporates the drop in the use of medical services from the price effect of the initial higher cost of defensive medicine.

43. For earlier critiques of this notion, see Nathan Hershey, "The Defensive Practice of Medicine: Myth or Reality," *Milbank Memorial Fund Quarterly* 131 (January 1972); Laurence R. Tancredi and Jeremiah A. Barondess, "The Problem of Defensive Medicine," 200 *Science* 879 (1978); Glen O. Robinson, "Rethinking the Allocation of Medical Malpractice Risk between Patients and Providers," 49 *Law and Contemporary Problems* 173, 177–180 (1986); and Stephen Zuckerman, Christopher F. Koller, and Randall R. Bovbjerg, "Information on Malpractice: A Review of Empirical Research on Major Policy Issues," 49 *Law and Contemporary Problems* 85, 107–109 (1986).

44. For a careful review of these surveys, see Deborah Lewis-Idema, "Medical Professional Liability and Access to Obstetrical Care: Is There a Crisis?" in Institute of Medicine, *Medical Professional Liability*, II, 78.

45. See Dana Hughes, Sara Rosenbaum, David Smith, and Cynthia Fader, ·"Obstetrical Care for Low-Income Women: The Effects of Medical Malpractice on Community Health Centers," in Institute of Medicine, *Medical Professional Liability*, II, 59; and Roger A. Rosenblatt and Craig L. Wright, "Rising Malpractice Premiums and Obstetric Practice Patterns: The Impact on Family Physicians in Washington State," 146 *Western Journal of Medicine* 246 (1987).

46. Thus, the study by Sloan et al., "Malpractice Experience," found that it was the doctors who had never been sued from 1975 through 1980 who were more likely to report retiring from or reducing their practice or moving out of state during the period 1981–1983—not the doctors who had been sued a little, and least of all the doctors who had been sued a lot in the earlier period.

47. A telling illustration of this problem was provided in testimony in the Hearings before the Subcommittee on Health and Environment of the Committee on Energy and Commerce, House of Representatives, 99th Congress, *Medical Malpractice* 7–8 (1986). A rural North Carolina clinic with seven doctors was engaged primarily in family practice. Its mal-

practice premiums for this work amounted to $28,000 a year. As soon as the clinic performed a single obstetrical delivery, its annual insurance premiums jumped to $140,000.

48. See Institute of Medicine, *Medical Professional Liability*, I, Table 4.2, pp. 61–62.

49. Again, it is noteworthy that although poor and minority patients bear the brunt of this side effect of the malpractice regime, they tend to sue physicians less, not more frequently: see Carol S. Weisman, Martha Ann Teitelbaum, and Laura L. Morlock, "Malpractice Claims Experience Associated with Fertility-Control Services among Young Obstetrician-Gynecologists," 26 *Medical Care* 298, 304 (1988).

50. See Morreim, "Cost Containment," and Robert C. Macaulay, Jr., "Health Care Cost Containment and Medical Malpractice: On a Collision Course," 21 *Suffolk University Law Review* 91 (1986).

51. For a helpful and detailed analysis of this example, see Stephen B. Thacker, "The Impact of Technology Assessment and Medical Malpractice on the Diffusion of Medical Technologies: The Case of Electronic Fetal Monitoring," in Institute of Medicine, *Medical Professional Liability*, II, 9. Since then a study has appeared that found no long-term benefits from electronic monitoring in the neurologic development of prematurely born babies: Kirkwood K. Shy, David A. Luthy, Forrest C. Bennett, Michael Whitfield, Eric B. Larson, Gerald von Belle, James P. Hughes, Judith A. Wilson, and Morton A. Stenchever, "Effects of Electronic Fetal-Heart-Rate Monitoring, as Compared with Periodic Auscultation, on the Neurologic Development of Premature Infants," 322 *New England Journal of Medicine* 588 (1990); see also the follow-up commentary by Roger Freeman, "Intrapartum Fetal Monitoring—A Disappointing Story," 322 *New England Journal of Medicine* 624 (1990).

52. This is the argument of Robinson, "Allocation of Medical Malpractice Risk."

53. See, e.g., Benjamin P. Sachs, "Is the Rising Rate of Cesarean Sections a Result of More Defensive Medicine?" in Institute of Medicine, *Medical Professional Liability*, II, 27–40, 37–38. Sachs concludes by emphatically agreeing with that position, notwithstanding the numerous qualifications that seem evident in the comparative data he presents in the body of his paper.

54. For a comprehensive picture of cesarean trends in the United States and other countries, see Paul J. Placek and Selma M. Taffel, "Recent Patterns in Cesarean Delivery in the United States," 15 *Obstetrics and Gynecology Clinics of North America* 607 (1988); and Francis C. Watson, Paul J. Placek, and Selma M. Taffel, "Comparison of National Cesarean Section Rates," 316 *New England Journal of Medicine* 386–389 (1987).

55. In particular, AMA survey data that was the basis for the major empirical study by Reynolds et al., "The Cost of Medical Professional Liability," simply asked doctors whether they were doing *more* of a variety of things—procedures, tests, visits, and record keeping—in response to

the growth in malpractice claims. The doctors were *not* asked whether any part of their altered practice patterns might actually be good for their patients.

56. A detailed description of the theory and initial results of our econometric analysis of malpractice deterrence can be found in Chapter 10 of the Harvard study. In the text I present the key findings of our reanalysis of this issue in the summer of 1990. A paper setting out scientifically the revised methodology and conclusions will appear in an economics journal in 1991.

57. See Reynolds et al., "The Cost of Medical Professional Liability."

5. The Alternative of No-Liability through Contract

1. Widespread contract waiver of doctors' *tort* liability need not imply the absence of any *legal* incentive for safe treatment of patients, even abstracting from the ethical and market incentives felt by doctors. The model of freedom of contract to reduce the burdens of tort litigation could, for example, be combined with a much more aggressive program of medical licensing, review, discipline, and license revocation in order to reduce the incidence of substandard medical care.

2. Tunkl v. Regents of the University of California, 383 P.2d 441 (Cal. 1963). The *Tunkl* case had certain unusual features. The plaintiff was a nonpaying charity patient who had signed a release while in pain, under sedation, and in need of immediate treatment at the hospital. In addition, California had a statutory provision that purported to specify the kinds of exculpatory provisions that would be legally unenforceable. However, the California Supreme Court used the *Tunkl* case as the occasion to sketch an array of policy factors that placed nonenforcement of contract waivers from malpractice liability generally in the "public interest." This broader judicial treatment of the problem has been a major influence on the subsequent course of this branch of the law, not only in California, but also in other jurisdictions without a similar statute.

3. See, for example, Emory University v. Porubiansky, 282 S.E.2d 903 (Ga. 1981) (a lower-cost university dental clinic). In Smith v. Hospital Authority of Walker, Dade and Catoosa Counties, 287 S.E.2d 99 (Ga. App. 1981), the Georgia Supreme Court held that its *Emory University* decision applied to the situation of a blood donor who, rather than needing treatment, was actually conferring a benefit on the hospital; therefore he presumably had some bargaining power about the terms of his donation. Among the cases in other jurisdictions that have uniformly struck down waivers of tort liability in the health care context are Meiman v. Rehabilitation Center, Inc., 444 S.W.2d 78 (Ky. App. 1969); Olson v. Molzen, 558 S.W.2d 429 (Tenn. 1977); and Tatham v. Hoke, 469 F.Supp. 914 (W.D.N.C. 1979). The last case is the only one I have found that involves a waiver other than a total waiver of all tort liability. In *Tatham* an abortion clinic simply imposed a $15,000 ceiling on its maximum liability.

4. The key decision was Henningsen v. Bloomfield Motors, Inc., 161 A.2d 69 (N.J. 1960), in which the New Jersey Supreme Court initially established strict liability for the benefit of consumers injured by defective products (a motor vehicle in this case), then held that such a warranty against personal injury could not be limited or waived by the manufacturer or dealer.

5. The significance of the judicial perception of the special human need for medical care, with its corollary of the presumed inability of patients to resist the imposition of blanket waivers of tort liability, becomes clearer by contrast with the way the courts tend to uphold such contract releases when the service in question seems to be a discretionary luxury (even if it is a risky one). See, e.g., Ciofalo v. Vic Tanney Gyms, Inc., 177 N.E.2d 925 (N.Y. 1961) (gym facility); Jones v. Dressel, 623 P.2d 370 (Colo. 1981) (sky-diving operation); Schlobohm v. Spa Petite, Inc., 326 N.W.2d 920 (Minn. 1982) (health spa); and McAtee v. Newhall Land and Farming, 216 Cal. Reptr. 465 (Cal. 1985) (motorcycle racing). Compare Wagenblast v. Odessa School District No. 105-157-166J, 758 P.2d 968 (Wash. 1988), holding that a public school system could not rely on waivers of liability for negligence as a condition of participation in interscholastic athletics.

6. The major scholarly piece to reintroduce the contract option to the malpractice debate in the mid-seventies was Richard A. Epstein, "Medical Malpractice: The Case for Contract," 1976 *American Bar Foundation Research Journal* 87. Epstein reiterated the core of his argument in "Medical Malpractice: Its Cause and Cure," in Simon Rottenberg, ed., *The Economics of Medical Malpractice* 245 (Washington, D.C.: American Enterprise Institute for Public Policy Research, 1978). In her general survey of the malpractice problem, Patricia M. Danzon, *Medical Malpractice: Theory, Evidence, and Public Policy* 209–213 (Cambridge, Mass.: Harvard University Press, 1985), also comments favorably (albeit with some reservations) on the potential value of contract as a vehicle for malpractice reform. But the most substantial and significant treatment of this idea in the eighties is the symposium edited by Randall R. Bovbjerg and Clark C. Havighurst, "Medical Malpractice: Can the Private Sector Find Relief?" 49 *Law and Contemporary Problems* 1 (1986). In that volume the important theoretical explorations of the possibilities of contract are Richard A. Epstein, "Medical Malpractice, Imperfect Information, and the Contractual Foundation for Medical Services," p. 201; Havighurst, "Private Reform of Tort-Law Dogma: Market Opportunities and Legal Obstacles," p. 143; and Glen O. Robinson, "Rethinking the Allocation of Medical Malpractice Risks between Patients and Providers," p. 173.

7. Intriguingly, although the general analysis by Epstein, Havighurst, and Robinson is clearly pertinent to this position, only Robinson, "Rethinking the Allocation of Medical Malpractice Risks," pp. 183ff., explicitly and systematically defends the possibility of no-tort liability through contractual agreement. Even he judges this option to be only intellectually supportable, not practically likely (see pp. 194 and 199). Havig-

hurst, "Private Reform of Tort-Law Dogma," pp. 52–53, is prepared to go no further than to elevate the trigger of physician liability from ordinary to gross negligence (see also Havighurst's other contribution to the symposium, "Altering the Applicable Standard of Care," p. 265). Richard Epstein has contemplated the possibility of no liability at all (in "Medical Malpractice: Its Cause and Cure," though not, so far as I could find, in his more extensive "Medical Malpractice: The Case for Contract"); however, in his latest exploration of this idea ("Medical Malpractice, Imperfect Information, and the Contractual Foundation for Medical Services"), Epstein concludes that imposing liability on doctors for failure to meet the customary practice standard is the most practical and efficient rule from the point of view of both tort doctrine and private contract (49 *Law and Contemporary Problems* 207).

8. For a description of some voluntary nineteenth-century precursors of mandatory workers' compensation for on-the-job injuries, see Richard A. Epstein, "The Historical Origins and Economic Structure of Workers' Compensation Law," 16 *Georgia Law Review* 775 (1982).

9. In Paul C. Weiler, *Governing the Workplace: The Future of Labor and Employment Law* 48–104 (Cambridge, Mass.: Harvard University Press, 1990), I discuss the implications of the almost universal prevalence of "at will" status for ordinary nonunion workers in America. The "at will" regime, produced by private employment contracts, has only recently come under the scrutiny of common law judges on account of a sharp upsurge in tort and quasi-tort litigation over wrongful dismissal. At several points in *Governing the Workplace,* I refer to insights about the virtues and vices of this new arrival on the employment litigation scene that judges might profitably draw from the world of medical malpractice.

10. Although I cannot cite any systematic scientific research to support this claim, the following personal anecdotal evidence amply supports that judgment. Recall the New York and California studies, which found that the risk of patient injury from hospitalization was about 1 in 25 cases, and that the risk of a negligently inflicted injury—in other words, a possible tort claim—was about 1 in 100. It was not until I began my research on medical malpractice and read the Mills California study that I had the slightest idea there was such a substantial risk of iatrogenic injury from medical treatment. Over the last several years I have frequently related these statistics in the classroom and in conversations with people interested in the malpractice question. Without exception, the reaction to the figures is astonishment that the risk of medical injury and the odds of malpractice litigation are of such an order of magnitude. This is admittedly a highly unscientific mode of research, but if I had to make an immediate commonsense policy judgment about the contract option, the safest assumption by far would be that American patients now have little idea of the significant likelihood that a tort will be committed in the course of their medical treatment.

11. Note in this example that the patient is an adult with full command of her faculties, and not in a medical emergency requiring immediate treat-

ment. Alter any one of these conditions and the pendulum swings even further toward the doctor's position on this issue.

12. By analogy, suppose that a worker would like to be hired now by a firm but insists on retaining the right to sue if he feels at some time in the future that he was unjustly fired. That worker would not likely get the job. As a result, *no* ordinary nonunion workers are currently able to insist on retaining the right to sue for wrongful dismissal in the future.

13. The argument that private contract will tilt away from any malpractice liability applies most strongly to the situation of the individual patient who seeks treatment from a fee-for-service doctor or hospital. A prominent theme in the recent scholarly effort to rehabilitate freedom of contract in the context of medical risks and liability (see the references cited in note 6 and the other contributions to the symposium in 49 *Law and Contemporary Problems*) is the important changes taking place in the organization of health care. Increasing numbers of patients are subscribing to institutions such as HMO's well before they actually need treatment, at a time when they may be prepared to shop around for the best available terms. Furthermore, much of this shopping is done for them by their employer (whether or not the workplace is unionized). Employers directly finance most health care insurance and regularly deal with groups or organizations of doctors to specify the terms on which health care will be provided to the work force. The assumption is that these developments on both the supply and demand sides of the medical marketplace have given patients the institutional perspective and leverage necessary to secure and select from a variety of liability arrangements that provide a better match for the diverse attitudes toward risk among the patient population.

Unquestionably, the transformation in the organization of modern medicine and the development of a much wider range of choices for consumers among competing providers has important implications for public policy toward medical accidents. For several reasons, though, I doubt that these changes will make much difference in the validity of my conclusion that unlimited freedom of contract tends to eliminate malpractice liability uniformly and across the board.

For one thing, the relationship between patient and individual fee-for-service doctor remains the major vehicle for the delivery of medical care; about 90 percent of practicing physicians still work in this mode (see American Medical Association Council Report, "Health Care in Transition: Consequences for Young Physicians," 256 *Journal of American Medical Association* 3384 [1986]), and this relationship generates nearly three-quarters of all malpractice claims (see *1984 Claims Closed Survey*).

Second, even in the case of HMO's and other organizations that employ doctors to supply medical services to subscribers, the intense interest of the physicians—major participants in the organizations' decision making—in avoiding the immediate prospect of litigation over the quality of their professional care would likely dominate the patients' interest in preserving a possible right to sue in the case of future medical accidents. Consequently the new, more competitive structure of the medical market would serve only to ensure that the cost savings produced by elimination of tort liability accrue to the benefit of the patient choosing between one provider and another. I recognize that these judgments are speculative, and that a brave new world of contract might turn out to be quite different from what I anticipate. But the fact is that there exists *no* past or present illustration of an HMO that has developed a more balanced alternative to the present tort system, so there is no example from which the risk-averse policymaker asked to grant *carte blanche* to private contractual innovation can draw any aid and comfort.

14. See Havighurst, "Private Reform of Tort Law Dogma," pp. 148–156; see also Clark C. Havighurst, "The Changing Locus of Decision Making in the Health Care System," 11 *Journal of Health Politics, Policy, and Law* 697 (1986), which puts this argument about malpractice law in the broader context of the trend from professional dominance to greater consumer control over health care decisions.

15. As I observed in Chapter 4, one feature of malpractice doctrine now being criticized from this perspective is the use of medical custom to define the standard of care. The typical legal critique of current deference to physicians' practice is that the medical profession may lag behind in adopting effective and feasible precautions, so courts should reserve the power to hold that customary medical standards are unreasonably *low*. The new economic critique, by contrast, contends that physicians' decisions about treatment take place in a setting in which patients typically have health insurance, which tends to produce customary standards of care that are too *high*—in the sense that the benefits of many tests and procedures are not worth the expense they entail when they are done routinely. See Danzon, *Medical Malpractice*, pp. 142–143. The implication is that when patients choose to utilize newer, more economical modes of care, they should also be permitted to contract with their providers to relieve them of the unduly burdensome requirements of traditional malpractice law.

16. To the same effect, see Patrick S. Atiyah, "Medical Malpractice and the Contract/Tort Boundary," 49 *Law and Contemporary Problems* 287 (1986). Atiyah argues that even though present-day American malpractice law is probably as burdensome as the contract proponents allege, this is not a reason for working through piecemeal and erratic contract negotiations, but rather a reason for seeking across-the-board legislative reform.

17. For explanations and defenses of this protectionist stance, each focusing on quite different problems and written from varying philosophical perspectives, see Duncan Kennedy, "Distributive and Paternalist Motives in Contract and Tort Law, with Special Reference to Compulsory Terms and Unequal Bargaining Power," 41 *Maryland Law Review* 563 (1982); Cass R. Sunstein, "Legal Interference with Private Preferences," 53 *University of Chicago Law Review* 1129 (1986); and Thomas H. Jackson, "The Fresh-Start Policy in Bankruptcy Law," 98 *Harvard Law Review* 1393

(1985). Both Sunstein, pp. 1166–1169, and Jackson, pp. 1410–1414, draw on a body of cognitive psychology research that provides some empirical footing for the proposition that people tend systematically to underestimate the incidence and significance of future accidents that may occur only rarely but that inflict severe injuries when they do. Robinson, "Rethinking the Allocation of Medical Malpractice Risks," pp. 188–193, also reviews this literature but concludes that it does not support the judicial antipathy in *Tunkl et al.* to patient waivers of malpractice liability. He argues that we have no reason to suppose that such cognitive biases will affect doctors any less than patients, and that in any event either or both parties might as easily overestimate as underestimate the true risks (leading people to buy too much rather than too little protection). My analysis in this section differs from Robinson's in underlining the fact that the doctor's concern is not the risk of future accidents but the immediate avoidance of the prospect of tort suits, about which he has a present awareness and intense aversion. The patient, by contrast, is asked to trade away a relatively remote option to sue his current doctor, an option whose potential use he is likely to underestimate (see note 10), and about which he is likely to feel ambivalent in any event. I suggested earlier that this sharp tilt in the incentives for both sides of this relationship would produce a systematic pattern of no malpractice liability if private contract were given full sway. The articles cited in this note explain why public policymakers—legislators and judges—need feel no embarrassment about refusing to honor voluntary agreements produced by this peculiar mix of awareness and attitudes.

18. See generally Paul C. Weiler, *Legal Policy For Workplace Injuries*, note 24 in Chapter 1.

19. Indeed, in my book on *Governing the Workplace*, pp. 78–104, I draw upon the less than happy experience in medical malpractice and other tort litigation to express serious reservations about the recent upsurge of wrongful dismissal litigation in the employment sphere.

20. Most of these statutes were enacted in the mid-seventies. A useful review and tabular synopsis of their provisions can be found in Irving Ladimer and Joel Solomon, "Medical Malpractice Arbitration: Laws, Programs, Cases," 615 *Insurance Law Journal* 335 (1977). An insightful survey of the case law interpreting the legislation as well as arbitration contracts signed under it is provided by James A. Henderson, Jr., "Agreements Changing the Forum for Resolving Malpractice Claims," 49 *Law and Contemporary Problems* 243 (1986). The limited body of empirical research on the impact of malpractice arbitration is summarized in Stephen Zuckerman, Christopher F. Koller, and Randall R. Bovbjerg, "Information on Malpractice: A Review of Empirical Research on Major Policy Issues," 49 *Law and Contemporary Problems* 85, 103–106 (1986).

21. The key cases are Doyle v. Giuliucci, 401 P.2d 1 (Cal. 1965); and Madden v. Kaiser Foundation Hospitals, 552 P.2d 1178 (Cal. 1976). California was the state in which malpractice arbitration began back around 1930, in a prepaid subscriber health system; the state is still the greatest source of

experience with this alternative forum. The other state that frequently utilizes medical arbitration is Michigan. After a decade of judicial struggle over its 1975 legislation, the Michigan Supreme Court upheld the validity of a statute that authorized contract waivers of the constitutional right to a jury trial in this context: see Morris v. Metriyakool, 344 N.W.2d 736 (Mich. 1984); see also Mary Bedikian, "Medical Malpractice Arbitration Act: Michigan's Experience with Arbitration," 10 *American Journal of Law and Medicine* 287 (1984) (reviewing the Michigan statute and the extensive case law that it provoked).

22. Indeed, the plaintiff in *Madden* was a state employee who in 1965 had enrolled in the defendant's medical care plan as one of the options paid for by her government employer. The arrangement for arbitration was not inserted in the plan until 1971, on the basis of negotiations between the state government and the Kaiser Foundation. Similarly, the plaintiff in *Doyle* was a minor whose parents were deemed to have validly waived their child's right to sue in court by participating in a group health insurance contract for the family. See also McKinstry v. Valley Obstetrics-Gynecology Clinic, 405 N.W.2d 88 (Mich. 1987), in which the expectant mother's waiver of the fetus's right to a jury trial was upheld. By contrast, in Beynon v. Garden Grove Medical Group, 161 Cal. Reptr. 146 (App. 1980), an adult subscriber was relieved from an arbitration clause that gave the doctor but not the patient the right to reject an unfavorable award and resubmit the case to a second arbitration panel, to be composed entirely of doctors. Clearly, the difference in the judicial verdict turned not on the quality of the voluntary consent but rather on the quality of adjudicative justice reflected in the respective arrangements.

23. See Irving Ladimer, Joel C. Solomon, and Michael Mulvihill, "Experience in Medical Malpractice Arbitration," 2 *Journal of Legal Medicine* 433 (1981). This study compared the experience in all cases referred to arbitration in Southern California from 1971 to 1981 with a matched sample of Southern California cases from the survey of NAIC closed claims from 1975 to 1978. The researchers were therefore able to control for the type of patient, nature of treatment and injury, and the type and number of defendants in order to isolate the differences made by the forum itself. At that time at least, the differences were not large in terms of either process or outcome.

24. A similar pattern is discernible in the more aggregated results of Danzon's econometric analysis; see Patricia M. Danzon, "The Frequency and Severity of Medical Malpractice Claims: New Evidence," 49 *Law and Contemporary Problems* 57, 77 (1986). She found that states which passed legislation that specifically permitted agreements for the voluntary arbitration of malpractice cases experienced 60 percent greater frequency of claims but 20 percent lower severity (in the larger group of claims) than would have been expected without such legislation. Actually, as Danzon herself concedes about her frequency finding, neither of these numbers can possibly be close to the real effects, because arbitration is used so rarely. It was employed in only 0.03 percent of the cases in the NAIC

survey of closed claims for 1975–1978, and there is no evidence of a marked increase since then. See Zuckerman, Koller, and Bovbjerg, "Information on Malpractice," p. 104, n. 4. Even if there were huge differences in the results in cases that actually went to arbitration (which Ladimer and Solomon, "Malpractice Arbitration," did *not* find), this would have had only a marginal impact on the results in the state's entire roster of malpractice cases.

25. At the same time, it is important to retain a healthy degree of skepticism about prescriptions of arbitration as a powerful antidote for the ailments of malpractice litigation. Legislators and judges have never been prepared to give *carte blanche* to arbitration of medical negligence cases. Instead, a typical statute would allow the patient a period in which to revoke the initial agreement to arbitrate (usually thirty to sixty days following the execution of the waiver or discharge from the hospital); a number of states (such as Michigan and California, though not for HMO's) prohibit the providers' making such patient agreements a condition to treatment. Even if the patient initially agrees and does not revoke the agreement within the prescribed time, the courts will meticulously scrutinize the circumstances of the original signing to ensure that the waiver of the patient's right to a jury trial was fully informed and voluntary (see Henderson, "Agreements Changing the Forum," on the California jurisprudence, and Bedikian, "Michigan's Experience with Arbitration," on Michigan). Such judicial practice has considerably undercut the possible gains from arbitration as an expeditious and economical procedure, and accounts at least in part for the modest differences found by researchers comparing the results of medical arbitration with those of litigation.

It is useful to speculate about why this has occurred. Voluntary arbitration functions best when it is part of an ongoing relationship between organizations—between labor and management, for example, or between two commercial enterprises—in which each side recognizes that it has more to gain from preserving the process than from winning any individual dispute; see generally Julius G. Getman, "Labor Arbitration and Dispute Resolution," 88 *Yale Law Journal* 916 (1979). The virtues of arbitration cannot be easily obtained by transplanting it into a setting in which appreciation of its advantages is not shared. A hospital or HMO may have a long-term interest in channeling all malpractice claims into such a private forum even if doing so is not conducive to the organization's winning any one case, whereas the dominant concern of the seriously injured patient is to win redress for the losses that he has already suffered. When the individual patient consults a personal injury lawyer (who will be needed to present an effective case in either forum), the lawyer is likely to be suspicious of arbitration and willing to fight for a chance to get to a jury if that seems advantageous to the case. Because the current law provides a favorable environment for challenges to arbitration clauses, such preliminary contests are increasingly undertaken— a development that causes arbitration to lose much of the comparative institutional advantage that it might otherwise have. For this reason, when it comes to seriously exploring alternatives to the jury trial in malpractice litigation, instead of private *ad hoc* arbitration I would opt for the concept of a public administrative tribunal, as recently proposed by the American Medical Association; see Chapter 6.

26. Indeed, in the context of workplace injuries the subrogated workers' compensation insurers have become a significant source of employee tort suits against third-party manufacturers, perhaps the most expensive form of tort litigation at present. See Paul C. Weiler, "Workers' Compensation and Product Liability: The Interaction of a Tort and Non-Tort Regime," 50 *Ohio State Law Journal* 825 (1989).

27. Two recent articles suggest different ways in which this limited contract adjustment to tort damages might be accomplished. In my summaries I adapt their proposals to the health context. The first piece, Alan Schwartz, "Proposals for Products Liability Reform: A Theoretical Synthesis," 97 *Yale Law Journal* 353, 407–408 (1988), suggests that the health care provider be entitled to offer medical treatment at a lower price in order to secure in exchange a waiver of tort liability from patients who can certify that they already have adequate first-party insurance for the medical costs and earnings losses from any disabling injuries (this insurance would likely be obtained through the patients' employment). Robert Cooter and Stephen D. Sugarman, "A Regulated Market in Unmatured Tort Claims: Tort Reform by Contract," in Walter Olson, ed., *New Directions in Liability Law* 174 (New York: Academy of Political Science, 1988), propose that a patient be able to sell his potential tort claim to his employer if the employer has provided adequate insurance for the economic losses from disability. In turn, the employer would be permitted to sell all its workers' tort claims to potential tortfeasors or liability insurers; the employer would be able to apply the proceeds of such sales to reduce the cost of its own first-party group insurance package.

   In each of these scenarios the contract waivers would produce a reduction in costly tort litigation, but only in situations in which there was some assurance that the basic economic needs of the victims would be taken care of. The difference between the two approaches is that Cooter and Sugarman would also ensure that the cost of the patient injuries would be shifted to the health care providers who were responsible for them. The purpose of this is to train a tort incentive on the health care system to take precautions that would prevent reasonably avoidable injuries. However, securing that incentive would generate an indeterminate level of administrative costs on account of the required negotiation and litigation between the numerous employers and tortfeasors potentially involved in the transactions. Whether the marginal gains in prevention would warrant the added administrative burden is an issue I shall not pursue here.

28. More precisely, compensation for the earnings losses from disabling injuries is not likely to be available. Although most Americans are insured for the bulk of their health care costs through a variety of public or private arrangements, a serious shortfall in long-term disability protection

remains. Using admittedly back-of-the envelope calculations, Kenneth S. Abraham, "Disability Insurance and Tort Reform" (American Law Institute Working Paper, 1987), estimates that only about $5 billion of private long-term disability insurance is written annually in this country (p. 4), a mere fraction of the approximately $100 billion of uncompensated earnings losses each year (p. 34). Abraham argues that the gap is the result of major systemic imperfections in the private market for disability insurance—the heuristic biases of potential victims that lead them to underestimate and to underinsure against such remote but severe injuries, and the problems of adverse selection and moral hazard faced by insurers with respect to individuals who choose to purchase such coverage. So however erratic, cumbersome, and costly it may be, the disability insurance now supplied through the tort system at least addresses the flaws in the free market that leave such a profound gap between these severe personal and social losses and the social mechanisms available to deal with them.

29. Recall the case described in Chapter 4, note 32, of the Harvard anesthesiologists who were prodded by the university hospitals' insurer to develop new practice standards and medical equipment to reduce the risks of something going wrong in anesthesia cases.

30. The best introduction to this theory and the body of supporting research is in W. Kip Viscusi, *Risk by Choice: Regulating Health and Safety in the Workplace* (Cambridge, Mass.: Harvard University Press, 1983). Viscusi reports the empirical data regarding compensating risk differentials (pp. 36–58) and then addresses the problems posed for the functioning of this market-for-risk by imperfect information available to workers (pp. 59–75). For a more recent and more general review of this literature, see Ted R. Miller, "Willingness to Pay Comes of Age: Will the System Survive?" 83 *Northwestern University Law Review* 876 (1989).

31. See U.S. Department of Health and Human Services, Health Care Financing Administration, *Medicare Hospital Mortality Information: 1986, 1987, 1988* (Washington, D.C.: U.S. Government Printing Office, 1989).

32. For a sample of the scientific literature, see Robert W. Dubois, William H. Rogers, John H. Morley, David Draper, and Robert H. Brook, "Hospital Inpatient Mortality: Is It a Predictor of Quality?" 317 *New England Journal of Medicine* 1674 (1987); Stephen F. Jencks, Deborah K. Williams, and Terrence L. Kay, "Assessing Hospital-Associated Death from Discharge Data: The Role of Length of Stay and Comorbidities," 260 *Journal of American Medical Association* 2240 (1988); Mark R. Chassin, Rolla Edward Park, Kathleen N. Lohr, Joan Keesey, and Robert H. Brook, "Differences among Hospitals in Medicare Patient Mortality," 24 *Health Services Research* 1 (1989); and Jesse Green, Neil Wintfeld, Phoebe Sharkey, and Leigh J. Passman, "The Importance of Severity of Illness in Assessing Hospital Mortality," 263 *Journal of American Medical Association* 241 (1990).

33. See Donald M. Berwick and David L. Wald, "Hospital Leaders' Opinions of the HCFA Mortality Data," 263 *Journal of American Medical Association* 247 (1990).

34. *HHS Report* contains a succinct but comprehensive review (pp. 55–103) of the medical credentialing process and its potential for reducing the incidence of substandard medical care. See also Gary L. Gaumer, "Regulating Health Professionals: A Review of the Empirical Literature," 62 *Health and Society* 380 (1984).

35. This enduring phenomenon was first described and analyzed by Robert C. Derbyshire, *Medical Licensure and Discipline in the United States* (Baltimore: Johns Hopkins University Press, 1969) (detailing the experience from 1963 to 1967); the research was updated to the period 1969–1978 in Robert C. Derbyshire, "How Effective Is Medical Self-Regulation?" 7 *Law and Human Behavior* 193 (1983). The issue has now become more salient in the contemporary debate over malpractice litigation and reform. See, e.g., Sidney M. Wolfe, Henry Bergman, and George Silver, *Medical Malpractice: The Need for Disciplinary Reform, Not Tort Reform* (Washington, D.C.: Public Citizen Health Research Group, 1985). In 1986 the Office of the Inspector General, U.S. Department of Health and Human Services, issued a report entitled *Medical Licensure and Discipline: An Overview,* which was reproduced in the House of Representatives Hearings on Medical Malpractice, No. 99-152 (March 18 and July 15, 1986), pp. 241–269, then summarized by its authors in Richard P. Kusserow, Elisabeth A. Handley, and Mark R. Yessian, "An Overview of State Medical Discipline," 257 *Journal of American Medical Association* 820 (1987). The article describes the state of medical discipline in 1984. The most recently reported figures for 1985 are summarized in a news story by Joel Brinkley, "State Medical Boards Disciplined Record Number of Doctors in '85," *New York Times,* p. 1, col. 1 (November 9, 1986). I draw upon these sources for the statistics reported in the text.

36. The level of activity by state licensing boards is far higher now than it was in the sixties, before the malpractice crisis first loomed on the horizon. Total disciplinary action by all state boards in the country averaged less than 200 cases a year in the mid-sixties. It rose gradually to about 400 cases a year in the mid-seventies, reached nearly 1,400 cases in 1984, then jumped to 2,108 disciplinary actions in 1985—a 60 percent increase in just one year. The state boards conventionally categorize their disciplinary actions as either serious (in cases of license revocation, suspension, and probation) or nonserious (practice restrictions, reprimands, and the like). Of the 2,108 actions taken in 1985, 406 were total revocations of a physician's license to practice, 235 were suspensions, and 491 were probations. The remaining 976 cases fell into the nonserious category. There was also a striking disparity in the rate of disciplinary activity across the states in that year, ranging from 19 and 17 per 1,000 doctors in Nevada and Arizona respectively, to fewer than 2 per 1,000 in states such as Connecticut and Nebraska, and less than 2 per 1,000 in New York and Massachusetts. The state board performance in the latter two states subsequently accelerated as a result of reforms introduced in 1985 and 1986.

37. See Chapter 1, note 38.

38. See Stephen Shavell, *Economic Analysis of Accident Law* 277–286 (Cambridge, Mass.: Harvard University Press, 1987), for a more general analytical comparison of the characteristic strengths and weaknesses of tort litigation and administrative regulation. The mode of analysis developed in Neil K. Komesar, "Injuries and Institutions: Tort Reform, Tort Theory, and Beyond," 65 *New York University Law Review* 23 (1990), is also highly illuminating for the health care context.

39. See Office of the Inspector General, HHS, *Medical Licensure and Discipline*, p. 15.

40. According to the *HHS Report*, p. 2, the total budget for all state licensing boards was $50 million in 1984, much of which was expended in the initial examination and credentialing process. It is within the constraints of their budgets that the boards must establish by "clear and convincing evidence" whether there was a lack of general competence sufficient to justify revoking or suspending a physician's license to practice. By contrast, patient tort lawyers in the same year were paid fees of nearly $900 million (one-third of the $2.6 billion indemnity payments to victorious plaintiffs: see *1984 Claims Closed Survey*, p. 18) simply to establish by the "preponderance of the evidence" that there was a lack of reasonable care by a doctor in a single situation.

41. See Chapter 4; see also William B. Schwartz and Daniel N. Mendelson, "The Role of Physician-Owned Insurance Companies in the Detection and Deterrence of Negligence," 262 *Journal of American Medical Association* 1342 (1989).

42. A valuable review of these reforms, focusing especially on the six states—California, Florida, Massachusetts, Michigan, New York, and Texas—is provided in a paper by a third-year student at Harvard Law School: Laura Keidan, "Physician Discipline: Cure for the Malpractice Crisis?" (1989). Keidan not only describes the statutory and administrative reforms, but she also presents statistics that compare rates of complaints and disciplinary action before and after the reforms went into effect. It is clear that significantly more board action is taking place in the wake of the reforms, especially in New York. However, comparing the level of board activity, particularly practice suspensions or revocations for alleged physician incompetence, to the total physician population and the number of tort claims indicates that there is a great distance yet to go.

How far is evidenced in a recent report from California; see Robert C. Fellmeth, *Physician Discipline in California—A Code Blue Emergency: An Initial Report on the Physician Discipline System of the Board of Medical Quality Assurance* (San Diego: Center for Public Interest Law, University of San Diego School of Law, 1989). As part of its 1975 overhaul of medical malpractice law, which pioneered in state legislative restrictions on patient suits, California instituted new physician discipline mechanisms that were expected to reduce the cost of medical injury without the need for litigation. In the 1987–88 fiscal year, in a state with 25 million people and 70,000 licensed physicians, a total of 12 physicians were the subject of any serious disciplinary action—probation, suspension, or revocation of license—for lack of competetence (see pp. 24–25).

43. See Mark A. Colantonio, "The Health Care Quality Improvement Act of 1986 and Its Impact on Hospital Law," 91 *West Virginia Law Review* 91 (1988), for a brief description of the law and its requirements.

44. The most systematic effort to identify and quantify the causes of increased state board disciplinary activity is Andrew K. Dolan and Nicole D. Urban, "The Determinants of the Effectiveness of Medical Disciplinary Boards: 1960–1977," 7 *Law and Human Behavior* 203 (1983). See also Derbyshire, "How Effective Is Medical Self-Regulation?"

45. See the articles cited in notes 38 and 39 to Chapter 4.

46. If the medical accident problem were largely attributable to a few bad apples in the profession, this single-minded emphasis would make some sense. But the sources of iatrogenic injuries are widespread. These injuries are the outgrowth of the techniques and mishaps of generally careful, conscientious doctors who must function in a highly risky and unforgiving physical environment. Therefore, more sophisticated policy instruments are required to reduce the chance of errors and to minimize the harm when they occur. Traditional medical licensing is simply not designed for this ambitious role.

47. See the discussion in Keidan, "Physician Discipline," about recent developments in New York State, Massachusetts, and Florida. Florida's program is also described in F. Townsend Hawkes, "The Second Reformation: Florida's Medical Malpractice Law," 13 *Florida State University Law Review* 747, 749–758 (1985).

48. The dominant OSHA-type model in Canada now utilizes such committees as the primary mechanism for improving workplace safety. For a brief description of the Canadian "internal responsibility" approach, see Paul C. Weiler, *Protecting the Worker from Disability: Challenges for the Eighties* 108–110 (Toronto: Government of Ontario, 1983), which contains references to more detailed Canadian literature on the subject.

49. In the next couple of pages I only scratch the surface of a topic that has become a cottage industry for law professors as well as lawyers. The scholarly articles on the subject that I have found most helpful are Philip C. Kissam, William L. Webber, Lawrence W. Bigus, and John R. Holzgraefe, "Antitrust and Hospital Privileges: Testing the Conventional Wisdom," 70 *California Law Review* 595 (1982); Clark C. Havighurst, "Doctors and Hospitals: An Antitrust Perspective on Traditional Relationships," 1984 *Duke Law Journal* 1071; James F. Blumstein and Frank A. Sloan, "Antitrust and Hospital Peer Review," 51 *Law and Contemporary Problems* 7 (1988); and Thomas E. Kauper, "The Role of Quality of Health Care Considerations in Antitrust Analysis," 51 *Law and Contemporary Problems* 273 (1988).

50. The trilogy of health care antitrust decisions consisted of Arizona v. Maricopa County Medical Society, 457 U.S. 332 (1982); Jefferson Parish Hospital District No. 2 v. Hyde, 466 U.S. 2 (1984); and Federal Trade Commission v. Indiana Federation of Dentists, 476 U.S. 447 (1986).

51. See Wilk v. American Medical Association, 671 F.Supp. 1465 (N.D. Ill. 1987) (chiropractors); Weiss v. York Hospital, 745 F.2d 786 (3d Cir. 1984) (osteopaths); Cooper v. Forsyth County Hospital Authority, 789 F.2d 278 (4th Cir. 1986) (podiatrists); and Nurse-Midwifery Associates v. Hibbett, 549 F.Supp. 1185 (M.D. Tenn. 1982) (nurse-midwives).

52. See Seglin v. Esau, 769 F.2d 1274 (7th Cir. 1985); and Pariser v. Christian Health Care Systems, Inc., 816 F.2d 1248 (8th Cir. 1987).

53. See Seidenstein v. National Medical Enterprises, Inc., 769 F.2d 1100 (5th Cir. 1985); and Goss v. Memorial Hospital System, 789 F.2d 353 (5th Cir. 1986).

54. See Nanavati v. Burdette Tomlin Memorial Hospital, 857 F.2d 96 (3d Cir. 1988).

55. 486 U.S. 94 (1988).

56. Among the appelate court decisions that upheld this defense were Marrese v. Interqual, Inc., 748 F.2d 373 (7th Cir. 1984); Doe v. St. Joseph's Hospital of Fort Wayne, 788 F.2d 411 (7th Cir. 1986); and the lower court in Patrick v. Burget itself (see 800 F.2d 1498 [9th Cir. 1986]).

57. For an extensive discussion of the HCQIA and its relationship to general antitrust doctrine, see Blumstein and Sloan, "Antitrust and Hospital Peer Review," pp. 70–89.

58. As was actually done in the case of Friedman v. Delaware County Memorial Hospital, 672 F.Supp. 171 (E.D. Pa. 1987), *affirmed*, 849 F.2d 600 (3d Cir. 1988). See, by contrast, Miller v. Indiana Hospital, 843 F.2d 139 (3d Cir. 1988); and Bolt v. Halifax Hospital Medical Center, 874 F.2d 755 (11th Cir. 1989), in which summary dismissal was denied.

59. See references in Chapter 2, note 23. The significance and possible extension of organizational liability will be developed in the next chapter.

60. See Hawkes, "Florida's Medical Malpractice Law," pp. 751–752.

6. No-Fault Patient Compensation

1. See the Report of the American Medical Association/Specialty Society Medical Liability Project, *A Proposed Alternative to the Civil Justice System for Resolving Medical Liability Disputes: A Fault-Based, Administrative System* (Chicago: AMA, 1987). A more accessible presentation of the proposal is Kirk B. Johnson, Carter G. Phillips, David Orentlicher, and Martin S. Hatlie, "A Fault-Based Administrative Alternative for Resolving Medical Malpractice Claims," 42 *Vanderbilt Law Review* 1365 (1989).

2. *1984 Claims Closed Survey* reported (at p. 82) that in 1984, although patients obtained some payment in 44 percent of all malpractice claims and in 70 percent of claims settled during trial, they won only 19 percent of the trial verdicts and 27 percent of the claims resolved at or after appeal (Table V.14). The substantial tilt in jury verdicts against the patient and in favor of the doctor accords with the results of the closed claims surveys from the late seventies, which also found that patients won only about a quarter of the cases that were tried to a verdict or beyond; see Patricia M. Danzon, *Medical Malpractice: Theory, Evidence, and Public Policy*

32, 38 (Cambridge, Mass.: Harvard University Press, 1985). Stephen Daniels and Lori Andrews, "The Shadow of the Law: Jury Decisions in Obstetrics and Gynecology," in Institute of Medicine, *Medical Professional Liability and the Delivery of Obstetrical Care*, 2 vols., ed. Victoria P. Rostow and Roger J. Bulger, II, 161–193 (Washington, D.C.: National Academy Press, 1989), reviewed a nationwide sample of malpractice jury verdicts from 1981 through 1985 and found that juries decided in favor of the plaintiff in 32 percent of the cases, versus 57 percent for civil plaintiffs generally (see p. 173). But if a patient does succeed in persuading a jury that the doctor was negligent, much higher damages will be awarded for the resulting injuries than would be awarded for a comparable injury in a motor vehicle or occupier's liability case. See Audrey Chin and Mark A. Peterson, *Deep Pockets, Empty Pockets: Who Wins in Cook County Jury Trials* (Santa Monica, Calif.: RAND Institute for Civil Justice, 1985). In that respect, malpractice defendants suffer from the same "deep pocket" syndrome that afflicts product manufacturers and employers defending themselves against tort litigation.

3. Apparently the expected recovery has to be on the order of at least $50,000 before any personal injury specialist will take a malpractice case: see U.S. General Accounting Office, *Medical Malpractice: A Framework for Action* 23 (Washington, D.C.: U.S. Government Printing Office, 1987). This factor, together with the great difficulty many patients have in even identifying a connection between their present disability and past medical treatment, explain why the Harvard study found that well under 10 percent of negligent injuries in the hospital ever produced a legal claim in the tort system.

4. See Chapter 2.

5. For the key components of the workers' compensation no-fault model, see Paul C. Weiler, "Legal Policy for Workplace Injuries" 5–22 (American Law Institute Working Paper, 1986). The corresponding responses of the malpractice regime to the same problems have been developed in earlier chapters of this book.

6. · See Chapter 3.

7. For an interesting review of the various ways in which medical practice standards are developed, see Eleanor D. Kinney and Marilyn M. Wilder, "Medical Standard Setting in the Current Malpractice Environment: Problems and Possibilities," 22 *U.C. Davis Law Review* 421 (1989).

8. On the same institutional theme in a different personal injury context, see Troyen A. Brennan, "Helping Courts with Toxic Torts: Some Proposals Regarding Alternative Methods for Presenting and Assessing Scientific Evidence in Common Law Courts," 51 *University of Pittsburgh Law Review* 1 (1989).

9. See Karin B. Nelson and Jonas H. Ellenberg, "Antecedents of Cerebral Palsy: Multivariate Analysis of Risk," 315 *New England Journal of Medicine* 81 (1986).

10. See George L. Priest, "The Invention of Enterprise Liability: A Critical History of the Intellectual Foundations of Modern Tort Law," 14 *Journal of Legal Studies* 461 (1985).

11. See George L. Priest, "The Current Insurance Crisis and Modern Tort Law," 96 *Yale Law Journal* 1521 (1987), in particular on product liability; and Kenneth S. Abraham, "Environmental Liability and the Limits of Insurance," 88 *Columbia Law Review* 942 (1988).

12. See *1984 Claims Closed Survey,* p. 25.

13. A number of recent cases and law review articles elaborating this history are cited in Chapter 2, note 23. For an illuminating historical account of the parallel relationship between hospital and physician in the health care system itself, see Rosemary Stevens, *In Sickness and in Wealth: American Hospitals in the Twentieth Century* (New York: Basic Books, 1989).

14. That litigation strategy has been facilitated by the evolution of "joint and several liability." This tort doctrine holds one party whose negligence helped cause a victim's injuries fully responsible for all the injuries (assuming one component of the injury cannot be isolated and attributed to just one actor), and leaves it to that defendant to collect whatever contribution it can from the other guilty party (something that clearly would not be feasible for hospitals faced with the seven-figure damage awards referred to in Chapters 1 and 2). For contrasting views on this controversial feature of modern tort law, see the illuminating exchange between Richard W. Wright and Aaron D. Twerski: Wright, "Allocating Liability among Multiple Responsible Causes: A Principled Defense of Joint and Several Liability for Actual Harm and Risk Exposure," 21 *U.C. Davis Law Review* 1141 (1988); Twerski, "The Joint Tortfeasor Legislative Revolt: A Rational Response to the Critics," 22 *U.C. Davis Law Review* 1125 (1989); Wright, "Throwing Out the Baby with the Bathwater: A Reply to Professor Twerski," ibid., 1147; and Twerski, "The Baby Swallowed the Bathwater: A Rejoinder to Professor Wright," ibid., 1161.

15. See Report of the New York State Insurance Department on Medical Malpractice, *A Balanced Prescription for Change* 53–54 (New York: 1988).

16. As I observed in Chapter 2, note 108, whether or not the presence of a cap on the patient compensation fund's responsibility would render unconstitutional the smaller cap on the negligent doctor's personal liability was the issue presented to but eventually avoided by the Louisiana Supreme Court in Williams v. Kushner, 549 So.2d 294 (La. 1989).

17. This was the rationale of the Florida Supreme Court when it upheld the constitutionality of the state's uncapped fund, in Florida Patient's Compensation Fund v. Von Stetina, 474 So.2d 783 (Fla. 1985). In a later case, Higley v. Florida Patient's Compensation Fund, 525 So.2d 865 (Fla. 1988), the court asserted that the presence of the fund absolved a negligent doctor, nurse, or other health care worker from any personal liability for an injury, even in the context of an indemnity action brought by the fund.

18. It might be tempting to go even further and make the hospital liable for all malpractice committed by its affiliated doctors, even for injuries that happen to occur in the doctors' own offices. Although this extension would create an even purer form of enterprise liability, it would also give rise to a number of philosophical and practical objections. For example, is it fair to subject a hospital to liability for events that occur completely

outside its premises and control? Which hospitals would be liable for the negligence of doctors who have admitting privileges at several institutions? Rather than try to devise answers to such thorny questions at this stage, it is better to focus on the somewhat less ambitious target described in the text, which would largely solve the real problem of excessively high premiums for the small number of critical specialties. Less than 13 percent of malpractice claims are now brought for events that occur in physicians' offices. The remaining claims stem from incidents in the hospital (81 percent) or in HMO's, nursing homes, and other institutions (see *1984 Claims Closed Survey,* p. 25). I suspect that the distribution of total dollars actually spent on claims (against surgeons and obstetricians, for example) is even more acutely tilted toward those that arise in an institutional setting.

19. See *1984 Claims Closed Survey,* p. 26.

20. As illustration, recall that New York State passed a law in 1985 requiring that hospitals in the state buy for their doctors excess insurance (that is, insurance for claims that exceed $1 million) for torts committed in the hospital. The state government has not yet persuaded the federal government to reimburse hospitals under the Medicare program for the additional expense attributable to the new insurance charge. See New York State Insurance Department, *A Balanced Prescription for Change,* p. 30.

21. For analyses from a law and economics perspective of whether such vicarious or enterprise liability is preferable to personal responsibility, see Lewis A. Kornhauser, "An Economic Analysis of the Choice between Enterprise and Personal Liability for Accidents," 70 *California Law Review* 1345 (1982), and Alan O. Sykes, "The Economics of Vicarious Liability," 93 *Yale Law Journal* 1231 (1984). Both the case law and the focus of these articles is on the employment context, within which the financial terms of the employer-employee relationship will adjust to the legal allocation of liability, albeit with considerable distortion, because the limited assets of the employee renders the employee judgment-proof against major tort claims. Because neither of these characteristics marks the hospital-doctor relationship, the optimal allocation of legal responsibility here must be judged in light of the most salient features of this specific setting.

22. See Frank A. Sloan and Mahmud Hassan, "Equity and Accuracy in Medical Malpractice Insurance Pricing," forthcoming in *Journal of Health Economics* (1990). Sloan and Hassan's calculations show how much more credible and powerful experience rating is when it is applied to the liability premiums of the entire medical staff of a hospital rather than solely to the premiums of the individual physician.

23. On the latter phenomenon, see Stevens, *In Sickness and in Wealth,* in particular, pp. 341–344, "Redefining the Workshop: Hospitals and Doctors."

24. During the first malpractice crisis of the mid-seventies, the no-fault alternative to tort liability was the subject of considerable discussion and debate. Among the major scholarly exponents of that idea were Clark C.

Havighurst and Laurence R. Tancredi, "'Medical Adversity Insurance'—A No-Fault Approach to Medical Malpractice and Quality Assurance," 613 *Insurance Law Journal* 69 (1974); and Jeffrey O'Connell, "No-Fault Insurance for Injuries Arising from Medical Treatment: A Proposal for Elective Coverage," 24 *Emory Law Journal* 21 (1975). The scholarly criticisms of the traditional tort regime and their exposition of the possibilities of some version of no-fault were reflected in legislation introduced in Congress in 1975 by Senators Inouye and Kennedy; see the description of this bill, S.215, in Note, "Comparative Approaches to Liability for Medical Maloccurrences," 84 *Yale Law Journal* 1141, 1158–1160 (1975); and in the recommendations of the State of New York Special Advisory Panel, *Report on Medical Malpractice* 4, 57–63 (New York: Government of New York, 1976). As I observe in the text, the specific form taken by the various fault proposals tended to differ considerably from the mandatory and comprehensive coverage characteristic of workers' compensation.

25. See Walter Gellhorn, "Medical Malpractice Litigation (U.S.)—Medical Mishap Compensation (N.Z.)," 73 *Cornell Law Review* 170 (1988).

26. The design and operation of the Swedish program is described in Marilynn M. Rosenthal, *Dealing with Medical Malpractice: The British and Swedish Experience* 174–186 (Durham, N.C.: Duke University Press, 1988); Jan Hellner, "Compensation for Personal Injury: The Swedish Alternative," 34 *American Journal of Comparative Law* 613 (1986); and Carl Oldertz, "Security Insurance, Patient Insurance, and Pharmaceutical Insurance in Sweden," 34 *American Journal of Comparative Law* 635 (1986).

27. A version of no-fault compensation did retain a foothold in the debate in connection with the "medical adversity insurance" plan developed and advocated by Clark Havighurst and Laurence Tancredi in numerous publications over the last decade. See, e.g., Clark Havighurst, "'Medical Adversity Insurance'—Has Its Time Come?" 1975 *Duke Law Journal* 1233; and Laurence R. Tancredi, "Designing a No-Fault Alternative," 49 *Law and Contemporary Problems* 277 (1986). In addition, the Commission on Medical Professional Liability of the American Bar Association issued the report *Designated Compensable Event System: A Feasibility Study* (Washington, D.C.: 1979). However, these different versions of the medical adversity insurance plan were significantly diluted forms of no-fault. Benefits would be paid only for a list of designated events, selected because they were deemed to be generally avoidable in normal medical circumstances, with fault litigation continuing to serve as the legal backdrop for all other cases. While medical adversity insurance would likely be an administratively useful refinement of the fault regime, it would rely on fault to a considerably greater extent than does even current tort liability for defective products. It would be worlds removed from the pure workers' compensation version of no-fault for workplace injuries. In effect, then, proponents of this insurance tacitly agreed with the critics of full-blown no-fault patient compensation that such a scheme would simply not be viable for medical accidents.

28. See Robert E. Keeton, "Compensation for Medical Accidents," 121 *University of Pennsylvania Law Review* 590 (1973); Guido Calabresi, "The Problem of Malpractice: Trying to Round Out the Circle," 27 *University of Toronto Law Journal* 131 (1977); and Richard A. Epstein, "Medical Malpractice: Its Cause and Cure," in Simon Rottenberg, ed., *The Economics of Medical Malpractice* 245–267 (Washington, D.C.: American Enterprise Institute for Public Policy, 1978).

29. For a useful description of Finland's program see Diana Brahams, "No Fault Compensation Finnish Style," *The Lancet* 733 (September 24, 1988).

30. See *Liability and Compensation in Health Care* (Toronto: University of Toronto Press, 1990).

31. The first of these enactments was the Virginia Birth-Related Neurological Compensation Act of 1987. The act instituted a program, effective January 1, 1988, that provides no-fault compensation to infants who suffer damage to the brain or spinal cord because of oxygen deprivation or mechanical injury during labor or delivery or in the immediate post-delivery period—damage that results in the total and permanent disability of the child. Compensation is awarded for all medical, hospital, rehabilitation, nursing, and custodial expenses that are not covered by other public or private insurance sources, and for a deemed loss of earnings from ages 18 to 65, based on half of the state average weekly wage. Obstetricians and hospitals are given the election of participating and contributing to this compensation fund, at an initial charge to the obstetrician of $5,000 a year and to the hospital of $50 per delivery. If the providers choose to participate, the program becomes the exclusive remedy for the infant and its family: all tort rights to sue are waived, except in cases in which there is clear and convincing evidence of intentional or willful injuries caused by the doctor or the hospital. The Virginia program, which had not yet received its first claim as of early 1990, has generated considerable scholarly commentary. For a detailed description of the background and design of the program, see Note, "Innovative No-Fault Tort Reform for an Endangered Specialty," 74 *Virginia Law Review* 1487 (1988). For contrasting views on this particular no-fault policy, see Richard A. Epstein, "Market and Regulatory Approaches to Medical Malpractice: The Virginia Obstetrical No-Fault Statute," 74 *Virginia Law Review* 1451 (1988); Jeffrey O'Connell, "Pragmatic Constraints on Market Approaches: A Response to Professor Epstein," 74 *Virginia Law Review* 1475 (1988); Cynthia L. Gallup, "Can No-Fault Compensation of Impaired Infants Alleviate the Malpractice Crisis in Obstetrics?" 14 *Journal of Health Politics, Policy, and Law* 691 (1989); and Andrew D. Freeman and John M. Freeman, "No-Fault Cerebral Palsy Insurance: An Alternative to the Obstetrical Malpractice Lottery," 14 *Journal of Health Politics, Policy, and Law* 707 (1989). The Florida provision, which is largely modeled on Virginia's, is described in Thomas R. Tedcastle and Marvin A. Dewar, "Medical Malpractice: A New Treatment for an Old Illness," 16 *Florida State University Law Review* 537, 582–590 (1988).

32. Danzon, *Medical Malpractice*, p. 169, estimates that 61 percent of tort damage verdicts are for economic losses, of which 23 percentage points (or a little over one-third of total financial losses) are for health care expenses.

33. See *Harvard Study*, Chapter 8, p. 54.

34. See *1984 Claims Closed*, p. 46, in which it is estimated that patient-victims with major or grave permanent total disabilities suffered average economic losses of approximately $1.7 million each.

35. See *Harvard Study*, Chapter 8, pp. 68–69.

36. Ibid., Chapter 8, pp. 78–79. I note that this calculation assumes that no-fault patient insurance would be a secondary payer to Medicare and Medicaid, a status that is unlikely unless the federal government agrees to relax its present insistence on subrogation claims to any liability insurance. Absent federal cooperation, the estimated cost of no-fault compensation for injured patients' health care expenses and lost earnings would rise another $250 million.

37. See Chapter 3.

38. My own calculations generate an estimated 15 to 20 percent administrative share of the workers' compensation claims-distribution dollar; see Paul C. Weiler, "Legal Policy for Workplace Injuries" (American Law Institute Working Paper, 1986). George Priest's figure is 21 percent; see "The Current Insurance Crisis," p. 1560.

39. See, for example, Herskovits v. Group Health Cooperative of Puget Sound, 664 P.2d 474 (Wash. 1983), and McKellips v. Saint Francis Hospital, Inc., 741 P.2d 467 (Okla. 1987); see also Joseph H. King, Jr., "Causation, Valuation, and Chance in Personal Injury Torts Involving Preexisting Conditions and Future Consequences," 90 *Yale Law Journal* 1353 (1981).

40. See *Harvard Study*, Chapter 6, pp. 19–20.

41. See the estimates by George Priest of the comparative administrative costs of no-fault, cause-based workers' compensation, and the various public and private loss insurance programs, in "The Current Insurance Crisis," p. 1560.

42. See note 31 above.

43. See Nelson and Ellenberg, "Antecedents of Cerebral Palsy."

44. This has recently been advocated for all cerebral palsy victims: see Freeman and Freeman, "No-Fault Cerebral Palsy Insurance."

45. On New Zealand, see Gellhorn, "Medical Malpractice Litigation," pp. 196–202; on Virginia, see Gallup, "Compensation of Impaired Infants," pp. 696–700.

46. See the latter sections of Chapter 4.

47. For a brief but helpful description of the Quebec plan, see Jeffrey O'Connell and Charles Tenser, "North America's Most Ambitious No-Fault Law: Quebec's Auto Insurance Act," 24 *San Diego Law Review* 917 (1987).

48. The two major studies are Marc Gaudry, "The Effects on Road Safety of the Compulsory Insurance, Flat Premium Rating and No-Fault Features

of the 1978 Quebec Automobile Act," in *Report of Inquiry into Motor Vehicle Accident Compensation in Ontario,* vol. 2 (Toronto: Queen's Printer for Ontario, 1988); and Rose Anne Devlin, "Liability versus No-Fault Automobile Insurance Regimes: An Analysis of the Experience in Quebec" (Ph.D. diss., University of Toronto, 1988). A brief but valuable review of the contrasting methodologies in these studies is Donald Dewees and Michael Trebilcock, "The Efficacy of the Tort System: A Review of the Empirical Evidence" 30–34 (American Law Institute Working Paper, 1989).

49. See Michael J. Moore and W. Kip Viscusi, *Compensation Mechanisms for Job Risks: Wages, Workers' Compensation, and Product Liability* 121–135 (Princeton: Princeton University Press, 1990); compare, using a somewhat different methodology, Michael J. Moore and W. Kip Viscusi, "Promoting Safety through Workers' Compensation: The Efficacy and Net Wage Costs of Injury Insurance," 20 *RAND Journal of Economics* 499 (1989).

50. For a revealing case study of the influence of workers' compensation premiums on employer health and safety policy, see Joseph V. Rees, *Reforming the Workplace: A Study of Self-Regulation in Occupational Safety* 72–80, 114–118 (Philadelphia: University of Pennsylvania Press, 1988).

51. The Swedish patient compensation system now operates along those lines. Systematic analyses of the first decade of claims appear in the professional literature, identifying higher-risk procedures and recommending alternatives. See, e.g., Rosenthal, "The British and Swedish Experience," pp. l84–l86. For this conception of the medical quality assurance problem, I have benefited from conversations with Dr. Donald M. Berwick, as well as his writings. See his "Continuous Improvement as an Ideal in Health Care," 320 *New England Journal of Medicine* 53 (1989). In the same vein, see Glenn Laffell and David Blumenthal, "The Case for Using Industrial Quality Management Science in Health Care Organizations," 262 *Journal of American Medical Association* 2869 (1989).

52. See Jeffrey O'Connell, "An Alternative to Abandoning Tort Liability: Elective No-Fault Insurance for Many Kinds of Injuries," 60 *Minnesota Law Review* 501 (1976). One might question whether and when a health care organization would consider it advantageous to adopt and pay for elective no-fault insurance in place of malpractice liability insurance for itself and its doctors. For an analytical exploration of the competing factors, see "Emerging Contractual Alternatives," Chapter 29 of the American Law Institute, *Compensation and Liability for Product and Process Injuries: Proposed Final Report,* vol. 2 (Philadelphia: ALI, 1991). This chapter was coauthored by Alan Schwartz, Kip Viscusi, and myself.

More recently Professor O'Connell has advocated a new option that he calls "neo-no-fault": see "Neo-No-Fault Remedies for Medical Injuries: Coordinated Statutory and Contractual Alternatives," 49 *Law and Contemporary Problems* 125 (1986). Under a neo-no-fault regime the legislature would empower health care providers to offer compensation for all net economic losses to already injured patients within 180 days of the filing of the tort claim. This compensation would forestall any further tort litigation on the case. This kind of one-way option, offered only to doctors, has acknowledged inherent problems; however, Professor O'Connell argues that this is the best way to move toward the more rational, more beneficial compensation scheme of no-fault without having to face the serious issues of cost and cause that come up in the medical context. Now that the Harvard study has developed data indicating that these problems may be manageable, I know that Professor O'Connell does favor experimentation with the bilateral elective option for true no-fault patient compensation.

53. As is evident from the many limitations and safeguards suggested for patient choice, I endorse only a qualified exercise of contractual freedom, not the blanket approval of wholesale tort waivers that I criticized in Chapter 5.

54. Interestingly, the Swedish no-fault scheme was adopted voluntarily in the health care system and still rests on a contractual basis. This has afforded the program the flexibility to adopt a variety of decision-making rules to be applied in difficult recurring cases—rules for deciding, for example, when infections should be treated as iatrogenic. (See references cited in note 26 of this chapter.)

55. Although not dramatically greater: see the estimates by Freeman and Freeman, "No-Fault Cerebral Palsy Insurance."

56. I should mention another possible target of such third-party litigation, the government or private health insurance programs that have undertaken closer monitoring of physician treatment to control unnecessary utilization of medical services. The legal viability of negligence suits against the administrators of such cost containment programs was sustained by a California appeals court in Wickline v. California, 228 Cal. Rptr. 661 (Cal. App. 1986), although the specific decision in that case held that the treating physician's discretion had not been constrained. While *Wickline* has triggered a number of scholarly analyses, e.g., John D. Blum, "An Analysis of Legal Liability in Health Care Utilization Review and Case Management," 26 *Houston Law Review* 191 (1989), I have been unable to find any later cases in which patient attorneys sought to take advantage of this opening.

57. 821 F.2d 1438 (10th Cir. 1987).

58. See, e.g., Reyes v. Wyeth Laboratories, 498 F.2d 1264 (5th Cir. 1974) (Sabin polio vaccine); and Abbott v. American Cyanamid Co., 844 F.2d 1108 (4th Cir. 1988) (diphtheria vaccine).

59. See, e.g., Kirk v. Michael Reese Hospital and Medical Center, 483 N.E.2d 906 (Ill. App. 1985) (thorazine); and Wooderson v. Ortho Pharmaceutical Corp., 681 P.2d 1038 (Kan. 1984) (oral contraceptives).

60. See Ohio Medical Products, Inc. v. Suber, 758 S.W.2d 870 (Tex. App. 1988) (anesthesia gas machine).

61. See Kozup v. Georgetown University, 663 F.Supp. 1048 (D.D.C. 1987) (AIDS-infected blood).

62. For this lament see Peter W. Huber, *Liability: The Legal Revolution and Its Consequences* 153–171 (New York: Basic Books, 1988).

63. See generally Paul C. Weiler, "Workers' Compensation and Product Liability: The Interaction of a Tort and Non-Tort Regime," 50 *Ohio State Law Journal* 825 (1989).
64. See Peter H. Schuck, *Agent Orange on Trial: Mass Toxic Disasters in the Courts* (Cambridge, Mass.: Harvard University Press, 1987).
65. See Oldertz, "Security Insurance, Patient Insurance, and Pharmaceutical Insurance in Sweden."
66. For a description of the background and design of this vaccine program, see Victor E. Schwartz and Liberty Mahshigian, "National Childhood Vaccine Injury Act of 1986: An Ad Hoc Remedy or a Window for the Future?" 48 *Ohio State Law Journal* 387 (1987). Further details of the process of funding and implementing this program are provided by Stephen D. Sugarman, *Doing Away with Tort Law: New Compensation Mechanisms for Victims, Consumers, and Business* 107–109 (New York: Quorum Books, 1989).
67. The workplace analogue to the *O'Gilvie* incident is Barker v. Lull Engineering Co., Inc., 573 P.2d 443 (Cal. 1978). In that case an employer directed a substitute employee to operate a piece of equipment on terrain that was so dangerous that the regular operator had refused to come to work in order to avoid the perilous assignment. The injured employee successfully sued the manufacturer for failing to incorporate in the machine safeguards that might have prevented his injuries.

Case Index

General Index